THE END OF GROWTH

JEFF RUBIN

—

THE END OF
GROWTH

UPDATED WITH A NEW AFTERWORD

VINTAGE CANADA

VINTAGE CANADA EDITION, 2013

Copyright © 2012 Jeff Rubin

Published in Canada by Vintage Canada, a division of Random House of Canada Limited, Toronto, in 2013. Originally published in hardcover in Canada by Random House Canada, a division of Random House of Canada Limited, in 2012. Distributed by Random House of Canada Limited.

Vintage Canada with colophon is a registered trademark.

www.randomhouse.ca

Library and Archives Canada Cataloguing in Publication

Rubin, Jeff
The end of growth / Jeff Rubin.

ISBN 978-0-307-36090-8

1. Economic development. 2. International economic relations. 3. Petroleum industry and trade—Economic aspects. 4. Economic forecasting. I. Title.

HD75.R82 2013   338.9'0090512   C2011-908175-X

Image credits: Valdis Torms/Shutterstock.com
Maps: Paul Dotey

Printed and bound in the United States of America

2 4 6 8 9 7 5 3 1

IN MEMORY OF MY PARENTS,
SHIRLEY ROSE RUBIN AND DR. LEON JULIUS RUBIN

[CONTENTS]

THE LAST MAJOR BARE-KNUCKLE prizefight in America happened in 1889. Shortly after midnight on July 8, John L. Sullivan knocked out Jake Kilrain in the seventy-fifth round, and with that an era was over.

And rightly so. Illegal in thirty-eight states at the time, bareknuckle matches were barbaric. Gloves became mandatory when boxing adopted the Marquess of Queensberry rules, a civilized turn that set the stage for the advent of great heavyweights like Jack Dempsey and Joe Louis. Although gloves helped usher in boxing's golden age, tossing out the London Prize Ring Rules that had governed bare-knuckle matches came at a cost. In the bare-knuckle days, fighters were so worried about breaking a hand that most of their punches were body shots. Today's fight crowds may love seeing heavyweights land knock-out punches to the head, but what's less thrilling is the number of brain-related injuries suffered by boxers. Repeated blows to the head can lead to something doctors call Dementia Pugilistica, a condition every bit as bad as it sounds.

Even changes made with the best intentions can have unintended consequences. More than a century ago, the powers that be intervened to do what they thought was best. They never dreamed that gloves could create any problems beyond putting a few bare-knuckle fighters out of work. And today, the folks pulling the levers of the global economy are making choices that are already costing us much more than you might think. When it comes to setting economic policy, trying to cushion the blow can sometimes be a whole lot worse than taking a few punches with the gloves off.

The economic recovery since the world officially crawled out of the last recession in 2009 has been wobbly at best. If you read the business section or listen to financial market pundits, you'll know that majority opinion suggests the roots of the financial crisis of 2008–9 lay in the debt-ridden wreckage of the United States housing market. The prescription resulting from that diagnosis involved taxpayers around the world opening up their wallets to bail out insolvent banks. The sums of money required were enormous, but we were told the ramifications of doing nothing would be even greater. Finance ministers and central bankers warned that government intervention was desperately required to save the global financial system from collapse and spare us from an economic fate worse than the Great Depression.

And so taxpayers underwrote the biggest bailout in the history of the financial industry.

If flaws in the global financial system were serious enough to jeopardize our economic future, then common sense dictates that deep reforms would unfold once the crisis passed. Since banks barely escaped insolvency as a result of carrying too much debt and exposure to poorly understood financial derivatives, it was fair to assume that regulators would soon put global banks on a much tighter leash. After shelling out trillions to prop them up, taxpayers reasonably expected to see new safeguards put in place to keep us from tumbling into the same mess ever again.

Well, guess again, because little has changed.

The global financial system is still as interconnected and full of risk as ever. A few familiar players are missing, such as Bear Stearns and Lehman Brothers, but the cast of characters is otherwise intact. And once again we're hearing ominous sounds from the financial markets. Only this time around, instead of the United States' housing sector being shaky, the deepest rumblings are emanating from across the Atlantic.

Europe is in the grip of a financial crisis. Greece is close to defaulting on its debt, and Portugal, Italy, Ireland and Spain aren't in much better shape. The European Central Bank is writing checks to keep these governments afloat and hold the euro-zone together. Meanwhile, German taxpayers, who are footing much of the bill to keep their neighbors solvent, are wondering what they're getting for their money and if they'll ever see any of it again.

In the world of modern finance, you don't have to live in Europe to be touched by what happens in Athens or Madrid, any more than you needed to own a home in Cleveland to feel the collapse of the subprime mortgage market. Thanks to our integrated global banking system, a financial market accident in one corner of the world now puts everyone at risk. An investment arm of your local bank could be exposed to a French bank, which in turn holds a big position in Greek bonds that are about to go horribly offside. When that happens, the pain ripples from Greece's bond market, to the French bank, to your regional investment dealer, and eventually onto your doorstep. Half a world away, you and millions of other depositors have a direct interest in Greek debt, even though none of you personally have invested a penny in Greece.

In this era of electronic trading, money travels at the speed of light across national borders with little regulation. The global financial system is an interconnected web that links our economic fates together as closely as our Facebook pages. When Greece or Italy can't pay their bills, there are few places to hide. We learned that lesson a few years ago when homeowners in Florida, Nevada and Arizona began missing their monthly mortgage payments.

There certainly wasn't any cover to be found inside the walls of a Canadian investment bank. Why do you think I'm an author now?

I spent nearly twenty years as chief economist of CIBC World Markets, a major Canadian investment bank with clients and operations around the world. It was certainly a good way to earn a living. Global investors are constantly grappling with changing financial conditions, which puts the services of a chief economist in high demand. One week you're advising sovereign wealth funds in exotic locales such as Kuwait or Singapore, and the next you're back in North America telling heavyweight pension funds how economic events will impact stocks, bonds and currencies. On other days, you're visiting global financial capitals and eating at nice restaurants with powerful portfolio managers and high-ranking government officials.

The press frequently chases you for comments, which opens up an entirely different aspect of the job. A chief economist is a de facto spokesperson for a bank's position, whether or not that's something either party really wants. Ultimately, it was that part of the job that forced me to rethink my two-decade-long career.

I remember the moment it dawned on me that big life changes could be on the way. It was a cold November night and I was flying back to Toronto on the bank's corporate plane with

Gerry McCaughey, CIBC's chief executive, and other senior bank officials. We had just left Montreal after hosting a dinner for the CEOs of some big Quebec corporate customers. A dozen or so top executives from prominent companies had come to a posh club in old Montreal to hear what we had to say. I led off with some opening thoughts about the economy. Then we went around the table to hear each CEO talk about what was happening with their firm and in their industry. After an elaborate meal (washed down with a memorable vintage Bordeaux), McCaughey concluded the evening with remarks on the bank's strategy and objectives. And then we headed for the airport.

Over the years, I'd crisscrossed the country on the corporate jet to speak at dozens of similar dinners. This time, though, I had a lot more on the line.

Earlier in the year, I had written an essay on the shifting pattern of global oil demand for an anthology about the future of energy consumption, and the publisher had asked me if I would be interested in turning it into a book. I figured I should take a crack at it, so for months leading up to that night in Montreal, most of my free time had been spent plugging away at a manuscript for a book on the global economy. I didn't know how it would turn out, but by the time I finished the manuscript, publishers in Canada, the United States and the United Kingdom were on board and I was excited about becoming a first-time author. But there was a hitch: I hadn't yet told anybody at CIBC what I was doing.

I had been thinking that CIBC might embrace my book, *Why Your World Is About to Get a Whole Lot Smaller*. I even thought the bank's brokerage arm, Wood Gundy, would be a natural marketing outlet. Prior to talking to McCaughey on the airplane, I had negotiated a bulk discount from my publisher in case any Wood Gundy brokers or other CIBC staff wanted to give a copy to clients. In retrospect, it was a naive expectation. I could tell from McCaughey's initial reaction as we flew through the night sky toward Toronto that I might have to seriously re-think my future.

I learned several things on the plane that night—among them, that you don't get to be CEO of a major Canadian bank without knowing how to turn a withering stare on an employee. After hearing my pitch, McCaughey replied curtly that I would need to get permission from the legal department. His icy look alone was enough to get me second-guessing my future at the bank.

I can't say I was surprised when the bank's lawyers sent down word four months later that permission would be denied. Economists at big banks do publish books, but most often the subject matter is along the lines of how your retirement savings can out-perform the stock market. Mine was about how triple-digit oil prices were going to reverse globalization. CIBC doesn't sell oil, and it sure doesn't sell de-globalization.

Looking back, I realize that McCaughey was only doing his job, which was to protect the bank's interests. But I didn't write the book so that it wouldn't get read. I'd been preaching its themes to whoever would listen at CIBC for years. It was time to take the message to a broader audience.

By the time I stepped away from the job, CIBC had much bigger things to worry about than my literary ambitions. At the time, the bank, like many financial institutions, was knee-deep in fancy financial market derivatives called collateralized debt obligations (CDOs). Prior to the housing market crash, CDOs, which are backed by assets such as homeowner subprime mort-gages, were making investors a ton of money. They also seemed to be relatively safe investments, at least according to rating agencies that granted many of these debt instruments gold-plated Triple-A status. But when mortgage holders who took on too much debt stopped making payments, the market imploded in a hurry. CIBC, for one, had to write down billions due to its CDO exposure.

How could so many smart bankers have stumbled down this path? One critical factor was losing sight of how rating agencies make money. They don't get paid by investors who base decisions on their ratings, but by the issuers of the securities that are being rated. Big agencies such as Standard & Poor's, Moody's and Fitch have a vested interest in keeping the folks who pay the bills happy. In economics we use the term *moral hazard* to describe a situation in which the interests of two parties entering into an agreement aren't aligned. The way debt rating agencies are compensated, they have an incentive to hand out generous ratings while at the same time they're insulated from the negative consequences of being wrong. That's a dangerous combination.

Investment bankers will tell you that steering clear of moral hazard requires keeping your head up and your eyes open. When the housing market crashed, CIBC and other financial institutions were caught skating across the ice with their heads down. They paid dearly for it on the bottom line. I must confess that CIBC's dwindling stock price, which shrank the value of the unvested bank shares and of the annual bonus I left behind, made my transition from long-serving Bay Street economist to fledgling author much easier to handle.

The experience also left me with a more jaded perspective on Canadian financial institutions than the one the country's politicians sell to the rest of the world. Canada's finance minister, Jim Flaherty, often holds up the nation's banks, and their regulatory supervision, as shining examples of why we don't need a radical reform of the global financial system. To be fair to Flaherty, other banks around the world had a more disastrous ride than Canadian institutions. My former bank may have sunk shareholders, but at least it didn't sink taxpayers. Nor did any of Canada's other big banks. Elsewhere, financial institutions such as the Anglo Irish Bank, based in Dublin, took part in blowing up entire national economies while leaving taxpayers to pick up the bill.

Discovering the nature of a disease is the first step to finding a cure. What's true for medicine also applies to the economy. Understanding the reasons for the last recession is critically important if we want to avoid another financial crisis.

—

I can still see Scott Stevens hitting Eric Lindros in game seven of the National Hockey League's Eastern Conference finals. Lindros carried the puck across the blue line with his head down and Stevens, maybe the hardest hitter of his generation, lowered his shoulder and delivered a check that's still talked about by hockey fans more than a decade later.

Lindros had been anointed as the next Wayne Gretzky while he was still playing minor hockey as a teenager. Even watching Lindros at fourteen, scouts knew his package of size, speed and skill made him a can't-miss prospect. And they were right. Lindros won a Memorial Cup with the Oshawa Generals, a pair of gold medals at the World Junior Hockey Championships, and an Olympic medal, all before lacing up his skates in the NHL. Selected first overall in the 1991 NHL entry draft, by the time Lindros landed with the Philadelphia Flyers he was on track to go down among the best ever to play the game.

But even before he lay crumpled on the ice after the Stevens hit, Lindros's career was already off the rails. He had just returned to the ice after missing thirty games with a concussion sustained in the regular season. Game seven was his second game back in uniform. His career lasted for several years after that hit, but many hockey fans believe he was never the same.

Pittsburgh Penguins captain Sidney Crosby was the next prodigious hockey talent to be ordained the new Gretzky. As they did with Lindros, fans have followed Crosby since he was a child. Like Lindros, he was also the first overall pick in the draft, and he became a national treasure after scoring the overtime goal against the United States that won the gold medal for Canada in the 2010 Vancouver Olympics. And like Lindros's career, Crosby's could be derailed by concussions. He's back at the top of the game now, but it's hard to forget how much he struggled to get back on the ice after suffering a concussion in early 2011. Some still say he should keep away from the game altogether for the good of his long-term health.

A rash of concussion-related misfortune has turned head trauma into a major issue for both the NHL and the National Football League. The summer of 2011 saw the deaths of three former or current NHL enforcers, each of whom battled problems stemming from concussions. The NFL is also dealing with several deaths that are being linked to concussions, including that of former star linebacker Junior Seau. The league is being sued by seventy-five former players who allege that it's been concealing the harmful effects of concussions since the 1920s.

Head injuries are now an unavoidable issue for both leagues. But concussions are only part of a much larger picture. The NHL and the NFL need to understand the true nature of the problem and take steps to change it. Players are bigger and faster than ever before. These days, kids are barely out of the womb before they're on sport-specific regimens that include weight training, protein-rich diets and missing school for far-flung road trips with their teams. A modern-day NFL safety hits like a human missile, often making helmet-to-helmet contact with a defenseless receiver. Likewise, a body check from a 230-pound NHL defenseman is like getting run over by a pickup truck.

Modern equipment that is lightweight and ultra-strong only amplifies the problem. Designed to offer protection from injury, today's shoulder pads, elbow pads and football helmets have actually turned players into weapons. As with the introduction of boxing gloves at the turn of the century, the evolution of professional sports has come with unforeseen consequences. Bigger, armor-padded combatants playing at faster speeds have made traumatic brain injuries systemic to sport. A season in a professional league is now a war of attrition; the question isn't if players will get hurt, but when.

So-called purists argue that big hits are part of the game. I've split a pair of season tickets to the Toronto Maple Leafs for years and enjoy a good hit as much as anyone, but when hardly a week passes without a professional athlete suffering a major head injury, it becomes clear that something is wrong. The leagues are reluctant to overhaul the rules for fear of alienating fans. But not recognizing that the world has changed is just sticking your head in the sand. Lindros played 813 games in the NHL, but most were sadly short of his full potential. Crosby's career may be abbreviated in his mid-twenties. How many more transcendent talents does the game need to lose before it wakes up?

The changes needed aren't just cosmetic. Over the years, players have lost a fundamental respect for their opponents. Does every off-balance skater have to be crushed into the boards? Do linebackers need to deliver kill shots to every helpless receiver who's going to the ground anyway? The Darwinian ethos of today's sports culture won't be easy to change. Professional leagues need to lead by example, and coaches must teach kids from an early age that winning is one thing, but winning at all costs is another. Concussions are a problem, but the real issues run much deeper.

What's true for professional sports applies equally to the world of international finance. To fully understand the precarious state of the global economy, the financial world needs to wake up to the idea that the last recession was much like a concussion: it hurt a lot, but it's not the real issue.

In *Why Your World Is About to Get a Whole Lot Smaller*, I argued that the US housing market wasn't responsible for blowing up the global economy. It was a symptom, not the cause. Federal Reserve chairman Alan Greenspan was spurred to hike interest rates by soaring oil prices, which were stirring inflation. Higher interest rates pricked the housing bubble, and the rest of the world was dragged down when the bubble burst.

The Fed's new chairman, Ben Bernanke, appears to be undeterred by the policy failures of his predecessor. His efforts to stimulate economic growth with rock-bottom interest rates and trillion-dollar quantitative easing programs will prove just as unsuccessful as Greenspan's attempts to keep the economy afloat. Bernanke believes that holding interest rates near zero will encourage Americans to spend money, particularly on new homes. But what's holding back the housing market isn't the cost of taking out a mortgage, but a lack of jobs and economic growth. And that has little to do with the Fed's monetary policy. The real culprit lies somewhere else.

The same factor that caused the last recession is ready to deep-six the global economy once again. And this time the economic shock will be greater than we saw last time around. The cost of oil is like an economic anchor. And make no mistake, higher energy prices aren't a symptom of our economic problems—they're the cause. The price of Brent crude, the de facto oil benchmark used in pricing almost three-quarters of the oil traded in the world, crossed the triple-digit threshold in early 2011, and it hasn't looked back since. Even West Texas Intermediate, the US-based price, is trading around $100 a barrel. And these oil prices won't fall until they trigger another global recession—one that will last much longer than just a few quarters.

Of course, there is at least one group that's content to see triple-digit prices, and that's Big Oil. High prices are inspiring oilmen to scour the earth like never before. They're drilling miles beneath the ocean floor, leveling boreal forests to dig up tar sands, and learning how to get at oil that's trapped in shale rock. Meanwhile, Western governments are swarming around the Middle East, even launching a couple of military invasions, in a bid to get their hands on every last drop of the region's treasure trove of oil before it too is sucked dry.

The cost of tapping the extra energy we need to fuel our econ-omies is mounting for both our wallets and the environment. Catastrophic environmental events, such as BP's Macondo well leak in the Gulf of Mexico or the nuclear accident at Fukushima, are happening with alarming frequency. Each one illustrates just how far we're pushing the limits of our energy consumption.

Even more unnerving, neither BP nor the Tokyo Electric Power Company (TEPCO) had any idea what to do when di-saster struck. At one point, BP engineers tried to plug the gush-ing Macondo well with golf balls. The multinational oil giant, regarded as one of the industry's best deepwater drillers, has yet to explain the advanced engineering theory behind that failed procedure. When the Fukushima reactors were flooded by a tsunami, TEPCO's nuclear technicians scrambled into nearby neighborhoods to borrow flashlights so they could read control panels. Such jerry-rigged operational responses hardly instill confidence in the failsafe nature of our global energy system.

How many once-in-a-century accidents have to happen before we recognize that they've become the norm and not the exception? And if we accept them as the norm, what does that say about our relentless quest for more energy?

We can't continue to increase our energy consumption exponentially without expecting to pay ever-greater costs. Even as our attempts become more desperate, it's easy to understand why we keep trying. When we stop finding new sources of energy, our economies stop growing.

Growth is the Holy Grail of modern societies. It's the common denominator underlying nearly every action taken by corporations and governments. Whether it's the sales manager at your local electronics store, the developer of a new housing project or a finance minister trying to close a huge budget deficit, each one prays at the altar of growth. Economic expansion comes in all shapes and sizes. It can be spotted in the building cranes above your city's skyline, in the bustle of shoppers at the mall on a busy Saturday and in the freshly turned sod of a new subdivision. All of this activity feeds into Gross Domestic Product (GDP), the total measure of what a country's economy produces each year.

Of course, growth also comes with a lot of costs. Without growth, we could stop building new highways for the burgeoning number of new vehicles that hit the road every year. We wouldn't have to build more nuclear energy facilities or coal-fired power plants to meet our expanding electricity needs. We could stop our cities from sprawling into the countryside to make room for new suburbanites. And we could cut back on the amount of greenhouse gases we emit into the atmosphere.

For the economics profession, the notion of a world without growth is pure science fiction. While most economists now acknowledge that expensive energy curtails GDP, the majority also believe that technological innovations will allow us to leap over the hurdles presented by resource scarcity.

Historians take a different view. The decline of the Roman Empire has captured the world's imagination for centuries, as has the collapse of Mayan society and the disappearance of people from Easter Island. Indeed, history is the story of the rise and fall of civilizations large and small. The exact reasons for social collapse are rarely known, but many theories cite resource scarcity as a contributing factor. Whether constraints on resources, such as food and water, is the driving reason behind societal failures will remain lost in the mists of time, but one thing is indisputable: civilizations that once flourished have eventually floundered. But most economists these days seem to have short memories. Viewed from the limited perspective of the postwar era, resource constraints, and a scarcity of fossil fuels in particular, appear to them to be no match for human ingenuity, which keeps finding ways to supply the world with more energy. However, rising resource prices are telling us that technological advancements are struggling to keep pace.

We could hardly pick a worse time for higher energy costs to start squeezing the growth out of the global economy. The modern world counts on economic growth to support population expansion, as well as satisfy the desire for higher incomes and all the extra things that money can buy. Since the last recession, the need for GDP growth has become even more urgent. Economic growth will provide the financial wherewithal that allows governments to service the debts accumulated during that downturn. Right now, though, the global economy is discovering that chasing growth is a catch-22. Our countries need GDP growth to repay the debt acquired during the last oil price–induced recession, but achieving that growth will bring back the same high prices that killed growth in the first place.

Finding the energy to fuel our economies is no longer enough; we need that energy to be affordable. That's why the oil industry is going to such lengths to tap the world's resources. That's why we're changing dictatorial regimes in Libya, propping up an absolutist monarchy in Saudi Arabia, digging up pristine forests in northern Alberta and drilling beneath the icy waters of the Arctic Ocean.

In the United States, the Obama administration, which just fined BP billions for the Macondo fiasco, is back issuing permits for deepwater exploration in the Gulf of Mexico. I guess the White House is betting other offshore drillers will have better luck contending with the ultrahigh pressures at the bottom of the ocean. On the other side of the world, China is building new nuclear plants in coastal areas that are prone to the same magnitude of earthquake that caused the Fukushima disaster. Beijing is undoubtedly hoping for a luckier roll of the dice when the next seismic event occurs.

The choice currently being made by most politicians simply to cross their fingers and hope for the best is hardly a sound way to deal with mounting energy costs. And in any event, the solution to higher energy prices won't come from finding larger oil reserves or building more nuclear plants. Nor will it come from a technological breakthrough in renewable energy. We aren't going to suddenly discover that solar panels or wind turbines hold a magic key that will power our economies. Instead, the solution to higher energy costs is quite simple: learn to use less energy. That doesn't mean returning to the Stone Age. As you'll see in this book, people in some countries, such as Denmark, live quite happily while also using a lot less energy. And you may be surprised to find out what's at the heart of that country's success.

The sooner more nations learn how to curb energy demand, the better it will be for everyone. In a world of energy scarcity, consuming more fuel comes at someone else's expense. One country's gain is another's loss. It's a pending reality that will affect how much oil everyone gets to burn from now on. And if you live in North America or western Europe, you can expect your fuel allotment to be much more modest than it's been for the last few decades.

The prospect of burning less oil may sound benign, but it carries profound economic consequences. Oil powers economic growth. That means if we cut back on oil, we cut back on growth. In a post-carbon world, our economies may run on a different fuel, but for now they're still critically dependent on oil, and will continue to be so for the foreseeable future.

Over time, our economies will become greener and more efficient. That's the hope, anyway. In the last forty years, we've made massive gains in fuel efficiency in places such as North America, western Europe and Japan. But at the same time, economic growth and a rising global population have meant that our total energy consumption has become greater than ever before. And now emerging economic giants such as China and India are looking to claim a larger share of global energy supply. Hundreds of millions of Chinese and Indians are moving from rural lives, where they consumed sparse amounts of fuel, to energy-intensive urban lifestyles. As these folks fill up the gas tanks of their brand-new cars and flip on light switches in their new apartments, how will the world keep pace with the fresh demand for energy?

One day, we may come up with a fuel alternative that will allow our energy consumption to increase by leaps and bounds. Renewable energy certainly has room to become a larger part of our power mix, and thanks to technological advances, that's exactly what's happening right now. But renewable energy won't come close to supplying the power we need to shelter us from the consequences of ever-higher oil prices. In the here and now, our economic fates are still unavoidably tied to fossil fuels.

No matter how much crude we're able to pull out of the ground, oil prices keep marching higher. Every year, the world notches more economic growth, which means each year the global economy needs more barrels of oil to keep running smoothly. As oil continues to get more expensive, the question is how much longer we can count on economic expansion to continue. And if growth grinds to a halt, what will that mean for the world? Will a static global economy cause our standard of living to regress? Or does this lurking new reality have other dimensions that might soften the blow?

Many folks are already questioning whether the boundless pursuit of personal consumption is really the key to a sense of well-being, particularly when we see the toll our ravenous lifestyles take on the planet. Countries that rank the highest on the United Nations' Index of Human Development don't have the largest or fastest-growing economies. Could there be a lesson there?

Maybe we can live with less GDP growth and not feel the poorer for it. The Germans have been learning to job-share, and it seems to be working fine for them. But that's in the developed world. In the developing world, millions of people struggle to put food on the table and keep a roof over their heads. These countries aren't working with much of a buffer. If GDP growth stagnates, what happens to the burgeoning populations inside the borders of poor nations?

What will China's and India's increasing consumption of the world's natural resources mean for them? Is their appetite for energy sustainable? And if it's not, what are the consequences for the amount of fuel left over for the rest of us? China and India are the locomotives of global economic growth. If they stall, how will that affect economies that have spent a decade riding on their coattails?

However uncertain the future appears, we know one thing for sure: a world of energy scarcity will be dramatically different from the world we have known. Yet when we look ahead, it's difficult to envision a future that offers such a stark contrast to our energy-abundant past. Ready or not, though, we'll soon have no choice.

The standard of living in the Western world has leapt far beyond what our parents and grandparents knew. In the coming years, it will be much more challenging for our children to achieve similar gains. Tomorrow's kids won't live in as many square feet of space, own as many flat-screen televisions or have as many cars in the driveway. But for all the material things they give up, they may be compensated in other ways.

Energy scarcity could become the environment's best friend. In the last few years, the world has been hit with record droughts that have pushed food prices sky-high. Could a permanent slow-down in economic growth be exactly what the climate change doctor ordered?

Of course, we'll still need to figure out how to feed the 10 billion people the UN forecasts will be sharing the planet by the end of the century. Will this projected human population meet a Malthusian fate, or can we navigate our way to a brighter future?

The shape of the world to come is still very much up for grabs. Living in a static economy will be much different than living in the world we've come to know. Even those of us in affluent countries in North America and Europe will have to start making real changes before long—and many Europeans are getting a taste of that future right now.

We'll undoubtedly encounter more than a few surprises along the way. I'm betting some of them will be big enough to change the way we judge this new world. The stakes are high, and we can't afford to lose, but we also have much to gain.

PART
ONE

CHANGING THE ECONOMIC SPEED LIMIT

THOSE WHO WERE AROUND IN THE 1970s will remember when speed limits were lowered in an attempt to stop drivers from burning so much gasoline. In the United States, the first OPEC oil shock spooked the president so much that he established a national speed limit of fifty-five miles per hour through the Emergency Energy Conservation Act. A slower speed limit didn't win Richard Nixon any fans among car-loving voters, but his hand was forced by oil prices that were punishing the US economy.

Well, speed limits aren't the only thing that can change when crude prices go up. Today's oil prices are changing the speed at which economies can grow. Just as people require food, economies require energy. The relationship is straightforward: economic growth is a function of energy consumption, full stop. And without question, the most important source of energy for the global economy is oil.

For most of the last century that worked out just fine. Cheap oil allowed global economic growth to keep marching higher. But in the last decade, that's all changed. Triple-digit oil prices are now forcing economies to downshift into a much lower gear. For some of the world's biggest economies, expensive oil means shifting all the way into park.

That's not a message most of us want to hear. Instead of making hard choices, we tinker around the edges. We order a new transmission, when it's the whole engine that's cooked. Making the wrong call on your car is bad enough; it's a whole lot worse when governments get the entire economic picture wrong. And right now that's exactly what's happening: governments around the world are being led astray by the belief that their economies are operating well short of their potential.

Sounds innocent enough, doesn't it? It's not. An economy's potential growth rate may be the single most important thing policymakers need to gauge. If they don't get it right, a lot of other things will go terribly wrong.

Central banks and finance ministries measure an economy's potential growth rate to help keep a country running smoothly. Economists look at two basic factors to gauge an economy's potential. The first is productivity growth, most often defined as the change in output per person. The second is labor force growth. Add the two together and you get an economy's potential growth rate.

It works like this. If productivity is growing at 2 percent a year and the labor force is growing at 1 percent a year, then the sum of the two numbers gives a sense of your country's potential rate of GDP growth. In this case, 1 percent plus 2 percent equals 3 percent. That means your economy can happily grow by 3 percent a year. Any higher and inflation will kick in; any lower and it's a good bet that more people will soon find themselves unemployed. The Federal Reserve Board pegs the US economy's potential growth rate at around 3 percent. Similarly, the Bank of Canada believes the Canadian economy can notch annual growth of 3 percent without running into problems.

When you hear Fed chairman Ben Bernanke or Mark Carney, the new head of the Bank of England and former Bank of Canada governor, talk about sustainability, they're not referring to an environmental initiative; they're discussing potential growth. These central bankers believe that an economy growing at less than its ideal rate means there's slack in the system. What do I mean by slack? Well, on the productivity side of the equation, it could mean that factories are working at less than full capacity. A weak order book, for example, could mean a plant runs one shift a day instead of two. Slack can also show up in the form of a company shelving plans for a new factory until sales improve. In terms of the labor force, slack means that more companies are laying off workers and fewer companies are hiring new ones. In an economy not working up to its potential, the unemployment rate will climb, while the jobs-wanted index shrinks.

If an economy is expanding above its potential growth rate, a whole other set of issues is created. On one hand, strong growth probably means the unemployment rate is falling, which is generally considered a good thing. But a fully employed population has a lot of cash to spend. That results in a lot of money chasing a limited supply of goods and services. In an economy cranking beyond its growth potential, factories are already working overtime, meaning the option to simply make more stuff to meet that demand isn't available.

Under these conditions, workers have the bargaining power to command top dollar from desperate employers, which only fuels inflation. Consider, for example, what happened in northern Alberta in the middle of the last decade. In a bid to take advantage of soaring oil prices, energy companies accelerated plans for billions of dollars' worth of construction projects in the province's tar sands. All that spending drew thousands of workers from around

Canada and the world to the city of Fort McMurray. Even with the influx of people, a limited pool of workers chasing an abundance of jobs sent wages through the roof. And it wasn't just oil-patch jobs proper; even kids pouring coffee at the local Tim Hortons were getting retention bonuses for staying more than three months. Fort McMurray's economy boomed past its potential growth rate, which pushed the cost of living beyond that of cities ten times its size. A zero percent vacancy rate in the city's rental market meant that transplanted workers, if they could find a room, were forced to pay triple what they would in Calgary, Vancouver or Toronto. Some new arrivals were even desperate enough to pay top dollar to rent out garage space from locals. Despite high wages, the numbers of the city's working poor swelled, as did the number of squatters living in the surrounding woods. In Fort McMurray, the insidious effects of inflation meant that some workers who relocated to take advantage of a seemingly can't-lose opportunity actually wound up in a situation that was economically untenable. Regardless of where you are in the world, when prices start rising faster than incomes, all those people working hard to get ahead are actually getting poorer.

For the economists who preside over a country's financial well-being, understanding where an economy is positioned in relation to its potential level of output is critical to determining how it should be managed. If there's slack, policymakers see a green light to add stimulus, which they believe will lead to growth without an undue risk of inflation. If an economy is already operating close to its potential, then stimulus measures will only bring about inflation rather than additional growth.

Here's where things get really interesting.

The difference between an economy's potential growth rate and what the economy is actually producing is known as an output gap. The bigger the gap, the more policymakers believe they need to step on the gas to try to close it. This is part of the economic theory behind the regular interest rate pronouncements you hear from such bankers as Bernanke and Carney. The Fed, for instance, estimates the US economy, in the wake of the 2008 recession, is operating as much as 6 percent below its potential level of GDP. Armed with a belief that the economy is underperforming, the Fed, in December 2012, took the unprecedented step of tying future interest rate decisions to job creation. Until unemployment, which is staying doggedly above 7 percent, drops to 6.5 percent, the Fed plans to keep rates unchanged. That means rates will likely stay near zero until at least 2015. The Fed is rarely so precise, typically preferring to use language that leaves more wiggle room to adapt to the ever-fluid conditions of the national economy. By assuring the market that rates will stay at zero percent (as long as inflation stays around 2 percent), the Fed is trying to instill borrowers with enough long-term confidence to take out loans that will be used to spur economic activity.

Conventional economic wisdom suggests that rock-bottom interest rates are the proper remedy for a struggling economy. And the Fed isn't alone in its prognosis. Judging by potential economic growth, many countries in Europe and North America appear to be struggling to close output gaps that are wide enough to drive a truck through. The culprit seems obvious: rising unemployment. Considering that jobless rates in some of the world's wealthiest nations, such as the thirty-four countries that belong to the Organisation for Economic Co-operation and Development (OECD), are almost double what they were a decade ago, it's easy to understand why so many government number crunchers believe there must be a tremendous amount of idle capacity in their economies.

But that thinking misses a crucial piece of the economic puzzle. A decade ago, oil cost $20 a barrel, a fraction of what it does today. Remember the equation for an economy's potential growth rate? The two components were productivity and labor. The price of oil doesn't enter into the calculations governments use to determine how much stimulus is needed to help stir a flagging economy. If it did, central bankers from Bernanke and Carney to Mario Draghi of the European Central Bank would be far less eager to use monetary policy to increase the amount of money circulating through the system. Politicians, meanwhile, would also be more hesitant to approve fiscal measures, such as stimulus packages and deficit spending, that are designed to boost employment and spur economic growth. All told, the economists pulling the levers on the global economy are unleashing a massive amount of stimulus into the world. But what if the game has changed? What if they're using the wrong tools for the task at hand?

Could the best-educated economic minds in the world really be so far off course? In a word—yes.

But it's not without good reason. Yardsticks such as potential economic output have helped OECD economies achieve an impressive track record of growth throughout the postwar era. A half century of success certainly helps to breed confidence. Throwing out what has been a winning formula is tough to do under the best of circumstances, let alone when the harsh new reality of world oil markets I'm about to describe may seem far from certain.

What we do know with certainty is that oil prices have quadrupled over the last ten years. You don't need to look any further than the nearest gas station for evidence of this sharp step change in the cost of energy. It's a shift that will permanently shackle the growth potential of the world's oil-burning economies.

Finance ministers and central bankers have already spent billions of your tax dollars to try to boost flagging economic growth. But the problem they're attempting to fix has been misdiagnosed using the wrong tools. When you change the price of oil, you change the economy's speed limit. Until we realize the implications of slower economic growth, we won't be able to make choices that will help us deal with this new reality.

THE CAUTION FLAG IS WAVING, BUT IS ANYONE PAYING ATTENTION?

So what do we know about this new world of higher energy costs?

To begin with, the countries guzzling the most oil are taking the biggest hits to potential economic growth. That's sobering news for the United States, which consumes almost a fifth of the oil used in the world every day. Not long ago, when oil was $20 a barrel, the United States was the locomotive of global economic growth. Washington was running budget surpluses. The jobless rate at the beginning of the last decade was at a forty-year low. Around the country, people slept soundly knowing that dreams of early retirement were almost in reach, as the value of their savings increased with each record high notched by the Dow.

That seems like a lifetime ago, not just ten years. Economic growth in the United States is now struggling to get off the mat. Its budget deficit is more than a trillion dollars and there are around 12 million Americans without jobs. At the same time as America's economy was deteriorating, world oil prices were quadrupling. This is not a coincidence.

And the United States isn't the only country getting squeezed by higher energy costs. From Europe to Japan, governments are scrambling to get GDP growth back on its feet. But the economic remedies being used are actually doing more harm than good, based as they are on a fundamental belief that economic growth can return to its former glory. During those salad days, it stands to be repeated, oil was around $20 a barrel. Leading central bankers and policymakers have failed to fully recognize the suffocating impact of $100-a-barrel oil on economic growth. Running huge budget deficits and keeping borrowing costs at record lows are only compounding current problems. It's throwing good money after bad.

Maybe it's hope or maybe it's denial, but world governments are still clinging to the idea that the good times of renewed and steady growth are right around the corner. And no country is hungrier for economic growth to resume than the United States. That desire is spurring Washington into running a trillion-dollar budget deficit, while leading the Fed to peg interest rates at zero in an attempt to induce an economic turnaround. By any historical benchmark, these are extreme actions. The US budget deficit, as a percentage of GDP, hasn't been this high since the country went into hock to fight the Second World War. There isn't much more the American public could ask the Treasury Department or the Fed to do that isn't already being done.

But neither huge budget deficits nor zero interest rates are long-term substitutes for cheap oil. In the end, an economy can't grow if it can no longer afford to burn the fuel it runs on. Of course, throw enough money at any situation and it will make a splash. When the water settles, though, nothing has really changed. The reality is that the price of oil has lowered the economy's speed limit. The Fed can continue printing American dollars at a dizzying clip, but no amount of monetary or fiscal pump-priming will change that basic economic reality. The sooner central bankers and finance ministers realize that, the better off we'll be.

Massive budget deficits and rock-bottom interest rates are the wrong prescription for the realities of the energy-constrained world we now live in. The US stimulus package in 2009 approved more than $700 billion in spending that was designed to kick-start a recovery. That money has put people to work and will help improve the country's infrastructure, but eventually it must be repaid. In the final analysis, the spending amounts to a very expensive short-term patch. Such policy measures, which are being enacted in the eurozone as well as the United States, are burdening national economies with a crushing amount of debt. If policymakers don't start making the right calls soon, an already bad economic situation will become that much worse.

ECONOMISTS ARE HOOKED ON GROWTH

I suppose it's only natural for central banks and finance departments to hold on tight to the idea of economic growth. For starters, growth is a top priority for politicians who, by definition, are constantly chasing reelection. A sick economy is a surefire way to lose voters.

But the bias toward chasing growth runs even deeper. Central banks and treasury departments are, after all, chock full of economists who are taught from the first day of class to treat growth as gospel. It's stamped into an economist's DNA. As an undergraduate student at the University of Toronto, nearly every economics exam I wrote dealt with the idea of maximizing economic growth. The tune stayed the same at McGill University, where I went to graduate school. It wasn't until I had years of real-world experience under my belt as chief economist of an investment bank that I began to understand what the textbooks were missing. The task of investing my own money is one thing, but the responsibility of guiding other people's investment decisions spurred me to challenge even my most basic economic assumptions. After watching GDP growth shrink in the face of steadily rising oil prices, I couldn't escape the notion that growth might someday become finite. During my formal training, steeped in conventional economic theory, the idea of static growth was never even considered. It doesn't matter which school of economic thought you subscribe to or where you belong on the ideological spectrum, the notion of growth is an unquestioned tenet of the discipline.

If you're from the University of Chicago, once home to the high priest of laissez-faire economics, Milton Friedman, you believe that a pause in economic growth, such as a recession, is a temporary event. Leave the market alone to do its work and the economy will get back on track. This was the line of thinking behind the economic policies of Ronald Reagan and Margaret Thatcher in the 1980s that drastically reduced the role of government. To free-market acolytes, an issue like rising joblessness isn't a problem so much as a hiccup. High unemployment rates force workers to lower wage demands until it becomes profitable for someone to hire them. It's the market (and certainly not tax-and-spend liberals in government) that will get an economy growing again, the thinking goes.

If you're from the Keynesian school of thought made famous at Cambridge University, you believe that recessions are remedied through government intervention. Modern-day Keynesians such as *New York Times* columnist and Princeton University professor Paul Krugman are outspoken proponents of stimulus spending. Krugman, for example, believes Obama's stimulus efforts are far too small to get the job done. He advocates even more government spending on new public works projects, such as bridges, highways and tunnels. Another path favored by Keynesians is slashing interest rates to encourage borrowing, which will lead to spending that will revive the national economy. Without such interventionist steps, Keynesian economists believe a recession can deepen into a long period of painful contraction, like the Great Depression of the 1930s.

Whether you're a free-market type or you believe in government intervention, your common ground with most economists is an unswerving belief in growth as the panacea of all economic ills. From the first page of your Economics 101 textbook to the last page of your Ph.D. dissertation, the discipline teaches you that an economy's trajectory is always upward.

The postwar era has given economists few reasons to doubt their faith in limitless economic expansion. Since the Second World War, the global economy has been in recession only 20 percent of the time. The rest of the time, it's been expanding. That's a pretty persuasive run. Over that stretch, each time a recession took hold, our economies found a way to start growing again. Consider what happened in the early 1980s during one of the worst recessions in recent US history. In a bid to fight inflation that was spiraling upward due to higher energy costs, Fed chairman Paul Volcker hiked interest rates to more than 20 percent. Inflation was eventually tamed, but the measures, which put the kibosh on lending and borrowing, also squeezed economic activity to the breaking point. Unemployment soared to the highest levels since the 1930s, home sales plummeted and GDP tumbled. By 1983, though, the economy was firmly back on track. The Fed dropped interest rates to single-digit levels and GDP grew steadily for the rest of the decade. That recession caused considerable pain, but it also followed the pattern we've all come to expect from the business cycle: an economy expands until it reaches a peak. It then contracts into a recession, hits a trough, and starts back on the road to recovery. That's what happened during the recession in the early 1990s and again in the first few years of the 2000s. In the postwar era, even the deepest recessions have rarely lasted more than a year.

But what happens if this new economic downturn isn't just one of those cyclical events? What if the global economy is entering an era where static growth is the new normal? In short, what will happen if our economies stop growing? Well, we're going to find out, because that scenario is about to unfold.

The end of economic growth means governments will need to radically change how economies are managed. Right now, fiscal and monetary policy are the two principal levers governments pull to keep economies growing at a healthy pace. But with oil prices around triple digits a barrel, yesterday's economic policy standbys won't work anymore. What's worse, those policies aren't just ineffective, but the soaring deficits actually burden our future with more debt. The fiscal pump-priming being implemented by finance departments and central banks simply buys us short reprieves. Any apparent financial recoveries are a mirage. When the smoke clears, oil prices will still be dictating the economic terms. Unfortunately, the huge deficits we've run up since the last recession are very real bills that will need to be paid.

Central banks are running printing presses almost nonstop to kick-start economic growth. In the United States, the Fed calls this tactic "quantitative easing"—a fancy way of saying the Fed is finding ways to pour as much new money into the system as it can. Typically, the Fed sticks to using its control over short-term interest rates to help strengthen the economy. But with those interest rates already at zero, Bernanke and Co. have needed to reach further into their bag of tricks. Under its program of quantitative easing, the Fed is buying longer-term government bonds in an attempt to inject new life into the economy. It works like this: By buying up US Treasury bonds, the Fed is trying to bring down long-term interest rates. A lower rate of return on long-term government bonds, considered a relatively safe haven in times of financial uncertainty, makes other investments more attractive by comparison. Investors typically park huge sums of cash in long-term US bonds in an attempt to ride out a financial storm. By lowering the returns on those bonds, the Fed is trying to steer money into other parts of the financial system where it can do more good for the economy.

As part of its quantitative easing program, the Fed also entered the market for mortgage-backed securities. Buying these securities allows the Fed to effectively lower mortgage rates, which reduces borrowing costs for potential homeowners, a move the Fed hopes will help to stimulate the housing market.

By engineering a more modest return on government bonds, the Fed is also trying to curb the giant appetite for US dollars among global bond investors. A decreased demand for US greenbacks naturally leads to a weaker currency, which is a boon for the country's export sector. It also favors products made in the USA over imported goods. When US goods become cheaper at home and abroad, factories start to hum, which gives rise to more manufacturing jobs.

The Fed believes that implementing such expansionary monetary policy will keep the United States from falling into an even deeper recession than the one faced in 2008. But quantitative easing is based on the conventional economic thinking that a return to growth is just around the corner. What's really standing in the way of growth is the cost of oil. And oil prices aren't coming down regardless of how much money is put into circulation. Fiscal and monetary policies need to be recalibrated to account for the economy's slower potential growth rate. But neither politicians nor average citizens want to hear that slower growth is here to stay. A booming economy makes for wonderful times. Jobs are plentiful. Property values rise. The stock market clocks double-digit gains. Wages go up. The world feels like your oyster. Why would we want to get off that ride if we don't have to?

OIL IS THE FUEL OF GROWTH

Why exactly is oil so special? For starters, it provides more than a third of the energy we use on the planet every day. That's more than any other energy source. But even that statistic doesn't come close to capturing oil's importance to the world. Where oil is truly indispensable to the global economy is as a transit fuel.

More than two-thirds of every barrel of oil produced goes toward transportation, whether it's in the form of gasoline, diesel, jet or bunker fuel. Planes, trains, cars, trucks, ships and even motorbikes all run on oil. Take away oil and we'll need to come up with another 6 billion ten-speeds and a whole lot of kayaks to help folks get around.

Just how unique is oil? Oil can be stored. It doesn't spoil. It can be easily moved through pipelines, trucks or tankers. It's found all over the world. It's used to make pop bottles and to power fighter jets. Most critically, it packs an unparalleled amount of energy into a tiny package. Given the same volume, oil contains more energy than natural gas and roughly twice as much as coal. We're making strides at developing alternative energy sources, but we still don't have anything close to a viable substitute that captures all of oil's magical properties.

The price of oil is the single most important ingredient in the outlook for the global economy. Feed the world cheap oil and it will run like a charm. Send prices to unaffordable levels and the engine of growth will immediately seize up.

You can draw a straight line between oil consumption and GDP growth. The more oil we burn, the faster the global economy grows. On average over the last four decades, a 1 percent bump in world oil consumption has led to a 2 percent increase in global GDP. That means if GDP increased by 4 percent a year—as it often did before the 2008 recession—oil consumption was increasing by 2 percent a year.

At $20 a barrel, boosting annual oil consumption by 2 percent seems reasonable enough. At $100 a barrel, it becomes easier to see how a 2 percent increase in fuel consumption is enough to make an economy keel over and collapse.

Fortunately, the reverse is also true. When our economies stop growing, less oil is needed. Shrink a country's economic activity enough and its oil intake suddenly becomes manageable again. For example, following the big downturn in 2008, global oil demand actually fell for the first time since 1983.

The relationship between oil and economic growth is a two-way street. Buying oil stocks, for example, is always a great idea when crude prices are going up. But when high oil prices trigger a recession that clobbers demand, crude prices come tumbling back down to earth, bringing those same oil stocks along for the ride.

That's why the best cure for high oil prices is high oil prices. When prices rise to a level that causes an economic crash, lower prices inevitably follow. Over the last four decades, each time oil prices have spiked, the global economy has rolled over into a recession. The problems may take different guises, such as stagflation in the 1970s or the financial market meltdown in 2008. Regardless of what story made the most headlines at the time, oil prices were lurking at the root of the problem.

Consider the first oil shock, created by the Organization of Petroleum Exporting Countries (OPEC) following the Yom Kippur War in 1973. Set off by this Arab-Israeli conflict, OPEC's Arab members turned off the taps on roughly 8 percent of the world's oil supply by cutting shipments to the United States and other Israeli allies. Crude prices spiked, and by 1974 real GDP in the United States had shrunk by 2.5 percent.

The second OPEC oil shock happened during Iran's revolution and the subsequent war with Iraq. Disruptions to Iranian production during the revolution sent crude prices higher, pushing the North American economy into a recession for the first half of 1980. At the same time, higher energy prices also spurred on the inflation that compelled Volcker to keep pushing interest rates higher. The economy notched a brief recovery, but a few months later Iran's war with Iraq shut off 6 percent of world oil production, sending North America into a double-dip recession that began in the spring of 1981.

When Saddam Hussein invaded Kuwait a decade later, oil prices doubled to $40 a barrel, an unheard-of level at the time. The First Gulf War disrupted nearly 10 percent of the world's oil supply, sending major oil-consuming countries into a recession in the fall of 1990.

Guess what oil prices were doing in 2008 when the world fell into the deepest recession since the 1930s? From trading around $30 a barrel in 2004, oil prices marched steadily higher before hitting a peak of $147 a barrel in the summer of 2008. Unlike past oil price shocks, this time there wasn't even a supply disruption to blame. The spigot was wide open. The problem was, we could no longer afford to buy what was flowing through it.

There are many ways an oil shock can deep-six an economy. When prices spike, most of us have little choice but to open our wallets and shell out more for what we burn. Unless we want to stop driving our cars or burning heating oil, what else can we do? Something has to give. Paying more for oil means we have less cash to spend on food, shelter, furniture, clothes, travel and pretty much anything else you can think of. A poll by the American Automobile Association in 2011 found that motorists still planned to hit the road for summer vacations, despite pump prices close to $4 a gallon. Americans, it seems, will always keep on truckin'. What changes is how much cash is left over to spend on hotels, restaurants and other holiday expenses. Soft consumer-demand numbers across the American economy confirm this same trend. Expensive oil, coupled with the average American's refusal to drive less, leaves a lot less money for the rest of the economy.

The International Energy Agency (IEA) is already warning that households are spending as much on energy as they have during past oil-induced recessions. There's only so much money to go around. When oil prices go north, consumer spending has no choice but to head south.

Expensive oil doesn't just curtail domestic spending; it also fosters a massive shift in wealth and power from countries that import oil to those that produce it. As oil prices ran higher between 2005 and 2007, OECD countries shipped nearly a trillion petrodollars to OPEC nations.

Think about the last story you heard about the extravagances of Middle Eastern oil sheikhs. An extra trillion dollars pays for a whole lot of indulgence. Consider Prince Alwaleed's plans for Kingdom City in Saudi Arabia. The prince recently commissioned a $1.2-billion construction project to erect the world's tallest building. His new tower will surpass the 160-floor Burj Khalifa (also built with oil money) in neighboring Dubai. What else but the price of oil could allow the world's tallest buildings to rise up from the desert sands?

The same petro-wealth allows billionaire Sheikh Hamad, a member of Abu Dhabi's ruling family, to emboss his name on an island he owns off the coast of the United Arab Emirates. The name HAMAD rises above the landscape in letters half a mile high and two miles across. It's immodest, certainly, but I suppose humility isn't a priority for someone whose name is now visible from space.

Fatih Birol, the chief economist at the International Energy Agency (IEA), the energy think tank of the OECD, estimates that annual revenues for OPEC's twelve members reached a trillion dollars for the first time in 2011. America, meanwhile, is running a trillion-dollar budget deficit to feed its oil-sucking economy. It might save everyone some time if the United States just shipped its stimulus spending straight to OPEC or directly into the pockets of oil-exporting dictators.

But the transfer of massive amounts of wealth isn't even the biggest issue. When oil prices go up, so does inflation. And when inflation goes up, central banks respond by raising interest rates to keep prices in check. Between 2004 and 2006, US energy inflation ran at 35 percent, according to the country's Consumer Price Index (CPI). In turn, overall inflation, as measured by the CPI, vaulted from 1 percent to nearly 6 percent. You'll remember what happened next. A fivefold bump in interest rates was the last straw for the massively leveraged US housing market. Higher rates popped the speculative housing bubble, which brought down not only several prominent Wall Street investment banks but also the entire global economy.

Unfortunately, history seems to be repeating itself right now. The same pattern of oil-driven inflation is with us again. And to rub more salt in the wound, world food prices are coming along for the ride. According to the food price index tracked by the United Nations Food and Agriculture Organization (FAO), the cost of food climbed by a third between 2009 and the beginning of 2013. Looking back even further, since 2002 the FAO's food price index, which measures a basket of five commodity groups (meat, dairy, cereals, oils and fats, and sugar), is up by roughly 130 percent.

A double whammy of rising oil and food prices means inflation will be here sooner than anyone would like to think. In India, the wholesale price index, the country's key inflation gauge averaged more than 9 percent in 2012. The situation is also a worry in China, where inflation hit a three-year high of 6.5 percent in July 2011, well above the government's stated goal of 4 percent. China is charting a difficult course, attempting to keep economic growth running at more than 8 percent while holding inflation in check at the same time.

When inflation rates rise in China and India it's a clear signal that those economies are growing at an unsustainable pace. China has made GDP growth of more than 8 percent a priority, but it needs to realize that higher energy prices have lowered the economic speed limit. The country will have to recalibrate its thinking on potential economic growth to recognize the dampening effects of high oil prices. Growth might not stall entirely, as it has in some countries in North America and Europe, but clocking double-digit gains is no longer feasible, at least without triggering a calamitous increase in inflation. If China and India, the new engines of global economic growth, are forced to adopt anti-inflationary monetary policies, the ripple effects for resource-based economies such as Canada, Australia and Brazil will be felt in a hurry.

China and India are painfully aware that Brent crude traded in triple digits for nearly all of 2012. Its recent high of $126 a barrel is only $20 off the 2008 oil price spike that brought eight years of global economic expansion to a screeching halt. Triple-digit prices will drive a stake through China's and India's lofty economic hopes, which hinge on burning more and more barrels of oil.

China and India are looking to achieve the same sort of sustained economic growth that North America and Europe enjoyed in the postwar era. That's entirely understandable, but there's an unavoidable obstacle that puts such ambitions out of reach: today's oil isn't flowing from the same places it did yesterday. More importantly, it's not flowing at the same cost.

That doesn't mean there won't be any more oil. New reserves are being found all the time in brand-new places. What the decline in conventional production does mean, though, is that future economic growth will be fueled by expensive oil from nonconventional sources such as the tar sands, offshore wells in the deep waters of the world's oceans, and even oil shales, which come with a long list of environmental costs that range from carbon dioxide emissions to potential groundwater contamination.

The arrival of these new sources of oil points to the same thing: oil will be getting more expensive. Where will that leave the global economy? Well, we know that when oil prices rise, economies eventually contract and roll over into a recession. The downturn then causes oil demand to drop and prices to plunge back down. But the minute the economy recovers, so too does demand, giving rise to the very same price hikes that trigger another recession. How does this ride end?

PEAK OIL IS REALLY ABOUT PRICES, NOT SUPPLY

When oil prices start to climb, the peak-oil debate inevitably moves back into the spotlight. In brief, the idea of peak oil holds that geological limits to the amount of oil that can be tapped means global oil production will eventually top out and then embark on an irreversible decline. It's a contentious topic. The message that oil's days are numbered is clearly not something the energy industry wants to hear. At the same time, the shrill tone taken by some peak-oil proponents, who see a coming oil crisis unleashing a doomsday scenario on us all, doesn't do their position any favors with the rest of the energy world.

I'll leave the geological argument to the geologists and petroleum engineers, where it belongs. What's important here is the link between oil prices and economic growth. Focusing on this relationship casts the debate in a very different light.

Like Mayan predictions for the end of days, predictions for peak oil come and go with some regularity. To the great consternation of peak-oil proponents, the oil industry continues to confound projections by getting better at pulling oil out of the ground. Better technology has kept the oil industry a step ahead of the best estimates of the peak-oil geologists.

That's a familiar story for the peak-oil movement, which got its start after an American geophysicist, M. King Hubbert, predicted in 1956 that conventional oil production in the lower forty-eight states would peak by the early 1970s. Hubbert was right, but subsequent projections have been derailed by the development of new sources of supply in Alaska and under the Gulf of Mexico. More recently, crude from Canada's tar sands and from shale deposits, such as the Bakken play in North Dakota, has kept the oil supply from following the same bell-shaped curve Hubbert used to describe the trajectory of conventional US production.

As new sources of oil are discovered, and the definition of what counts as oil has expanded to include new sources of supply such as bitumen from the tar sands, the peak crowd has been forced to roll back predictions for the dreaded peak to points further in the future. A popular view now held by many peak-oil advocates sees oil production reaching an undulating plateau, sparing the world from the sharp drop-off in production foreseen in earlier predictions.

It's easy to get caught up in the semantics of the peak-oil debate. Just what is oil? Are new sources of supply really producing effective substitutes for the conventional oil we're losing to depletion? But the issue that should be at the forefront of peak-oil discussions isn't physical supply but economic cost. World supply may continue to defy peak-oil predictions, but that's just a geological sideshow. What matters to the economy is the price it takes to get new supply flowing. It's not enough for the global energy industry simply to find new caches of oil; the crude they find must be affordable. Triple-digit prices make it profitable to tap ever more expensive sources of oil, but the prices needed to pull this crude out of the ground will throw our economies right back into recession.

What geologists don't get is that peak oil isn't about supply: higher prices will always fetch more oil supply. It may not be exactly what purists think of as oil, but hey, if it burns, it'll do. Peak oil is really a demand phenomenon rooted in economics, not geology. It doesn't matter if billions of barrels are waiting to be tapped in unconventional plays such as the tar sands or oil shales if the cost of extraction is beyond our capacity to pay. In other words, the only peak that matters is the one determined by what we can afford, not by how much we can drill. Potential oil resources are only meaningful if we have the money to actually pay for the fuel. Otherwise, who really cares if we can pump it out of the ground?

The energy industry's task is not simply to find oil, but to find stuff we can afford to burn. And that's where the industry is failing the global economy. Prices have more than quadrupled over the last ten years. Each new barrel we pull out of the ground is costing us more than the last. The resources may be there for the taking, but our economies are already telling us we can't afford the cost.

Today, the world burns about 90 million barrels of oil a day. What if that's enough? If our economies are no longer growing, maybe we won't need any more than that. We might even need less. Maybe the oil trapped in the tar sands or under the Arctic Ocean can stay where nature put it.

Some people might call that an oil peak. Others might just call it the end of growth.

CHAPTER 2

DEBT IS ENERGY INTENSIVE

THOSE LUCKY ENOUGH TO TRAVEL down the Italian coast will tell you that the ruins at Pompeii are not to be missed. Uncovered in the 1700s, Pompeii is a snapshot of what Roman life was like circa AD 79. It's also a plucky little set of ruins. In the last two thousand years, Pompeii has survived the eruption of Mount Vesuvius, the fall of the Roman Empire, the Dark Ages and a pair of world wars.

And right now, the ruins are falling apart.

Exhibit A is the House of the Gladiators, a stone building on Pompeii's main street thought to have been a training ground for fighters. The Gladiator House made it through volcanoes and Allied bombers, but in the end Italy's debt problems turned out to be too much for it to withstand. It unceremoniously collapsed into a pile of rubble in late 2010.

And it's not just Pompeii. Archeologists are sounding alarm bells about other national treasures, including the Grand Canal in Venice and Florence's Duomo. The deteriorating state of historical sites has worried Italians for years. But only now are austerity measures forcing such deep cuts to the country's culture budget that there's no government money for ancient monuments. Italy is now pinning its hopes on wealthy philanthropists stepping in with cash to help preserve cultural treasures, including the Colosseum.

Italy's crumbling landmarks are only the tip of the iceberg.

Take a look around Europe. Whether you're Italian, Greek, Irish, Spanish, Portuguese or even British, it must be painfully clear that your economic future is full of IOUs. Look no farther than Greece. Each one of its 11 million citizens owes the equivalent of 30,000 euros. It doesn't matter that Greek citizens didn't personally sign loan papers, their government borrowed the money on their behalf. But no one gets a free ride. Greece's problems are exacerbated by a culture of tax evasion that forced the government to rack up massive budget deficits to fund public services. Now, one way or another, the Greek people will end up paying for that debt.

In the aftermath of the financial crisis of 2008, Greece was not alone. Governments around the world piled up debt in a double-barreled attempt to fight the recession and save a global banking system on the edge of collapse. And now countries are left with huge budget shortfalls that dwarf anything we've seen in the postwar era.

At its worst, Ireland's annual budget deficit accounted for nearly a third of its GDP. Spain's deficit last year was more than 6 percent, well above its austerity-driven target of 4.5 percent. In Greece, intensely unpopular austerity measures have shrunk the annual budgetary shortfall from a high of 15 percent in 2009 to 6.6 percent in 2012. To put those numbers in perspective, the European Monetary Union (EMU) sets a ceiling on budget deficits of 3 percent of GDP as part of its criteria for inclusion in the eurozone.

Annual deficits, of course, don't simply go away when the calendar turns the page. Budget deficits pile up on each other, compounding into mountains of national debt that can become bigger than the economies they're financing every year. Japan's national debt, for instance, is now more than twice as large as its annual GDP. Greece's total debt is expected to reach 190 percent of GDP in 2013. Italy's debt is roughly double its GDP. That's nearly twice as much as the threshold set out for inclusion in the EMU, which requires that a country's debt-to-GDP ratio doesn't exceed 60 percent. In the United States, the Obama administration is running a budget deficit of more than a trillion dollars. That's caused the country's debt-to-GDP ratio to nearly double in the last few years to around 70 percent, as Washington has strung together a series of record deficits to help fight the effects of the recession.

Nearly every OECD country is drowning in red ink these days. Governments are counting on an economic recovery to act as a life preserver. But bringing economies to life, as we saw in the last chapter, requires burning more oil. Economic growth and oil consumption are joined at the hip, a relationship that casts government debt in a brand-new light—one with a decidedly oily sheen.

We know that servicing debt is very energy intensive. We also know there's an ocean of debt out there. What's not clear, from Athens to Washington, is exactly how governments will pay back an already crushing debt load that's only getting bigger. Whether it's the taxes you pay or the public services you depend upon, it doesn't take long before your government's financial problems are knocking on your door. In the United States, that could mean cuts to Medicare. It certainly means the federal government can transfer less money to each state, which is bad news for education, among other things. Older schools get closed, new schools don't get built, class sizes go up and kids are sent to schools that are farther away from home. The burden of servicing the national debt means everything else gets the short end of the stick, as costs are passed from Washington to the state level and on down to municipalities. Streets are patrolled by fewer police officers. Snow is plowed less often in the winter. Cities can run fewer buses and the ones that do roll by cost more to hop on.

In Europe, the consequences of the fiscal problems are even more severe. In the UK, record budget deficits, and the accompanying austerity measures that include crippling increases in university tuition, contributed to a widespread dissatisfaction among young people that fueled some of the worst rioting in years. The images of violence, looting and arson that broke out in cities across England in 2011 left an indelible impression. In Athens and Madrid, general strikes are now routine, as are the ensuing clashes between police and protesters, many of whom are now packing everything from stones to petrol bombs.

Saddling a worried electorate with debt and budget cutbacks is a time-tested way for a government to find itself out of work when the polls close. Ireland is a case in point. In February 2011, the incumbent party, Fianna Fáil, suffered the worst election defeat for a sitting Irish government since 1918. In Greece, President George Papandreou found his country caught between meeting the ever more draconian fiscal demands of its foreign creditors and a rising resistance to austerity measures among its citizens. His government collapsed, forcing Papandreou's resignation. In Italy, Prime Minister Silvio Berlusconi, who had managed to survive corruption charges and salacious sex scandals, couldn't outlast his country's debt crisis. He resigned in November 2011, after seventeen years as the dominant force in Italian politics. Even Germany's Angela Merkel, whose country remains the economic stalwart of the EU, is looking over her shoulder as opponents make political hay criticizing the country's outsized role in back-stopping the monetary union.

Europe is stuck in a quagmire of austerity measures, budget deficits and financial bailouts. As its political leaders are finding out, it's a situation fraught with the likelihood of debt default, social upheaval and political change. The economic hopes of an entire continent are wrapped up in a single magic bullet: growth. Were a strong-enough economic rebound to take hold, it could slay the deficit and spare the EU. A sharp rebound in economic growth would fill government coffers with tax revenues that could be used to pay back the huge amounts owed to creditors. At the same time, a turnaround in the EU's financial fortunes would spare citizens from suffering through more income-sucking tax increases and bone-deep cuts to social spending. The debt-strapped countries borrowing the money, the bondholders on the hook for billions, and the EU taxpayers footing the rest of the bill could all come out okay if Europe's economy recovers.

But pulling off such a recovery will take copious amounts of energy. The question that needs to be asked is whether the global economy can afford the fuel bill.

The pace of economic growth needed to allow a heavily in-debted country such as Greece to service its debt means burning an incredible amount of oil. German taxpayers and the bondholders funding EU bailouts may not realize it yet, but the debt being accumulated in countries such as Greece and Portugal might as well be denominated in barrels of oil. If the eurozone needs economic expansion to pay back debt and that growth can only happen by burning more fuel, the price of oil starts to loom pretty large.

Global oil consumption in 2000 was roughly 76 million barrels a day, with Brent crude averaging $28.50 a barrel; the world's

annual oil bill was $791 billion. Skip ahead to 2010. World con-
sumption was up to 87 million barrels a day, with Brent averaging $79.50 a barrel. The combination of higher prices and more
demand had quadrupled the annual fuel bill to $2.5 trillion. Only
a year later, Brent crude was averaging more than $100 a barrel.
That price increase alone added more than $500 billion to what
the world spends each year to keep the wheels turning.

The extra money didn't fall from the sky. The cost is footed
by the world's major oil-consuming economies, and the cash is
shipped into the outstretched arms of oil-exporting nations like
Saudi Arabia, Russia and Canada.

When the world's annual fuel bill was less than $800 billion,
oil-importing nations like the United States clocked healthy
economic growth year after year. Now that the world is spending
more than $3 trillion a year on oil, those same economies are
floundering.

This isn't a coincidence.

Triple-digit oil prices turn the sovereign debt market into something resembling a giant Ponzi scheme. The investors who are
buying the bonds that allow governments to roll over the debt
amassing in the financial system are essentially making larger and
larger bets on future economic growth. But as oil prices climb
higher, the prospects for that growth become ever more tenuous.
It's like doubling down just as the odds are turning against you.

Think about buying a 30-year government bond today. In effect, you're betting a country's tax base will expand for the next
three decades. Remember, though, that the economy's speed limit
changes along with the price of oil. What happens if an economy,
denied the cheap energy it needs, can only grow at a fraction of its
previous pace, if at all? How would tax revenues increase enough
for a government to make debt payments? And if a country can't

make those payments, what happens to the value of your 30-year bond? In order to avoid default, will governments try to reschedule much longer repayment terms than were initially agreed to by the bondholder? And if so, how receptive do you imagine the bond market would be to the next government debt issue?

The relationship between growth and debt suddenly shows up in very stark terms. If investors can no longer count on growth, what happens to the appetite for government bonds? The nasty kicker in all this for a government is the timing: just when a stagnant economy makes a government's borrowing needs the most urgent, the doors to new money start to close.

If you're wondering why governments are continuously borrowing money, it's a good question. Governments don't pay off debt the way you pay down your mortgage. Although they make constant debt payments to creditors that have lent them money in the past, governments are continually writing more IOUs to finance current deficits. Government debt is really a revolving door.

The bigger a country's economy, the more debt it can carry. The idea is similar to a bank calculating the size of your mortgage by looking at your income. In addition, the credit ratings handed out by agencies such as Standard & Poor's and Moody's play a role in determining how much it costs governments to borrow money. These agencies closely monitor national balance sheets and then advise investors about a country's fiscal health. The amount of debt a country already has on the books in relation to the size of its economy is key in judging a country's creditworthiness. The massive accumulation of US debt since the 2008 recession, for instance, didn't do the country any favors with ratings agencies. Standard & Poor's—troubled by the increasing size of the national debt, the pace of government spending and a rocky outlook for the US economy—downgraded the country's credit rating in August 2011. The United States had maintained S&P's coveted Triple-A rating since 1941.

Governments that sport a low debt-to-GDP ratio have the luxury of borrowing at a cheap interest rate. The lower the interest rate, the fewer tax dollars need to be devoted to servicing the national debt. That leaves more money for things such as education, health care and the other social services we all hope governments can provide. In contrast, a high debt-to-GDP ratio leads to a low credit rating. By some estimates, S&P's downgrade of US debt will cost the country tens of billions of dollars a year. The higher borrowing costs leave Washington with that much less money to spend on everything else.

Consider what happens if your country's economic growth flat-lines. In a static economy, only one half of the debt-to-GDP ratio is going up—the wrong half. If debt continues to increase and GDP stays the same, one of the key ratios used to determine borrowing costs starts to look pretty shaky. That means your government will have to start paying a higher interest rate if it wants to continue financing its debt. But that's not all. What it costs you to borrow money from your bank is pegged to your government's borrowing costs. If your government has a sterling Triple-A credit rating, it's able to borrow money from the bond market at the cheapest possible rates. Those low borrowing costs trickle down to your country's banks and on to you. Conversely, when a country's debt-to-GDP ratio goes in the wrong direction, governments are forced to dangle higher interest rates to entice bond investors to assume a greater degree of risk. When your government pays more to the bond market, it eventually means that you and everyone you know will pay more to take out a loan. This cycle of higher borrowing costs only makes it that much harder for your economy to grow.

Start piling on debt without economic growth and pretty soon a government's borrowing rate will go through the roof. At the height of its financial crisis in 2011–12, Greece was forced to pay more than 30 percent interest to borrow from the bond market. That's why bailout funds from the EU are so desperately needed. Without those emergency funds, Greece is at the mercy of the bond market and its usurious interest rates. In the event that growth comes to a complete standstill, persuading creditors to keep financing government deficits becomes a hard sell.

Static growth means the revolving door of government debt could stop revolving. If your government can't keep rolling over its debt in the financial markets, that's bad news for everyone. The national debt will quickly start to feel like your personal debt, since governments will have few choices but to raise taxes to service the debt. You can figure out what that means for your after-tax income—if you still have an income. The inevitable budget cuts will put a lot of workers, particularly those in government, on the breadlines. In the United States, for instance, the public sector is taking a beating. Cash-strapped state and local governments cut more than 140,000 jobs in 2011, according to the Labor Department. That's on top of the 200,000 jobs eliminated in 2010. All told, more than 500,000 public-sector jobs have been shed in the States since the recession began in 2008.

Digging out from under this situation is a tall order that requires governments to raise a lot of cash. Of course, the more a government flirts with a debt default, the more compensation investors require to entice them into the bond market. Not that investors in government bonds aren't used to facing risk. Over the course of a 30-year bond, it's only natural for an economy to stumble through a few rough patches. After all, which country hasn't had a recession in the last three decades? Historically, bond investors have been willing to ride out the cyclical bumps, secure in the belief that recessions are temporary events and eventually an economy will get back to growing. Even during the downtimes, they'll keep financing government debt, knowing the payoff will come when the economy perks up.

But what happens if a bond investor loses faith in a country's economy? The prospect of static growth puts a chill on investors that have bought bonds expecting to receive a steady stream of interest payments for the next thirty years. Again, take Greece as a test case. Its economy is suffocating beneath the weight of the draconian budget measures demanded by its creditors. Its economy is shrinking and a turnaround is nowhere in sight. All of that means the country's debt-to-GDP ratio will keep deteriorating, which will lead to even higher borrowing costs. Meanwhile, austerity measures and budget restraints will become even harsher in an attempt to appease the European taxpayers funding its bailout. A partial list of these measures, which are designed to drastically reduce the size and role of the Greek government, includes: tax increases, public-sector wage cuts, reduced health care spending, school closures, cuts to social security for seniors, and the privatization of state-run enterprises such as airports and electrical utilities.

Greece is trapped in a brutal downward spiral. Any confidence that its economy will recover is being propped up by Draghi and the ECB.

And soon it won't just be Greece's economy that isn't growing. The cheap energy that allowed for economic growth in the past is gone, and it's not coming back. It's a relic of a different time. The world's bond markets have yet to fully absorb the financial risks of slower growth, but they will soon. As economic growth slows to a crawl, it will become more expensive for governments to issue bonds. If a government is looking to assign blame for the higher costs, it won't need to look any further than the price of oil.

The European countries in the worst financial shape all share the expensive distinction of having little or no domestic oil production. It should come as no surprise that Portugal, Ireland, Italy, Greece and Spain are at the bottom of the EU's fiscal totem pole. Known by the unflattering acronym PIIGS, these countries are most at risk of economic collapse due at least in part to the misfortune of missing out on the geological lottery. Unlucky as that may be, the reality of triple-digit oil prices leaves these countries little room for fiscal optimism.

When a debt-laden country finds its economy choking on the punitive cost of oil, it has two choices. The first is to squeeze a teetering economy even harder in the hope of cutting a path back to prosperity. The second choice is to default on its debt.

The first option, as Greece makes abundantly clear, isn't working. In a vacuum, tax hikes and spending cuts can allow a country to reduce its budget deficit. But in the real world, those tactics can easily become self-defeating. The more brutal the fiscal austerity measures, the greater their economic impact, which only deepens the recession. Any deficit reduction achieved through spending cuts is more than offset by the negative fiscal consequences of a deeper economic slowdown.

The amount of money collected from taxes is a function of economic activity. Less activity shrinks tax revenues. It seems straightforward enough, but it's not a tune EU creditor nations want to hear. Before they open the purse strings and offer emergency funding, they want to know that politicians won't spend it like drunken sailors. It's an understandable position. If I lend you $100 until tomorrow, I want some assurance you don't plan to spend $500 today.

Greece is bending over backwards to meet the EU demands. As a result, the only sure thing is that the bailout money won't be repaid. Right now, Greece's economy is contracting by roughly 5 percent a year. The EU can demand all the austerity measures it wants, but at that rate Greece's debt is only going to get bigger.

CAN THE EUROPEAN MONETARY UNION SURVIVE?

Greece will likely still do what Greece has always done, which is default. It's nothing new for the country. Over the last two hundred years, Greece has been in a state of default more than half the time. With such a storied track record of delinquent borrowing, it shouldn't come as a shock to its partners in the EMU that Greece will once again look to wipe the slate clean with a default.

And this time Greece has company. Ireland and Portugal are facing massive fiscal problems, as are the major eurozone economies of Spain and Italy. Chunks of stone aren't falling from the Colosseum because Rome wants it to happen. Italy's economy is on the ropes, the country is crumbling, and Italians can do little but watch.

It wasn't always like this. In the past, European countries had an escape hatch that could save a bankrupt government from officially entering into default. But membership in the European Monetary Union took that option away. The seventeen countries in the EMU traded the freedom of autonomous currencies for the combined economic strength of the euro. And for much of the last decade, a strong euro made that look like a good bargain. Now that tough times are here again, though, a drowning country like Greece is nostalgic for the bygone days of the drachma. Prior to adopting the euro, if Greece found itself in a fiscal mess, it would invariably devalue its exchange rate. For Greece, in particular, this was an especially effective tactic. A plunging drachma would breathe new life into tourism, Greece's most important industry. Over time, a pickup in tourism spending would send more tax dollars to Greece's government, helping the country back onto its feet.

But now Greece has no choice but to look to its European partners for a bailout. In practice, that means German taxpayers end up sending welfare checks to Athens. In the old days of a plunging drachma, Germans would pay less money and get a holiday in Santorini for the trouble of helping Greece out.

So why would Germany saddle itself with the problems of a southern neighbor? It turns out Germans get much more for their money than a holiday in the Greek islands. The weak economies of the PIIGS help to hold down the value of the euro. For Germany, the world's second-largest exporter, a weaker euro translates into jobs and profits for domestic industries, as German companies do booming business around the world. If you're wondering about the advantages of holding the euro down against competing currencies such as the US greenback or the Japanese yen, just ask Volkswagen, Adidas, Mercedes-Benz, Siemens, Henckels or Audi. Better yet, just walk down a city street and see how long it takes before a Volkswagen rolls by or someone with three stripes on their shoes walks past. Easier still, check your kitchen. I'm betting you have at least one Henckels knife in a drawer, if not a whole block on the counter.

The question Germany must now ask itself is whether the substantial benefits of a weaker euro are worth the costs of backstopping such bailouts. As the economic woes continue in Greece and other struggling eurozone economies, the folks in the Bundestag are staying up at night trying to figure out an answer.

The longer creditor countries such as Germany try to save the PIIGS, the closer the European debt crisis comes to washing up on the home front. Standard & Poor's now considers only four members of the EMU—Germany, Finland, Luxembourg and the Netherlands—worthy of its top credit rating. And the agency recently put even those economies on credit watch, a step that's often a prelude to a downgrade. If that happens, those countries will have to spend more money financing their own debt, leaving less to contribute to emergency funds for their neighbors.

IT REALLY ISN'T ABOUT GREECE

If Germans finally tire of sending welfare checks to Greece and force the country to bolt from the euro, it won't be leaving on its own. Its expulsion from the monetary union would trigger a domino effect among its fellow PIIGS. Economists call this contagion—just like a virus spreading from one person to another. Contagion is the real reason the EU is so worried about Greece. It's also the reason Draghi has pledged to do whatever it takes to keep Greece in the monetary union and preserve the euro. The ECB has managed to staunch the worst of the bleeding for now, but the eurozone debt crisis remains far from resolved.

Much like Greece, Portugal depends heavily on tourism to make its economy go. And also like its Hellenic neighbor, Portugal is getting billions of euros from bailout packages funded by its EU partners. But if Greece dumps the euro and brings back the drachma, Portugal's tourism industry will be at a huge disadvantage. If the price of a holiday in Santorini is cut in half due to a devalued drachma, can the beaches of the Algarve compete when tourists are still being charged prices in expensive euros? Politicians in Lisbon will quickly realize they can't.

Portugal's most sensible option will be to follow Greece's lead and leave the monetary union. A return to the escudo will allow Portugal to say hello to tourism dollars and goodbye to the austerity measures being demanded by Angela Merkel, the International Monetary Fund and the European Central Bank. It will lose bailout funding, but given its current situation, Portugal must ask how much it will really lose in the long run.

If Greece and Portugal leave the monetary union, can Spain and Italy be far behind? Before you know it, a road trip through western Europe will once again fill your pockets with the bright colors and confusing denominations of stand-alone currencies. The political dreams of pan-Europeanism will soon give way to the imperatives of economic reality. The euro will survive, but by shedding the weaker southern economies, its value will strengthen. German automakers, to name one group, won't welcome this news. A stronger euro will boost the sticker price of German-made cars around the world, making Fords or Subarus that much more attractive in comparison. The currency union will continue, but it will shrink to a handful of northern European countries, including France, the Netherlands and Germany.

Many will argue that the EMU should have taken that shape from the start—that throwing the PIIGS into a currency union with Germany and France was an unnatural configuration similar to putting Mexico into a currency union with the United States and Canada. When economic times are good, Mexico would be fine. But when the business cycle turned down, it would be an entirely different story. Without the ability to devalue the peso and juice its economy, Mexico's situation would soon turn just as desperate as Greece's is today.

What will the European Union look like in the event of a monetary divorce? The currency sphere is only part of the picture. If the monetary union unwinds, can the EU's free-trade zone be far behind?

One of the core arguments in establishing the euro was to prevent countries from devaluing currencies to gain a competitive edge over neighboring states. Being in a monetary union stopped a country like Spain from weakening the peseta and shifting its economic problems elsewhere. All other things being equal, a weak peseta makes Spain's exports look more attractive than goods coming from places such as Germany and France. The currency gap allows Spain to effectively ship its unemployment to surrounding countries. That's great if you're a Spanish worker. Not so much if you're looking for a job in Marseille or Hamburg.

The lure of currency depreciation has seldom been more attractive for countries such as Spain and Greece than it is today. National unemployment rates are trending as high as 20 percent. Youth unemployment is even worse, bumping over 50 percent in Spain and Greece, and stoking worries about a lost generation of young people. With one out of every five workers on the street, politicians in Athens and Madrid have plenty of incentive to walk away from the euro. If the weak sisters do indeed leave the monetary union, it remains an open question whether they would be allowed to stay in the free-trade zone.

If it were to leave the EMU, Greece's drachma is forecast to drop as much as 40 percent against the euro. That's hardly a level playing field for a free-trade zone. Factories in Athens would start taking business from plants in Munich and Amsterdam. Tolerance for such beggar-thy-neighbor currency depreciation wears thin in a hurry, particularly when unemployment is already a problem in most countries in Europe. That's one of the reasons why tariffs are erected in the first place: to protect domestic economies from cheaper goods supported by devalued currencies.

In the light of such a competitive imbalance, can European free trade survive? And if the free-trade zone is altered, what will that mean for labor markets? Will workers from fiscally wayward countries that abandon the euro retain the right to work throughout the EU? While mobility has benefited an expanding European economy, allowing workers to find jobs and employers to find staff, it won't look nearly as attractive when the continent's economy contracts.

But even broader implications exist for Europe.

Any sovereign debt default by an existing EU member will surely raise the bar for future entrants into the monetary union. How will applications from places such as Albania, Serbia and Turkey be viewed in light of a defection by countries in southern Europe? Former Eastern bloc nations such as Romania, Poland and Hungary have long hoped that membership in the EMU will help stabilize their shaky economies. With the experience of Greece and Portugal still fresh, do you think existing members of the monetary union will be excited to throw open the door to new applicants? Such questions are easy to muse about in the abstract. But if you're an unemployed worker in Kraków, your day-to-day life hinges on the answers, as do your family's prospects.

These questions also affect the balance of power throughout the region. Rejecting the applications of former Eastern bloc nations will be considered a bad move by those in the EU who believe a unified Europe will give the region the clout needed to compete in the global economy in the coming decades. In other places, though, the move would be welcomed. Russia would be happy to see EU expansion grind to a halt. Moscow's traditional sphere of influence in eastern Europe has already been eroded by the pull of the EU and NATO. The Cold War may be over, but that doesn't mean Russia has stopped being a major player on the world stage.

If Europe's influence shrinks, it leaves room for Russia's to expand.

The stakes at play in sovereign debt defaults go well beyond the euro. A breakup of the monetary union opens the door for all kinds of economic and political shifts. You can bet the Europe of tomorrow will look very different from the Europe of today.

ARE WE BAILING OUT COUNTRIES
OR ARE WE BAILING OUT BANKS?

America's mortgage crisis didn't stay American for long. Because of the deep interconnectedness of the global financial system, the United States' problems quickly became the world's problems. And that's what worries the powers that be in Europe today. When the subprime crisis unfolded in 2008, the US government quickly stepped into the fray. Ostensibly, Washington was looking out for homeowners. The real impetus for the government bailout money was saving the banks. Saving a few voters' houses was just an ancillary benefit.

Exposure to Greece's economic problems cut the market value of French banks in half. Two of the country's banking giants, Société Générale and Crédit Agricole, own Greek bank subsidiaries. By comparison, German banks have less direct exposure to Greece. That would seem to make the situation less serious for Germany than for France. But it doesn't. What matters to Germany is the fate of French banks. Germany's financial sector is inextricably bound to France's, and as a result, bankers in both countries are terrified of a Greek default. So while it appears that Berlin is trying to prop up a failing Greek economy to help save the eurozone, what's really at stake is the solvency of Europe's biggest banks.

A sovereign debt default would send shock waves throughout Europe's banking system. Massive write-downs at banks would be followed by even bigger bailout checks to help save those same financial institutions. And the fallout won't be limited to Europe. That was the great lesson of the US subprime crisis: no one is safe. A Greek default might start in Athens, but it would quickly spread to Paris, Berlin, New York and Tokyo. Today's interconnected financial market gives everyone exposure to everyone else.

Will taxpayers be asked to finance another massive bank bailout? Will protest movements such as Occupy Wall Street morph into a broader-based political opposition that will demand far more in return for the next round of bailouts than the free ride the banks got the last time around? The Occupy movement has been dismissed by the conservative establishment as mere fringe groups of young people camping in city parks. But what if they're simply the most vocal representation of a deeper current of dissatisfaction among citizens? Could other changes be on the way?

The financial industry is overdue for a deep structural overhaul that will help to eliminate some of the conflicts of interest that led to the 2008 financial crisis. During the Great Depression, for instance, US lawmakers adopted the Glass-Steagall Act, legislation that separated the different parts of a bank's business. Under the act, a bank's traditional deposit-taking business was walled off from the proprietary trading desks that make huge leveraged bets in stock, bond and currency markets. Separating bankers lending money from traders investing money, the thinking went, would help to mitigate the type of rampant speculation that led to the stock market crash of 1929. Wall Street, of course, chafed at having its wings clipped. The financial industry argued that too many rules limited its global competitiveness. Buoyed by a culture of deregulation that took hold in the 1980s, Wall Street was able to get

Glass-Steagall repealed in 1999. The recent carnage in the banking industry has led to calls for a return to tighter regulations. Of course, in the United States, which takes pride in its freewheeling business culture, regulation is almost a dirty word. So far, a push back toward the days of Glass-Steagall has been rebuffed.

Until changes are made, however, don't expect to see taxpayer-funded bank bailouts end anytime soon. Consider what happened at Swiss-based UBS, one of the world's largest and most reputable banks. In September 2011, a mid-level employee on the bank's proprietary trading desk racked up a $2.3-billion loss. That was a hard hit to UBS's bottom line. But it's even worse for the Swiss taxpayers who will end up bailing out the banking giant in the event of another credit crisis. But can any of us really expect anything different in a system that rewards risk takers with annual bonus checks in the seven figures and leaves taxpayers to backstop the losses when big bets go horribly wrong?

Simply resurrecting old barriers between deposit-taking institutions and investment banking may not go far enough to fix our banks. In countries where another round of bailouts would mean taxpayers become the de facto owners of banks, outright nationalization could be the end result. The hue and cry that would go up from the corridors of financial power would be deafening. But putting investment bankers on civil service salaries might actually bring about the types of reforms needed in the financial services industry without the bother of passing new legislation to rewrite the rules for financial markets. That's not in the cards for Wall Street or Bay Street, but it is a possibility in smaller countries where rounds of taxpayer-funded bank bailouts have destroyed the financial industry's political capital.

Without the giant bonuses that motivate bankers to take big gambles with other people's money, maybe the world's banks would go back to doing what they used to do, which was to prudently lend out depositors' money to customers. Whatever shape it takes, the coming European banking crisis, following so closely on the heels of the subprime mortgage crisis, is about to push the pendulum back to ever greater government regulation of financial markets.

WILL AMERICA DEFAULT?

The financially strapped PIIGS aren't the only countries at risk of default.

If America's annual budget deficit drops to $845 billion in 2013, as projected, it will be the first time in five years that the gap between tax revenue and spending has dipped below $1 trillion. While the country's budget deficit is no longer in the same league as Greece, America also doesn't have the same deep-pocketed neighbours to turn to in times of need. While Greece can look to its friends in the EU for cash, America's biggest lender also happens to be its biggest political adversary.

It's no small irony that in a post–Cold War global economy, the last bastion of Communism has become the banker to capitalism's fallen angel. Economics makes for strange bedfellows. Irony aside, though, the People's Bank of China is the institution that keeps funding America's monstrous budget deficits. And it has been doing so for some time. Nearly every month, China's central bank allows Uncle Sam to pay his bills by showing up and buying bonds at the US treasuries auction. These regular public auctions are held by the US Treasury Department, which sells a range of securities to raise money for the country. For example, a Treasury bill, or T-bill, is a short-term debt obligation backed by the US government that carries a maturity of less than a year. Throughout the year, the Treasury holds different auctions for 3-month, 6-month and 52-week T-bills. Similarly, the Treasury also sells T-bonds, which are long-term securities with maturities of ten years or more, and T-notes, an intermediate security with a maturity between one and ten years. China is the single largest holder of US treasuries. All told, Communist China holds more than $3 trillion in foreign reserves, more than half of which are in US assets.

If China wakes up one day and decides to stop lending to the United States, the world's largest economy could soon join the PIIGS.

Of course, China's willingness to fund America's huge budget deficit isn't an act of charity. The People's Bank of China buys US Treasury bonds to help keep its currency from rising against the US dollar. China's demand for treasuries is tantamount to a demand for US currency. In foreign exchange markets, such demand is what allows a currency to hold its value. For the last decade, the relationship between a cheap yuan and a strong US greenback has been a fundamental component of the global economy.

Globalization allowed for a mutual dependence to develop between America and China. Poles apart on an ideological level, economically the pair has made sweet music together. A rapacious American consumer has dined on cheap labor from China for years. Meanwhile, China's central bank has cycled the savings of these same workers into US treasuries, an investment that allows Americans to keep buying Chinese goods. This self-reinforcing cycle of trade and capital flows defined the apex of the global economic model. Americans were able to purchase more for every dollar of income, since just about everything they consumed came from a sweatshop halfway around the world. With a nation of eager buyers across the Pacific ready for its goods, China became the world's factory.

But China achieved that position in a different world from the one we live in today. In order to staff its factories, China uprooted millions of peasants from traditional lives of rural farming and put them to work. The sheer size of China's massive labor force, combined with rock-bottom wages, gave China an economic advantage over all comers. China could make things cheaper and faster than any other country, a capacity that led to a line of customers out the door. A world that still seemed to enjoy an abundance of natural resources also helped. China's plants could run all day on cheap power from coal-fired plants, while affordable oil made the cost of shipping goods to faraway markets an incidental expense.

But a new landscape of energy scarcity means distance now costs money. Shipping a crate of dollar-store bobbles across an ocean doesn't make as much financial sense when oil is at $100 a barrel. Rising salaries are also cutting into China's wage advantage, one of the growing pains, party leaders are finding, of its turn toward capitalism. Workers are now agitating for higher salaries and better working conditions. So far, Beijing is supporting the push for higher wages. Better pay not only helps to allay worker concerns, it also boosts activity in the domestic economy. An increase in domestic spending reduces China's reliance on foreign exports as a means to expand the country's economy. Still, higher wages also mitigate China's competitive advantage over its Asian neighbors and countries in the developing world that are vying for the same customers. In short, new dynamics are in play, which are loosening the glue that holds China and the United States together.

Changes to the economic landscape will soon demand different policy responses from Beijing. China's economic priorities are shifting away from supplying the American market with cheap goods and toward battling the inflation that's taking hold inside its own borders. At times in the last few years, Chinese inflation, as we saw in the last chapter, has verged on getting away from the country, running higher than 6 percent for part of 2011. One way for China to tame such inflationary pressures would be to let the value of its currency rise.

Faced with the menace of inflation, the prospect of spending billions on US treasuries in order to hold down the value of the yuan may start to seem like the wrong move. If China allows the yuan to strengthen against the US dollar, that would effectively reduce the prices China pays on imported goods such as oil and corn. Along with collaring inflation on imports, a stronger yuan would also give Chinese consumers more purchasing power. Replacing foreign customers with domestic ones is already part of China's long-term economic plans, so it's easy to envision the country hastening the process. And putting the Chinese consumer in the driver's seat of the country's economic growth could seem like a good idea to Beijing right about now, given the economic plight of Europe and North America.

The time isn't far away when selling goods to the rest of the world will simply be gravy for China, which has 1.3 billion consumers inside its own borders. Look no further than its booming auto sector for an indication of how superfluous the rest of the world could soon become. The Chinese car market is now the biggest in the world, about a third larger last year than the market for vehicles in the United States. The global auto industry knows which way the wind is blowing, and it's digging in for the long haul. Recently, German automakers BMW and Audi became the latest companies to announce big spending plans for new Chinese factories. And China isn't even an auto-exporting nation. Someday that may change, but right now these new plants are being built to service domestic demand. Auto ownership in the country is still less than a tenth of what it is in the United States, meaning the Chinese market has plenty of room to run.

Allowing the yuan to rise would give prospective Chinese drivers more buying power to purchase vehicles made in domestic factories. So far, the People's Bank of China has resisted the idea of letting the yuan strengthen as a means of battling inflation. Instead, the bank has chosen to fight inflation using a combination of interest rate hikes and tighter lending requirements for its banks. These moves are designed to put the brakes on economic activity, which helps keep prices from rising. But it also forces China's economy to bear the full brunt of the country's inflation. If China wants to share some of that economic pain, it could decide to export part of the burden to the United States.

If China wants to strengthen its currency, all it needs to do is stop buying US treasuries. Cutting its participation in Treasury auctions would decrease the demand for US dollars in global currency markets, causing the US greenback to weaken against other currencies. If China wanted to further accelerate the yuan's rise against the US dollar, it could also start selling down its massive holdings of US treasuries. Flooding the market with treasuries would shrink the universal appetite for buying US bonds at future Treasury auctions, depressing the dollar even further.

That's an uncomfortable amount of power for one country to hold over another.

If the People's Bank of China decides to skip the next US Treasury auction, it wouldn't take long for Americans to notice. The huge pool of savings that China's central bank invests in the United States helps to hold down America's borrowing costs. Without China's backing, the USA would have to pay higher interest rates on every bond it sells. What would this mean for the average American? Well, everything from the price a bank charges for a car loan to mortgage rates are benchmarked to the Treasury's borrowing rate. If China decides it's better off with a stronger yuan, that rate will inevitably rise—and the consequences will touch every American who holds any debt.

Of course, the Fed could try to counteract the loss of Chinese demand for treasuries by cranking up the printing presses even further. That's essentially what Fed chairman Bernanke has done with the rounds of quantitative easing he's employed since 2008. By stepping into the market and buying treasuries on its own, the Fed has infused the US economy with cash. Buying its own bonds offers a reasonable facsimile of Chinese demand that helps hold down borrowing costs. At least for a while.

But when a government starts printing money to finance its own debt, isn't that just another form of default?

I bet the Greek government wishes it could do that right about now. But unfortunately, Greece doesn't have a currency of its own. (And even if the drachma were around, who would want to hold a Greek bond?) But the United States isn't Greece. Not only does America have its own currency, but the US dollar is also the world's reserve currency. That means the United States can borrow money from all over the world and then repay foreign lenders with US dollars. Nothing too tricky about that. But consider what happens to the value of that debt if the United States decides to devalue its currency by printing money to buy its own bonds. Sure, the United States still repays its loans, but the actual value of the payments isn't worth as much. That's a good spot to be in if you're the United States. Not so much for lenders.

When the concept of a default comes to mind, you may be picturing a deadbeat who won't repay his creditors. Maybe he refuses to make interest payments or perhaps even tries to skip out on the full value of a loan. But those are only some of the ways a default can occur. In the old days of metallic money, a sneaky form of default could come about when a country attempted to debase its currency by putting less gold or silver into each coin. More recently, a country that runs into hard economic times might decide to change the promise of value made by its currency. The US government used this tactic on two occasions. In the days of the gold standard, paper currency could be physically exchanged for gold bullion. During the American Civil War, the government suspended the convertibility of the American dollar into gold. And during the Great Depression, in 1933, Washington once again stepped into the currency market, reducing the amount of gold that backed each US dollar.

In the modern world of fiat currency (the term for the paper money we all know and use), old-time currency debasement has been replaced by exchange rate depreciation. Instead of a sovereign ruler instructing the royal mint to use less gold in each coin, governments now tell central bankers to print more money. A surplus of a currency in the market lowers its value in relation to the currencies of other countries. It's supply and demand in action.

Printing more money to lower the value of your currency may not technically be called a default. But if something walks like a duck and quacks like a duck, does it really matter what it's called?

If China stops attending US Treasury auctions, forcing the Fed to print more money to make up the shortfall, then the increase in the amount of US currency in circulation will lead to a devaluation of the dollar. While the United States will be able to keep making loan payments, those payments will be much less valuable to creditors.

Japanese investors found this out the hard way. In the 1970s, the Japanese, who helped fund the deficits created by US involvement in the Vietnam War by buying US bonds, were taken to the cleaners by a plunging greenback. Between 1971 and 1981, the US dollar dropped 40 percent against the yen. That meant that for every dollar Japan invested in US treasuries, it only received 60 cents in return.

So what would happen if the US dollar fell by 40 percent against the yuan? On one hand, an argument could be made that a weak US dollar would boost exports. But exports carry a relatively small overall weight in the US economy. As a share of GDP, exports from the US account for about a quarter of what they represent for countries such as Germany and Canada, which rely much more heavily on selling goods to the rest of the world. What's more, any gains from boosting exports would be more than offset by the rising price of imports.

Which brings me back to oil. No import is more important to America's economy than oil. And the more it costs the United States to import oil, the harder it becomes for the country's economy to grow. The United States accounts for about a fifth of the oil consumed in the world every day. That's an expensive tab at the best of times, let alone when the dollar is weak.

As I've just said, a shift in China's monetary policy toward a strong yuan would force the United States to fund more of its debt at home. Part of that responsibility would be borne by the Fed's printing presses. No doubt Bernanke has many more tranches of quantitative easing up his sleeve for the days ahead. The rest of the adjustment would come from cutting government spending and raising taxes to reduce the size of the deficits that must be funded.

The pending battle to pare down America's huge budget deficits won't be limited to showdowns in Congress, like the ones over the debt ceiling that rocked markets during the summer of 2011 and again at the end of 2012. It's likely to spill over into the streets, just as it has in Europe. In Wisconsin, that has already happened, after the Republican governor rescinded the collective bargaining rights of state employees, claiming the state's fiscal crisis was so severe that taxpayers could no longer afford to give state workers the right to strike. Demonstrations by disenfranchised workers on the steps of the Capitol building in Madison looked eerily similar to protests on the other side of the Atlantic. North of the border, Canada's federal government, which has yet to face a debt crisis, has nevertheless already attempted to short-circuit the right to strike for federal civil servants, as well as airline and postal workers.

Ideology guides different politicians to take different approaches to managing debt. For Tea Party Republicans, busting public-sector unions is a fitting response to a state fiscal crisis. If you're a Democrat, you're more inclined to go after special tax breaks given to the oil industry or look to raise the amount millionaires pay in personal income tax. Left wing or right wing, politicians and governments are now living in a radically different financial reality than they've known in the past. Triple-digit oil prices mean there's simply less money to go around. Sacred cows are about to get slaughtered on both sides of the political divide as financial austerity replaces fiscal largesse.

STIMULUS NO LONGER ON THE TABLE

Say what you will about stimulus packages, governments were able to marshal a massive amount of cash to battle the financial crisis in 2008. Governments threw so much money into getting us out of the last mess, there's hardly any ammunition left to fight another recession. The massive coordinated fiscal stimulus deployed by countries such as the United States, Great Britain and Japan last time around has left those nations far too broke to pull the same thing off again.

While it may look as if a lack of political will is standing in the way of international action to resolve the eurozone's financial problems, it's actually a lack of available cash. Neither governments nor taxpayers have the wherewithal to bail out any more troubled banks. Even worse, the IOUs written to pull us out of the last recession need to be repaid. That's a tall order for any government. Instead of riding a new wave of economic growth, countries are struggling under the twin burdens of massive debt and triple-digit oil prices.

The actions taken to stave off the last recession will make it that much harder to stay afloat during the next downturn. National balance sheets are drowning in red ink. Governments can only hope the next recession is far enough away to give the world time to get its fiscal house back in order. A decade or so of economic growth would do nicely. But triple-digit oil prices combined with the trillions of dollars of debt that have just been racked up make a return to the days of robust growth a nonstarter.

Even worse, the situation in the Middle East, home to the world's cheapest oil, is becoming ever more volatile. Instability in the region threatens to disrupt oil supplies and send energy prices even higher. If that happens, then the next recession may be just around the corner.

[CHAPTER 3]

THE ARAB REVOLT

THE I-405 IS THE BUSIEST ROAD IN AMERICA. Every day, some 400,000 vehicles crawl along the freeway's twelve lanes before spreading out across Los Angeles and the rest of southern California.

Doing the math, that's nearly 3 million cars a week, or 145 million a year. And that's just one highway. America's 2.7 million miles of paved roads is the largest network in the world. Consider the endless gallons of gasoline burned by the cars that fill up those roads and it's easy to understand how America guzzles more oil than any other country.

I'd like to say that America's huge appetite for oil is why you should care about the supply still buried under the Saudi Arabia desert. But it's not only American appetites we need to worry about here. In the last five years, China has spent more than $700 billion on transportation infrastructure, more than twice as much as the United States. Construction of twelve national highways there was recently completed, roughly thirteen years ahead of schedule. China's expressways, most of them less than ten years old, now cover the same distance as the US Interstate system, which took three decades to build.

All those new roads will soon be carrying a whole country full of new drivers. You can guess what the added demand will do to oil prices. If you've ever wondered why you should worry about the future of the Middle Eastern oil supply, all those roads in China are your answer.

REGIME CHANGE NEVER HELPS OIL PRODUCTION

The world's oil-consuming powers have long coveted the treasure trove of petroleum wealth in the Middle East. And those powers aren't shy about safeguarding the region's oil production, even if it means direct military intervention or staging a coup d'état.

The British began angling for political control of the region and its vast crude reserves in 1908, when the Anglo-Persian Oil Company made the first discovery there. In the lead-up to the First World War, Persian supplies became vital to Winston Churchill's plan to replace coal with oil as the fuel of the British Empire's navy. In 1914, Churchill moved to secure the Royal Navy's oil supply, gaining a 51 percent stake in Anglo-Persian through a £2.2-million investment that effectively nationalized the company. During the Second World War, Churchill then engineered the replacement of Persia's pro-German ruler, Reza Shah Pahlavi, by his more British-friendly 21-year-old son, Muhammad Reza Pahlavi.

A decade later, Western powers once again intervened to protect oil interests in the region after Mohammed Mossadegh, the new prime minister, nationalized the Anglo-Iranian Oil Company, bringing the country's oil reserves under Iranian control for the first time. Mossadegh's political grip on the country effectively marginalized the Shah's power. In 1953, the Shah, with the help of the CIA, attempted a countercoup. Mossadegh caught wind of the plot and the Shah was forced to flee the country, eventually landing in Rome. The Shah didn't know that the apparently failed coup had actually rallied key factions of the military to his cause. Faced with an upsurge of support for the Shah, Mossadegh fled, and the younger Pahlavi returned from his brief exile to regain his throne.

The Shah protected British and American oil interests in Iran until 1979, when he was overthrown by a popular revolution and replaced by an Islamic fundamentalist regime led by Ayatollah Khomeini. Until his downfall, the Shah's decades-long rule of Iran was marked by the same brutality that defined Moammar Gadhafi's regime in Libya and Hosni Mubarak's years in Egypt. Now deposed, these three rulers also shared another trait: each made sure the oil kept flowing into world markets. For years, these regimes counted on steady oil production to bring cash into the country and keep Western powers so happy that they would tolerate what these men were doing to their own citizens.

And for years, they were successful. Before the Iranian revolution of the late 1970s, the country was pumping almost 6 million barrels a day. Some forty years later, Iran's production is still below 4 million barrels a day.

Regime change has never been good for local oil production in the Middle East, no matter which leader gets ousted or who enters the picture after he's gone. Even when Western powers go so far as to occupy a Middle Eastern country, oil production still doesn't respond the way invaders would presumably hope. Take the most recent American invasion of Iraq, for instance. When Iraqi dictator Saddam Hussein ran the show in Baghdad, during its peak years in the 1980s the state-owned Iraq Petroleum Company cranked out more than 3.5 million barrels a day. Almost a decade after the United States invaded the country and toppled Hussein's regime, Iraq's production is still less than it was twenty-five years ago by roughly 500,000 barrels a day. Of course, the Bush administrations never acknowledged that their motive for going to war against Iraq, not once but twice, was oil, just as the Eisenhower administration didn't own up to the CIA's involvement in the overthrown Iranian government in the 1950s. But it hardly seems like a coincidence that the first site American troops secured when they reached Baghdad in the Second Gulf War was the Oil Industry building. Were they expecting to find weapons of mass destruction there?

Likewise, the Brits still aren't confessing to their real reasons for joining the US-led invasion, nor to harboring their own ambitious plans for the country's oil sector. Despite then prime minister Tony Blair's denials that access to Iraq's oil fields motivated British involvement, minutes of meetings between government officials and domestic energy firms show that oil was indeed considered in pre-invasion deliberations.

With Saddam removed from power, Iraq's oil resources were thrown open to the world's biggest energy companies. It didn't take long to divvy up the spoils. In one of the largest land grabs in the history of the oil industry, the new Iraqi government handed out twenty-year production contracts to multinational energy giants including BP, Exxon and Shell. Foreign corporations now control half of Iraq's 112 billion barrels of oil reserves.

Iraq's massive oil reserves stoke endless optimism about the country's potential output. After the invasion, the US Department of Energy predicted Iraqi production would reach 3.5 million barrels a day by 2005 and as much as 4 million barrels a day by 2010. Instead, the Sunni insurgency broke out. Pipelines and oil facilities were sabotaged, oil workers captured, and suicide bombers targeted foreign engineers. Before a period of relative calm descended in 2009, Iraq's output was often below 2 million barrels a day. By the end of 2012, the country's daily production was holding at a twenty-year high of around 3 million barrels. Still, that's a long way off the Iraqi government's forecast that the country will produce a world-leading 12 million barrels a day by 2017.

Iraq undoubtedly does contain vast unexploited oil reserves, but fearless predictions for spectacular production gains overlook both the region's history and its present reality. The country's oil industry is an obvious target for sectarian violence, which has roots that long predate the formation of modern Iraq. For centuries, the portion of the Ottoman Empire that we now call Iraq comprised three separate and distinct provinces, Mosul, Baghdad and Basra. Following the First World War, the victors combined these provinces into a single country. Removing the borders, though, didn't alter deep divisions between Kurds, Sunnis and Shiites. In 1920, Britain imposed a foreigner who had never seen the country, Faisal I, of the Hashemite Monarchy that today rules Jordan, as king of Iraq.

Nearly a dozen coups later, one of which included the beheading of King Faisal II in 1958, Saddam Hussein rose to power in 1979. His brutal methods worked to keep Iraq together in name, but the people remained no more unified than the ethnically diverse comrades forced together by Joseph Stalin under the banner of the USSR.

Undeterred by their failure to pump more oil out of Iraq, Western powers were still game to enter Libya in 2011. The coalition of NATO forces that intervened in Libya's civil war did help put an end to a brutal forty-year dictatorial regime. But it's also hard to ignore that Libya is home to the largest oil production and reserves in North Africa.

Once again, Western nations claim oil had nothing to do with intervening in Libya, just as oil had nothing to do with deposing Saddam Hussein. Instead, NATO described its involvement as a humanitarian mission. But if protecting a defenseless population from a ruthless dictator was the reason for going into Libya, why isn't NATO knocking on other doors as well? Syria and Yemen, to name just two countries, are home to dictators just as brutal as Gadhafi. Is it a coincidence that oil production in those countries is insignificant compared with Libya's?

Like Iraq, modern Libya is a postcolonial concoction, created when Italy amalgamated the three historically distinct areas of Tripolitania, Cyrenaica and the Fezzan. Establishing a cohesive federal state from those divisions, while negotiating a myriad of underlying tribal alliances, will be as much of a challenge in Libya as it is in Iraq. In that light, the lessons of past experience in the region suggest global energy markets should temper expectations for the stability of future Libyan oil exports.

In the Middle East, oil and totalitarianism are a familiar pair. Military dictatorships have controlled Egypt, Libya, Tunisia and Algeria for years, while absolutist monarchic rule exists in Oman, Bahrain and Saudi Arabia. Each of those countries is either a major oil producer or has strategic control over a vital oil-transit choke point such as the Suez Canal or the Strait of Hormuz, through which some 16 million barrels of oil pass every day.

An implicit quid pro quo has existed between Western democracies and Arab dictatorships: in exchange for a steady flow of oil to global markets, Western governments turn a blind eye to the measures Middle Eastern regimes take to stay in power. Since 9/11, the fact that the West has been fighting the terrorist threat from al-Qaeda only makes it easier for governments to justify increased military, financial and political support for such regimes.

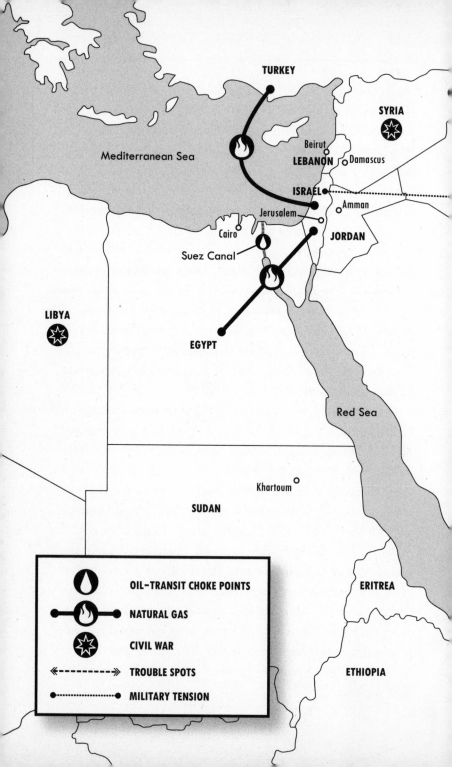

TURKEY

SYRIA

Mediterranean Sea

Beirut

LEBANON   Damascus

ISRAEL

Jerusalem   Amman

Cairo

Suez Canal   JORDAN

EGYPT

LIBYA

Red Sea

Khartoum

SUDAN

ERITREA

ETHIOPIA

OIL-TRANSIT CHOKE POINTS

NATURAL GAS

CIVIL WAR

TROUBLE SPOTS

MILITARY TENSION

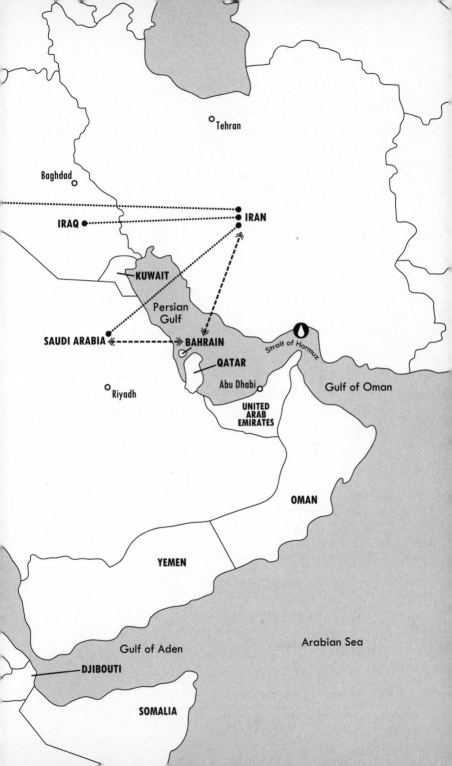

Consider American foreign policy in the Middle East, which runs the gamut from inconsistent to contradictory. On one hand, President Obama spent the first half of 2011 applauding the democratic impulse behind the Arab Spring. On the other hand, only a year earlier, the White House announced the largest military deal in US history, a $60-billion arms sale to Saudi Arabia. The infusion of new weaponry will no doubt buttress the military capacity of a strategic ally in the Middle East. Still, before approving the sale, White House decision makers clearly had to come to terms with the House of Saud's long track record of human rights violations. It's a tradeoff familiar to every American president since Franklin Roosevelt. And if a constant flow of arms to those countries isn't sufficient, America offers its allies in the region further protection, mostly from a possible Iranian attack, by maintaining military bases in Qatar, Bahrain and the UAE.

Even the best efforts of the United States, which include Operation Desert Storm and Operation Iraqi Freedom, may not be enough to hold together the old order in the Middle East. The shaky patchwork of dynastic absolute monarchies and military dictatorships, funded by petrodollars and armed by oil-consuming powers, is crumbling from within. Despite fears in the West about the disruptive potential of al-Qaeda and Islamic fundamentalism, neither the terrorist organization nor hard-line Muslims were behind the revolts against repressive regimes in Tunisia, Egypt and Libya. The real catalyst turned out to be hunger.

The Middle East is fortunate that it can export more oil than any other place, because desert sands are ill suited to raising crops. For years, a steady stream of petrodollars has made it possible to swap hydrocarbons for carbohydrates. That's a workable trade when oil prices are rising faster than food prices. But when food prices take off, the system breaks down. Throw in a global recession that sends oil prices tumbling and the oil-for-food arrangement becomes even more strained. Nothing sends a person into the street quite like an empty stomach.

Food supply isn't the only thing struggling to keep pace with a burgeoning population in the Middle East. So is employment. Double-digit youth unemployment is systemic in the region. A hungry population full of young people unable to find enough work to put food on the table only promises to keep stoking unrest throughout the Arab world.

As more regimes topple in North Africa and across the Middle East, the West will be sincere in its efforts to help new democracies take root. Ending decades of oppression, though, doesn't change the cold truth that regime change isn't good for oil production. That awareness is uppermost in the minds of Saudi Arabia's oil customers in the West. Oil markets get jittery about uprisings in countries such as Libya, Egypt or Syria, but the prospect of a revolt in Saudi Arabia is the energy world's worst-case scenario. The kingdom not only produces more than 9 million barrels of oil a day, it also keeps enough spare capacity in reserve to make up for shortfalls when production falters elsewhere in the region.

It's no coincidence that the forthright President Obama will call for dictators elsewhere in the Middle East to stand down but remains silent about the need for political reform in the Kingdom of Saudi Arabia. The deep and tangled ties between America and Saudi Arabia are laden with decades of hypocrisy. Still, the long-standing economic relationship ranks among the most important between any two countries in the world today. A disruption to production in Saudi Arabia, the world's second-largest oil producer after Russia, would make the loss of Libyan output, or that of any other OPEC producer for that matter, look minor by comparison.

Concerns about Saudi Arabia aren't just theoretical. In neighboring Bahrain, an absolutist monarchy sits tenuously atop a country divided by fundamental religious and economic differences. A Sunni elite minority lives in glass towers in the capital city of Manama, while a politically disenfranchised Shiite working class is ghettoized in suburban slums, shut out from high-paying jobs in government, the military and the private sector.

A former British colony, the island kingdom of Bahrain was supposed to be a constitutional monarchy run by an elected parliament. At least, that was the plan when Britain turned over the island to home rule. Instead, in 1975 the monarch, Isa bin Salman Al Khalifa, suspended parliament and imposed an autocratic rule that remains in full force today.

The Arab Spring has created a crisis for Bahrain's ruling class. Inspired by the success of popular revolts in surrounding countries, the Shiite majority—held in check for decades—is calling for the abolition of the Sunni monarchy. Protesters numbering in the hundreds of thousands have taken to the streets in a bid to replace the king with a democratically elected government, and have been brutally put down.

Only a short causeway separates Bahrain from Saudi Arabia. The proximity to the Saudi kingdom, coupled with Bahrain's historic ties to Iran, make Bahrain a key pawn in the ongoing cold war between the Saudi and Iranian regimes. Much of Bahrain's Shiite population has Iranian roots, a cultural heritage that troubles Saudi rulers. Bahrain's political importance and strategic location in the Persian Gulf also aren't lost on America, which keeps the US Fifth Fleet parked offshore from its naval base on the desert island kingdom.

Recent events have done little to calm Saudi concerns about Bahrain. If social and political upheaval jumps across the border, it wouldn't be the first time. In the mid-1990s, rioting in Bahrain stirred the sympathies of Shiite activists who oppose the Saudi regime. Any renewed calls for democracy in Bahrain are sure to echo in the kingdom once again, forcing the House of Saud to quell any opposition to its authority. Although Saudi Arabia's Shiite population remains a disenfranchised minority, several million do live in the oil-rich eastern provinces, a region critical to the petro-wealth that keeps the House of Saud in power.

That's why the Saudis were quick to dispatch troops to Bahrain to help the Sunni ruler contain the local ripples of the Arab Spring. It's also why King Abdullah, Saudi Arabia's octogenarian monarch, is loosening the purse strings like never before. Some $130 billion in additional spending has already been dished out to shore up support among the Sunni majority. The largesse includes the creation of tens of thousands of new public-sector jobs, one-time bonus payments for existing civil servants and the construction of some 500,000 new houses.

If the royal patronage works to head off potential unrest inside the kingdom, it will be money well spent for King Abdullah. However, any apparent kindness shouldn't be confused with a softening of the House of Saud. The country's totalitarian leadership is facing unprecedented challenges to its power structure in both the short and medium term.

The Kingdom has enjoyed a peaceful transition of power for going on six decades, but age and infirmity may soon force changes to the status quo. Since the death of King Abdul Aziz, known as Ibn Saud, in 1953, the throne has shifted only among his sons. The first generation of his offspring, however, is getting older. Crown Prince Nayef died in 2012, which followed the passing of Crown Prince Sultan a year earlier. The new royal successor, Prince Salman, is nearly eighty and also reportedly in poor health.

Next in line for the throne is Prince Muqrin, who in early 2013 was appointed second deputy Prime Minister, a role that historically tabs him as successor to the crown prince. His ascension, however, isn't guaranteed. Saudi Arabia lacks formal rules for succession beyond the current crown prince. While Prince Muqrin, born in 1945, is the most likely candidate, after him the sons of Ibn Saud are not only old, but dwindling in number. At some point, the line of succession will have to pass to one of his grandsons.

The House of Saud may be able to negotiate this transition smoothly. Then again, it may not. Saudi Arabia is rife with potential fault lines. The number of Saudis living below the poverty line is increasing, an ominous situation in a country where 60 percent of the population is under 30 years old. The ruling family doesn't have to look far for examples of what happens when a large and disaffected generation of young people takes to the streets.

Are the billions of dollars in fresh handouts from the Saudi government a sign of a regime on its last legs? Could Abdullah's death eventually lead to an internecine power struggle as the legitimacy of the ruling leader is called into question? Could that be a catalyst for another populist revolt? Will the House of Saud become another name on the list of deposed Middle Eastern despots? Perhaps, but if so, it bears asking: what might take its place?

A long history of autocratic rule in Saudi Arabia has left a social and political vacuum. Saudi Arabia, like other countries in the region, has limited exposure to democracy. Only recently have women been given the right to vote in municipal elections, the only kind that exist in the country. A step toward universal suffrage is positive, no doubt, but it should be noted that Saudi women still need a male escort to drive them to the polling station.

If the House of Saud does fall, it's hardly certain that a Western-style democracy will rise in its place. A country such as the United States has had more than two hundred years to develop its democratic system of checks and balances, and organized political parties. In the wake of a revolution, Saudi Arabia would be lucky to have twenty days in which to do the same thing. What's more, the established institutions best equipped to fill the political void are hardly synonymous with the notion of civil liberties. One option is Islamic fundamentalism, which has deep roots across the Middle East. In Saudi Arabia, Wahhabi clerics are already a well-organized political entity with the wherewithal to rule the country. And while secular government is considered the most progressive option by Western political standards, in the Middle East secular hasn't meant a separation of Church and State; it has meant military dictatorships. Whether it was the Baath party's dictatorial rule in Iraq or Syria, or strongman dictatorships in Egypt, Libya, Tunisia and Algeria, the region has known little else. Israel and Turkey are the only countries in the area where a government can be voted out of power. Suffice to say, it's unlikely the Arab world will look to the Jewish state as a role model.

I'm not saying that democracy can't work in the Middle East, only pointing out that a popular uprising won't necessarily result in the best-case scenario dreamed up by a liberal-thinking West. A post-Gadhafi Libya, for example, is already taking a fundamentalist turn, as evidenced by the calls now being heard for the imposition of Sharia law.

But what if democracy does take hold? That would certainly advance the cause of freedom in the Middle East, but, speaking solely from an economics perspective, new governance wouldn't necessarily translate into more oil exports. And I suspect that without the promise of increased oil flow, Western nations really won't stay that concerned about what form of government evolves in the region.

In fact, the pursuit of democratic forms of government could lead to less oil, not more. Democracy would give ordinary people who have never had a say in resource management a vote on what should be done with their hydrocarbon reserves. When the polls open, the newly enfranchised masses might elect leaders who want to sell fewer barrels to Western oil consumers.

In Egypt, the voices of the Arab Spring have already closed one important energy supply line. The fall of Mubarak's regime meant an end to Egyptian natural gas flowing to Israel and Jordan, since, not surprisingly, that supply arrangement was unpopular among the Egyptian people. The pipeline that runs from the Sinai Peninsula into Israel, and on to Jordan, has now been repeatedly bombed, an act that would have been unthinkable when the country was under Mubarak's iron grip.

That's bad news for Israel, which relies on the pipeline for about 40 percent of its natural gas. The news is even worse for Jordan, which counts on the same pipeline to supply the gas used to generate roughly 80 percent of its power. Ironically, losing the pipeline may force Jordan, a longtime Egyptian ally, into the arms of Iran, which has offered to replace the lost gas supply.

More importantly, the loss of Egyptian gas has put Israel and Turkey on a collision course. It will certainly expedite Israel's efforts to tap large gas fields under the eastern Mediterranean, which Turkey has its own plans to develop—plans that include military escorts for drilling ships.

For oil consumers in the West, the takeaway from the Arab Spring is that regime change can lead to dramatic shifts in energy policy. In the Middle East, you can never tell exactly how the dominoes will fall. In one instant, Mubarak's reign is ending to applause from all, and in the next, Israel and Turkey are bumping into each other in the Mediterranean. And of course there's also the international showdown brewing over Iran's nuclear program, which promises to open up another frightening can of worms.

At the very least, we know that energy supply in the region is politically fickle. Will new leaders feel compelled to listen to the voices on the street that swept them to power? The answer feels like yes. And if the answer is yes, what will that mean for supply contracts inked by deposed rulers? New regimes born in the aftermath of the Arab Spring may be less inclined to supply oil to customers in Europe or North America. Production contracts could instead be granted to energy-hungry countries such as China and India, both of which have massive sovereign wealth funds looking for opportunities to invest in energy.

No matter what form political change may take, the region's history makes it abundantly clear that, for world energy markets, social upheaval invariably leads to less supply.

OPEC CAPACITY IS TAPPED OUT

Events taking place above the ground aren't the only thing you should worry about in the Middle East. Apart from the inherent political instability, the global economy has other reasons to expect less oil from the region in the future. Beneath the ground, the Middle East's legendary oil reserves are showing signs of mortality.

The twelve members of OPEC supply roughly a third of the world's oil needs. That's about 30 million barrels a day, of which OPEC's Middle Eastern members, including Saudi Arabia, Iran and Iraq, account for approximately two-thirds. After decades of the region pumping countless barrels, geologists and economists are wondering how much longer Middle Eastern oil reserves will be able to continue to support such a heavy drain.

It's a contentious point. As the big dog of OPEC oil supply, Saudi Arabia's reserves have drawn the most scrutiny. The kingdom currently pumps more than 9 million barrels of oil a day, a figure it claims it could ramp up to 13 million barrels if the global economy needed the production. The Saudi energy minister and Saudi Aramco, the country's state-run oil company, routinely dismiss concerns that the country's actual production capacity would fall short of those levels if put to the test.

Saudi Arabia's argument is essentially threefold. When it comes to current production, Saudi Aramco argues the giant fields that have served the country for decades still have considerable headroom to pump out more barrels. What's more, the Saudis say they've yet to turn to new extraction methods developed in the last decade, which have helped extend the life of older fields around the world. When output does waver, the kingdom says it has proven reserves it is waiting to tap. When pressed, the Saudis also point out that the country remains underexplored. The seemingly limitless production from existing finds like Ghawar, a prolific field unmatched by any other in the world, has made spending on further exploration largely unnecessary.

But should these Saudi claims be trusted? The Saudis keep industry data behind the curtain of a totalitarian regime. Outside engineers and geologists haven't been granted an opportunity to verify Saudi assertions about future capacity. That leaves us reading the tea leaves to get a sense of what's unfolding behind the walls of the world's most important oil producer.

As an economist, I put more weight on what a country actually produces than on what it says it can produce. Saudi Aramco claims daily production can be quickly lifted if the world needs it to turn up the volume. But the country hasn't sustained output of 10 million barrels since the early 1970s. When oil prices marched to triple digits in the last decade, the Saudis knew full well the devastating effect such a rise in cost would have on the global economy. The offices of Saudi Aramco are full of people with advanced degrees from top business schools such as Oxford and Wharton. So why didn't the Saudis ramp up production to bring oil prices down to more affordable levels? It's been suggested the Saudis withheld production to boost revenues from high prices. But the well-trained economists at Saudi Aramco know that thinking is shortsighted.

The immediate effect of triple-digit oil prices is to put a damper on economic growth. Plunging the world into a recession sends oil prices tumbling and keeps petrodollars out of Saudi coffers. No country in the world is more invested in keeping the global oil market healthy. The House of Saud has literally thousands of members, who depend on a steady diet of oil revenues to feed their lifestyle. More importantly, oil money allows the royal family to buy off an increasingly rebellious populace with billions in handouts. Without wads of cash available to mollify an alienated and largely unemployed population of Arab youth, the House of Saud is just as vulnerable to the internal revolts of the disaffected that brought down Mubarak and Gadhafi.

If Saudi Arabia could prevent oil prices from rising to levels that induce a recession, the regime's survival instincts alone would seem to demand that its national oil company try to pump every possible drop. But that's not what's happened. When President George W. Bush came to his ally King Abdullah with hat in hand in 2008, he knew that more Saudi production could help stave off a dire economic decline. And what did King Abdullah do for his friend? Saudi Arabia boosted production by a scant 300,000 barrels a day, most of which was of a heavy sour variety that most refineries can't process. Why didn't King Abdullah ride to the rescue in a white hat with guns blazing?

The recession that followed destroyed demand for millions of barrels of oil. That was just as bad for Saudi Arabia as it was for the United States. Meanwhile, the global economy continues to shudder from the aftershocks of that recession. Europe's post-recession struggles, for one, might have been softened if the Saudis had increased production at the time. Instead, Europe's debt crisis seems likely to send the world into another recession, which, in turn, will take a heavy toll on oil demand and prices.

Of course, American motorists don't want to hear about the intricacies of the oil markets when they shell out four dollars a gallon at the pump. And so US politicians take the easy route, and blame foreign suppliers for high gas prices. That scores more points with voters, particularly when the bad guys are in the Middle East, than actually facing the unpleasant realities of global supply and demand.

None of which means Saudi Arabia isn't still critical to global oil markets. That's why President Obama continues to support the House of Saud, while turning his back on other dictatorial regimes. Saudi production is critical to keeping prices from soaring higher. If the Arab Spring sweeps the House of Saud from power, the world will face a supply disruption that will send prices rocketing to unheard-of heights.

When it comes to lowering oil prices from current levels, however, the Saudis are now much less influential than in the past. All evidence suggests the Saudis lack the capacity to ramp up production to keep prices from moving higher. Whether it's a supply disruption from another country or simply an increase in world demand, Saudi Arabia doesn't have a trump card left to play. That's troubling news for the rest of us, who have not only counted on Saudi production for years but still need it to be there for decades to come.

Unfortunately, there is an even bigger threat to Saudi crude exports: the country's own insatiable thirst for oil.

RUNAWAY FUEL CONSUMPTION CANNIBALIZING EXPORT CAPACITY

Go outside Riyadh into the desert and you'll hear the sound of roaring engines. Young Saudis spend entire nights drag racing under the desert stars. When gasoline costs 12 cents a liter, less even than bottled water, it's a relatively cheap pastime. Egregiously subsidized fuel prices are the most tangible way Saudi Arabia's average citizens benefit from the country's petro-wealth. And what better way to take advantage of cheap gas than by turning loose 400-horsepower engines on desert drag strips?

With the Arab Spring sweeping across the region, you can bet fuel subsidies will be the last thing cut by a Saudi regime already nervously looking over its shoulder. Add up all that fuel consumption, though, and pretty soon it's a bigger threat to global oil supply than the depletion of Saudi's aging oil fields.

Oil-consuming countries need to appreciate the ramifications of the quickening pace of oil consumption in the Middle East. In the final analysis, the world doesn't care how much oil is produced by Saudi Arabia or any other OPEC nation; what matters is how much of it gets exported. And every year that number is becoming a smaller portion of the region's output.

Saudi Arabia's daily oil exports, around 7.5 million barrels in 2005, fell to less than 6 million barrels in 2010. Whenever

OPEC announces a production increase, oil-importing countries assume that the higher output will translate into more exports. In reality, the exact opposite has occurred for most of the last decade. When Saudi Arabia ramped up production in 2011, it used more than half the increase to meet its own surging power demands.

Domestic oil consumption is increasing more than 5 percent a year in Saudi Arabia and elsewhere in the Middle East to meet domestic demand that stems from subsidized gasoline that costs roughly a tenth of what drivers pay in North America. It's a sweet deal for Saudi motorists, but the discounts don't stop there: Saudi citizens enjoy the cheapest power rates in the world.

As with any good deal, there's a catch. How do you suppose Middle Eastern countries generate electricity? There's no coal in the region to speak of. Hydroelectric dams aren't exactly abundant in the desert. Western governments, meanwhile, frown upon Middle Eastern states building nuclear power plants (although Iran doesn't seem to be asking permission). So power in the Middle East comes from oil and natural gas, the same hydrocarbons the West wants to see exported to global markets.

It shouldn't come as a surprise that rock-bottom power prices mean electricity demand is increasing by leaps and bounds throughout the Middle East. In Saudi Arabia, power-generation capacity is increasing 10 percent a year. At that rate, the size of the country's electrical grid will double to 68,000 megawatts by 2018. Even the Saudis recognize the downside of feeding such an immense appetite for oil-fired power. Saudi Aramco's chief executive warned in 2010 that domestic oil consumption, if left unchecked, would hit a staggering 8.3 million barrels a day by 2028. That's an untenable amount, nearly matching current Saudi production.

Of course, several practical constraints make that type of linear growth in domestic demand unlikely to occur. Saudi Arabia will continue to use a tremendous amount of oil for power generation, but the country's rulers know that export revenues are the alpha and omega of their wealth. Whether it's the thousands of members of the House of Saud who need stipends or the generous spending required to keep citizens from pouring into the streets, the royal family is beholden to export dollars to retain authority. Dwindling exports would also reduce the country's importance to the United States, an uncomfortable outcome for the House of Saud, whose members know that American military support is the kingdom's best chance for survival. Saudi Arabia won't continue generating power at the expense of exports indefinitely.

Nevertheless, the trend of Saudi power demand clearly points upward. And the more oil Saudis burn to generate electricity, the more expensive it will be to fill your tank.

Cheap power rates and subsidized gas are only partially responsible for Saudi Arabia's growing domestic oil appetite. The rest is being driven by thirst. Whether or not you believe that Saudi Arabia is running out of oil, the country is most certainly running low on water. Rainfall in the desert kingdom averages about four inches a year, and water is consumed at a rate fifteen to twenty times greater than natural replenishment. The country's aquifers, the so-called "fossil water" composed of rainfall from thousands of years ago, are already about 80 percent depleted.

Saudi Arabia, like most countries, uses more water for agriculture than for any other activity. For more than twenty years, the country's aquifers have allowed the country to be a self-sufficient producer of wheat. But farming a desert isn't easy. Agriculture accounts for more than three-quarters of total water consumption, a burden now too much for Saudi aquifers to handle. Since 2008, the country's annual wheat harvests have collapsed from 3 million tons to about 1 million. Meanwhile, wheat consumption in the country continues to increase by about 5 percent a year.

To make up the shortfall, the Saudis have turned to imports. To avoid the vagaries of world food markets, the kingdom has put its petro-wealth to work, snapping up agricultural land in places such as Ethiopia and Sudan, and now wheat grown in those countries is ending up on the tables of Saudi households. As the developing world grapples with food shortages, it remains to be seen how much longer Saudi Arabia can expect those countries to export wheat when local populations are staging food riots.

Drinking water is an even more acute issue for the region. To battle the problem, wealthy countries such as Saudi Arabia and the UAE are spending billions constructing giant desalination plants to turn seawater into fresh water. Saudi Arabia already gets nearly 70 percent of its drinking water from these plants. The Saline Water Conversion Corporation produces 3.36 million cubic meters of desalinated water a day, yet it's not keeping pace with a demand for fresh water that's tearing ahead at 7 percent a year. Water, like oil, is massively subsidized by the Saudi government. That allows the average Saudi to use 950 cubic meters of water a year, nearly twice the global average.

Running a desalination plant consumes a huge amount of energy. So much so that the Saudis are essentially trading oil for water. The country is reportedly burning more than a million barrels a day in its network of desalination facilities. To meet projected increases in water usage in the coming years, the kingdom will need to build more plants, which means burning even more oil.

So much energy is required by the desalination process that Saudi Arabia has been forced to invest billions in nuclear power plants and solar energy projects. By 2030, the kingdom plans to have sixteen nuclear reactors on line to help meet its energy needs. To witness Saudi Arabia, whose oil reserves have long been the envy of the world, embrace nuclear power is disconcerting. Yet that's exactly what's happening.

What are the ramifications for Saudi's oil customers in the West? Chances are that less of the world's oil supply will be coming from OPEC, which will only make every other barrel of global production that much more expensive.

Whether it's because of social unrest, a lack of spare production capacity or a swelling appetite for its own product, the Middle East's wherewithal to lift oil output in the coming years is looking ever more fragile. Yet the International Energy Agency (IEA) is now counting on the Middle East and North Africa to supply as much as 90 percent of the additional oil the world will burn in the next decade. If that oil doesn't flow, it's far from obvious where we'll find the fuel to power tomorrow's economic growth.

HITTING THE ENERGY CEILING

THE COLDEST BOTTLE OF WHISKY in the world can be found on a desolate chunk of rock near the North Pole.

A few years ago, this frozen bottle of Canadian Club became the cocktail of choice on Hans Island, replacing a high-end bottle of Danish schnapps that had been there since 2004. The island is nestled in a remote strait between Greenland and Ellesmere Island, and dropping by isn't like taking a weekend breather to the Bahamas. Nevertheless, Danish icebreakers and Canadian helicopters periodically make the trek into the High Arctic for a visit. Once there, a handful of dutiful soldiers will disembark and spend a few hours stomping around the island's barren half a square mile before planting a fresh flag and going home—but not before leaving behind their national libation of choice.

This Arctic bottle swap is part of a low-key turf war between Canada and Denmark. While not exactly India versus Pakistan over the Kashmir, the territorial dispute, now four decades old, is more than just a frivolous patriotic flap between global light-weights. Both sides will tell you it's about Arctic sovereignty.

Really, it's about oil.

When pundits like me say the era of expensive oil is upon us, Arctic exploration is what we're talking about. It's hard to imagine a worse place to work than the Arctic Ocean. The cost, not to mention the logistics, of towing a massive drilling platform through iceberg-filled waters is staggering. And then a crew has to be flown in to drill several kilometers into the frozen seabed before any oil is even produced or shipped. It's not for the faint of heart. If oil companies had any other choice, they wouldn't be there. The Arctic is, quite literally, the end of the earth. And that's exactly where the energy industry is being forced to search for oil to keep the global economy humming.

Exxon, the world's largest oil company, signed a deal with Russia in 2011 to explore in the Arctic. According to President Vladimir Putin, Russia and Exxon could spend as much as $500 billion over the life of the deal. Granted, Putin is known to talk a big game, but even the suggestion that they are signed up to spend half a trillion dollars shows how much oil companies are now forced to shell out to find deposits big enough to supply the world's energy needs.

Here's the catch: for those oil resources to become tomorrow's fuel supply, oil prices have to keep climbing. The extraction economics—towing drilling platforms into the High Arctic, conducting environmental assessments, paying skilled workers, operating in subzero temperatures, maintaining icebreakers to bring tankers through frozen waters, not to mention actually drilling into the ocean floor—simply won't work otherwise. But higher prices, as we saw in chapter 1, also kill demand. As I wrote in that chapter, that's the dilemma we face with the world's remaining oil supply: we can't afford the prices needed to lift it out of the ground.

The difference between what the oil industry calls a resource and what it calls a reserve helps to shed light on this predicament.

The first term is used to account for what's in the ground. The second refers to what can be economically extracted. Canada's tar sands, for example, contain more than 170 billion barrels of proven oil reserves, giving the country the third-largest reserves in the world, behind only Saudi Arabia and Venezuela. It's a big number, but it's dwarfed by estimates of the resource held in the deposit, which are in the ballpark of 1.6 trillion barrels. That's more than the current assessment of the total proven reserves held by every country in the world. Calculating the number is also a largely esoteric exercise, since prices won't ever climb high enough to make it worthwhile to extract the vast majority of the resource.

From a geological standpoint, you can always boost production by accessing increasingly costly or environmentally hazardous sources of new supply. Canada's tar sands are a case in point, as are the oil industry's expensive forays into the deep waters of the Gulf of Mexico, offshore from west Africa and into the High Arctic. The higher crude prices go, the more oil the industry will extract from the bowels of the earth.

Oil is a big-money game. As long as there are profits to be made, the energy industry will keep finding ways to pull more oil out of the ground. But make no mistake—technological breakthroughs you may have read about, like hydraulic fracturing, which are helping the industry increase production, aren't a magic bullet that will solve the world's energy needs. Fracking, for example, involves injecting an oil and gas formation with a high-pressure mixture of water, chemicals and sand to help increase the porosity of the subsurface rocks that hold the resource. The more space that can be created between the rocks, the more oil or gas is able to flow up through the wellbore. The technique has been around for decades, but it's only in the last ten years that rising commodity prices have provided enough incentive for the industry to get serious about its use. In some jurisdictions, concerns that fracking could contaminate water supplies have put the industry at odds with landowners and environmental groups. Controversy aside, from a strict supply perspective fracking is not going to allow the global industry to boost production enough to prevent prices from climbing ever higher. For the world to meet its future energy needs, significant production gains will also be needed from sources such as the deposits of bitumen and heavy oil found in Canada and Venezuela. Higher oil prices and improvements in production efficiency recently allowed Venezuela to categorize more of the resources contained in its Orinoco heavy oil belt as proven reserves. The Orinoco belt, or Faja as it's known locally, is now credited with 297 billion barrels of reserves, up from 211 billion. That's more than the 265 billion barrels stored under the oil-rich deserts of Saudi Arabia and the 170 billion in Canada's tar sands.

No one is saying the size of these resources isn't impressive. But when it comes to the health of the global economy, size doesn't really matter; the issue is the price per barrel we'll need to pay to justify hauling that oil out of the ground.

The huge caches of oil found in Canada and Venezuela are what are known as unconventional resources. Compared to conventional oil, which is the stuff you might think of as flowing out of the ground Beverly Hillbillies style, unconventional oil is much harder to get at. How hard? you ask.

Take the Alberta tar sands as an example. Oil-soaked sand must first be dug up and trucked to giant industrial plants called up-graders. The sand is then blasted with intense heat to separate the oil from the sand; the oil is then mixed with other chemicals to produce what's called synthetic crude. This mixture is shipped to a refinery, where it's further processed into a product we can use, such as gasoline or diesel fuel. Since the tar sands are in northern Canada, this work is done in temperatures that in the long winters routinely dip to 40 degrees below freezing, and it uses the biggest trucks and heavy equipment ever built. The remoteness of the mines even spurs some companies, such as Canadian Natural Resources, to build airstrips to ferry workers in and out on Boeing 737s.

Compare that effort and expense with Spindletop, the conventional discovery credited with kicking off the Texas oil boom in 1901. At its peak, easy-to-refine crude from Spindletop literally gushed out of the ground at the astounding rate of 75,000 barrels a day. To put that in perspective, in 2010 the average daily production of a Texas oil well was 6 barrels. In total, the state's 158,000 wells produce just shy of 1 million barrels a day. After a hundred years of exploration, there are no Spindletops left to find. Instead, the global energy industry is spending hundreds of billions pulling oil out of places such as Canada's tar sands and the Faja. That's just the cost of doing business these days.

Unfortunately, Big Oil's bottom line isn't the only place taking a hit—it's bad for you too. No one knows this better than the International Energy Agency. Every year, IEA economists issue a voluminous report called the *World Energy Outlook*, in which they attempt to reassure anxious energy consumers in the West that future energy supplies will be there when needed. The 2012 report was a home run in this regard. The resurgence of US oil and gas production is, in the words of the IEA, nothing short of spectacular. So-called tight oil reserves that were previously uneconomic to drill are now contributing hundreds of thousands of barrels a day to US production.

Output from North Dakota's Bakken play, for example, has

more than tripled since 2009 to more than 700,000 barrels a day. In Texas, the Eagle Ford basin is producing north of 300,000 barrels a day, more than double the output from 2011. Backed by an expectation that production from these and other tight oil plays will continue to increase by leaps and bounds, the IEA is now forecasting the US will pass Saudi Arabia to become the world's largest oil producer by 2017.

It's a remarkable turnaround for the energy fortunes of the world's biggest energy consumer. But it must also be noted that the advances in horizontal drilling and hydraulic fracturing behind this energy renaissance don't come cheap.

Environmental advocates, for one, are sounding loud alarm bells about the harm being caused by such a swift ramp up in industrial activity. Indeed, the oil boom in North Dakota is now so big it can be seen from space. A decade ago, nighttime pictures taken from the International Space Station show the US Midwest as a black void of rural darkness. Now, though, the hundreds of flare stacks burning off unwanted natural gas from the prolific Bakken fields have created a new light source that rivals nearby Chicago.

The IEA is calling for production from US tight oil plays to triple in the next few decades to more than 3 million barrels a day. That will put even more of a strain on water supplies. Fracking a single well typically takes many millions of gallons of water. As the number of wells goes up, the demand for water will naturally follow. And that doesn't even account for related issues, such as potential groundwater contamination and managing the industrial wastewater that's kicked off as a byproduct. If US oil production eventually does reach the IEA's forecast, it's certain the energy industry will have managed to maneuver around some serious obstacles along the way.

Such issues aside, for the global economy what matters more than supply is price. The sources of oil now being tapped are becoming ever more costly. According to the IEA, the oil and gas industry spent more than $600 billion in 2012 on exploration and production. That's up more than 20 percent since 2008 and a fivefold increase since 2000.

The good news is that the global oil industry is astoundingly good at finding new reserves and bringing on new production. The bad news is that the low-cost oil we can afford to burn is being replaced by more expensive sources. Even if technology allows us to outpace the treadmill of depletion, continually swapping out cheap conventional crude with more expensive unconventional oil is shifting the industry's cost curve to a place our economies simply can't afford.

The cheapest oil, and much of the new production the world will need in the coming decades, will continue to come from the very same OPEC countries that are currently bubbling over with social unrest. I'm all for populist rebellions against brutal government repression, but if the region's history has taught the economist in me one thing, it's that oil production, as we saw in the last chapter, doesn't increase during a revolution—or after.

Even accounting for the turning tide of US energy output, Saudi Arabia remains the key player in global oil flows. While the IEA remains confident that OPEC has enough spare pumping capacity to keep the world economy running smoothly, its forecast that future Saudi production will reach 14.5 million barrels per day is higher than even Saudi Aramco's best guess at its future capacity. Saudi Arabia is still OPEC's kingpin, but that doesn't change the reality that Saudi oil production is below where it was in the 1970s.

OLD KING COAL—AN EXPENSIVE OLD SOUL

Oil isn't the only vital resource that's getting uncomfortably pricey for the global economy. Cheap coal has been one of our energy staples, but assuming that we still have an abundant supply of coal may be no more valid than our earlier belief in the abundance of cheap oil.

Oil may be the world's transit fuel, but coal is the world's principal source of electric power, particularly in countries such as China, where power demand is growing at double-digit annual rates. Some 40 percent of all the electric power in the world is generated from burning coal. It's second only to oil in terms of its total contribution to global energy use.

And affordable coal may soon be running out just as fast as affordable oil is.

No matter how plentiful it once was, no resource can withstand the pressure of an exponential growth in demand. China burned 3.7 billion tons of coal in 2010, according to the US Energy Information Agency, compared with 1.2 billion tons in 2000. Most everyone knows that oil prices have quadrupled in the last decade. Given such a dramatic rise in China's coal consumption, it shouldn't come as a surprise that coal prices have increased just as quickly.

China may still consume only half as much oil as America, but the Chinese economy has long surpassed the United States in coal consumption. In fact, China burns nearly twice as much coal as the United States while only possessing half of its coal reserves. A burgeoning Chinese vehicle fleet is still powered by oil, but coal is behind China's world-leading economic growth, accounting for more than three-quarters of the country's power. An ever-increasing supply of coal is needed to keep China's factories humming, its lights on and, most of all, its GDP growing.

China is acutely aware that coal, like oil, is getting more expensive to burn all the time. Just as oil prices hit unprecedented highs a few years ago, so too did the price of its hydrocarbon cousin. Newcastle coal, named for the Australian port from which much of it is shipped, is the benchmark coal price for Asia. At the peak of the boom in global commodity demand in 2008, coal prices rose to almost $200 a metric ton, a price matching the lofty $147-per-barrel perch reached by oil prices at the time. Only record coal prices didn't get nearly as much public notoriety as record oil prices. (If drivers were forced to fill up at the local coal pump every week, the Newcastle price would draw much more attention.)

Oil prices tumbled a drastic 70 percent when the recession hit. Though coal didn't fall as dramatically, its price still dropped by more than half. And, like oil, coal prices perked up again along with the global economic recovery.

In today's economy, in order to expand their GDP, countries need to burn more hydrocarbons. That's why China is digging up its coal reserves at a pace never before seen. China's official growth plan calls for burning as much as 5 billion tons per year, more than a third higher than recent consumption. The country already accounts for almost half of global coal production, yet it holds less than 15 percent of the world's coal reserves. The country now uses more coal each year than the USA and Europe combined. Once a coal exporter, its massive consumption now forces China to be a net importer. Something has to give. At the current rate, China's coal reserves will be depleted sooner than anyone had previously imagined.

It's easy to see why most climate change scientists worry that China's ambitious coal consumption targets will throw off enough carbon emissions to cook the atmosphere and trigger cataclysmic climate change: it is already a world-leading carbon emitter. But as we'll explore later on, before global warming spells the end of the world, those same climate change scientists need to ask where China is going to get all the coal it's expecting to burn. To fulfill the carbon emission projections made by groups like the Intergovernmental Panel on Climate Change (IPCC), the Chinese economy may need to burn through the coal supplies of several planets.

A few doors west, India's fuel demands are also bolting higher. Overall, world coal consumption, according to the IPCC, is forecast to double over the next two decades. That covers the demand side of the equation. But we still need to ask where we'll get all this coal.

As growing power shortages across the country will attest, China is already struggling to come up with the 3.7 billion tons of coal it burns each year. That's why Chinese companies are scouring the world looking for new coal reserves. State-run Chinese firms shelled out more than $32 billion to acquire foreign mining companies between 2005 and 2010. The biggest splash came in 2008 when Aluminum Corporation of China, a state-run mining firm known as Chinalco, paid $14 billion for a 9 percent stake in Anglo-Australian mining giant Rio Tinto.

If you ask the world coal industry, experts will tell you that enough coal exists to fuel the generation of electricity for the next two hundred years. In one sense, the coal industry experts are probably right. The world will never geologically run out of coal, just as it will never run out of oil. But just as the world is rapidly running out of affordable oil, the same constraint is being felt in the world coal market.

As it turns out, our supply of economically viable coal is a lot smaller than we think. At least, that's true for the high-grade coal in demand around the world. Not all coal is created equal. Energy content is critical when it comes to what kind of coal is worth the trouble of shipping and what coal stays home. The highest grades, such as anthracite and bituminous coal, can have as much as five times the energy content of other "brown" varieties, such as sub-bituminous and lignite. If you have to ship five times as much low-grade coal to match the energy content of high-grade coal, it's evident why it makes little sense to transport low-grade coal to faraway power plants.

Unfortunately for the world's economy, the most abundant forms of coal are those so-called brown coals with a low energy density. The world has a lot of brown coal, but shipping it is another story. It's not worth loading brown coal onto a boat when the bunker fuel used to cross the ocean is worth more than the cargo. Not surprisingly, the type of coal with the highest energy density, anthracite, has been depleted far more rapidly than coal with lower energy content. Its percentage of total coal production has fallen steadily, while the percentage of lower-grade coal has risen.

Because of huge differences in energy content between coal grades, physical tonnage can offer a misleading picture of energy supply. For example, coal production in the United States, which boasts the world's largest reserves, has never been greater. But from the standpoint of how much energy is produced, coal peaked in 1998. While physical production has grown since then, the substitution of lower-grade coal for higher grades has resulted in a reduction in actual energy content. In fact, America's production of high-grade anthracite has been steadily declining for more than sixty years. Annual production is now less than a quarter of its 1950 level. Production of the next-highest grade of coal, bituminous, peaked in 1990 and has since been declining as well. But despite a drop-off in high-quality production, the total coal output from US mines has increased by roughly 20 million tons per year. All that coal, though, packs a smaller energy punch than less tonnage of better quality did years ago.

Less energy for more tons mined—just another example of the concept of diminishing returns that's now common in our energy landscape.

What makes the depletion of high-quality coal reserves even more troubling is that most coal doesn't leave home. The vast majority of coal production, some 85 percent, is burned in the country where it's mined. That leaves only 15 percent of global coal production available for export. The lion's share of coal is concentrated in only seven countries: China, America, Russia, South Africa, Australia, India and Indonesia. By and large, the coal these countries mine goes to a captive domestic audience. The exception is Australia, which exports three-quarters of its production. Because Australia's domestic power market is relatively small, only needing to serve 20 million people spread across a coal-rich continent, Australia can ship most of its coal to China and Japan, and on its own accounts for about 40 percent of global exports.

Imagine if 85 percent of the world's *oil* was burned where it was produced, and only 15 percent of global production was available for export. The global economic map would look a lot different than it does today. The US economy, for one, would be dramatically altered. The United States burns two to three times as much oil as it produces every day. If it couldn't secure daily oil imports of 8 to 10 million barrels, it wouldn't be the world's largest economy. If the United States had to rely on homegrown fuel, its GDP would shrink to a shadow of what it is right now.

Scary as it might sound to a US trucker on the I-90, that's precisely where the American economy would be if oil were more like coal. But the reality of the energy world is that oil is a good traveler. For coal, proximity is the name of the game.

When you consider that oil and coal are the two most important fuels in the world, accounting for almost two-thirds of all the energy consumed each day, it's hard not to recognize that oil and coal that cost more have sobering implications for global economic growth. Perhaps, in a post-carbon world, we'll discover new ways of harnessing energy that free us from the constraint of the planet's increasingly finite supply of economically usable hydrocarbons. But that day is still in the distance. In the meantime, we're staring at the depletion of the resources that power the global economy. And that can't help but have a huge impact on the pace at which our economies will be able to grow in the future.

TOMORROW'S POWER?

In some circles, there's one energy source that does offer a potentially viable alternative to oil and coal. But every time nuclear gets a foot in the door, the world gets an unpleasant reminder of why no one wants to see a reactor outside their living room window.

The meltdown of three reactors at a nuclear power station in Japan in early 2011 marked the latest setback to nuclear energy's chances of becoming the fuel of tomorrow. News of three damaged reactors at the Tokyo Electric Power Company (TEPCO) nuclear plant didn't take long to reverberate around the world. Before the accident at Fukushima, the nuclear industry was coming off a good run. Concerns about carbon emissions had translated into a new receptiveness toward the nuclear industry, which almost had its ducks in a row for an aggressive global expansion. That completely changed in the hours after the tsunami struck the Japanese coast in March 2011. Uranium prices plunged, as did the shares of uranium producers such as Saskatchewan-based Cameco. Firms that build reactors, such as France's Areva, and engineering companies that design nuclear power plants, such as Montreal's SNC-Lavalin, also took a hit. Investors quickly sold off everything that had anything to do with generating nuclear power.

Governments were also bailing out on the industry, even those who'd been counting on nuclear to play a bigger role in a carbon-constrained future energy mix. The dull thud of future business hitting the floor is a familiar sound to nuclear industry veterans. It was last heard after Chernobyl. Before that, it was Three Mile Island.

Global warming may pose far greater dangers down the road than a reactor meltdown, but nothing scares people more than radiation. And not just in Japan, which suffered nuclear horrors during the Second World War. Halfway around the world, people in Boston were measuring for trace fallout in rainwater. On the west coast of North America, folks from Los Angeles to Vancouver worried that radioactive discharge would wash ashore from thousands of miles away. Ships were diverted from Tokyo Bay to avoid possible radiation exposure. Even the United States Navy ordered vessels to redeploy to the leeward side of the Japanese islands.

No matter how exaggerated the fear, Japan's nuclear accident became the world's nuclear accident. It was another kick in the teeth for the nuclear industry and the countries that depend on splitting the atom to power their electrical grids.

Of course, countries don't just randomly decide that they're going to invest in nuclear technology. Generally, the countries who are betting big either lack domestic hydrocarbon resources, like France, or have an enormous energy appetite that dwarfs domestic energy production, like the United States. The fact that Japan would rely so extensively on nuclear power is a compelling example of how basic economic imperatives are hard to ignore. A little more than half a century after Hiroshima and Nagasaki, Japan trails only the United States and France in nuclear power usage.

If you look at the country's bill for fuel imports, it's easy to see why nuclear plays such a big role in its energy grid. Japan's economy burns roughly 4.5 million barrels of oil every day, ranking it third in the world behind the United States and China. That's a pretty big appetite for a country that has less than 150,000 barrels a day of domestic oil production. The rest of those barrels have to come from somewhere, which leaves Japan at the mercy of import prices.

Its dependence on foreign oil bit Japan hard during the first OPEC oil shocks. Not even the United States suffered as much as Japan during the oil embargo of the 1970s. After seeing the economic damage that an oil price shock could unleash, Japan made a concerted national push toward nuclear energy, which now accounts for nearly a third of its power supply. Even so, Japan still relies on oil for nearly half of its energy needs. Japanese motorists, in particular, depend almost exclusively on imported oil, which makes buying even more oil on world markets to fuel power plants the last thing Japan wants to do.

Yet if history is any guide, Japan's hydrocarbon fuel bill will be significantly greater in a post-Fukushima economy than ever before. Like the accident at Three Mile Island in 1979, the impact of the Fukushima meltdown will be felt for decades. Overnight, the accident in Pennsylvania undermined American confidence in the safety of nuclear power. There wasn't a brand-new reactor built in the United States for decades. And judging from the public reaction to the accident in North America, Fukushima will put the kibosh on any budding hopes for a nuclear renaissance in Canada and the United States for years to come.

In Japan, the nuclear industry's very existence is now at stake. Its key player, TEPCO, is developing a public persona comparable to the one BP now enjoys in Louisiana following the Macondo well disaster in the Gulf of Mexico. As with BP, the aftermath has been nearly as upsetting as the actual event. It took months for TEPCO to admit its reactors experienced core meltdowns, when in fact those events occurred almost immediately after the plant was swamped by the tsunami. An international team sent by the World Atomic Energy Commission also found that the radiation released in the early stages of the disaster was double what TEPCO had previously admitted.

If you check TEPCO's track record, you won't be surprised by the lack of candor. Like BP, TEPCO is no angel. Between 1977 and 2002, TEPCO was found to have falsified nuclear safety data on at least two hundred separate occasions. In 2005, public disclosure of the firm's nuclear indiscretions forced the resignation of the company's president and several board members. Safety concerns were so rampant that the Japanese government forced TEPCO to shut down seventeen of its reactors for inspection. And TEPCO's problems didn't end there. In 2007, only two years after TEPCO was allowed to restart these reactors, an earthquake forced the company to admit that its reactor in the Chuetsu-oki region was not built to withstand such tremors. The government subsequently ordered TEPCO to shut down that plant.

More recently, yet another TEPCO president resigned after the firm posted the largest loss in Japanese corporate history. Since Fukushima, TEPCO's shares have fallen more than 80 percent. Future liabilities, meanwhile, are staggering. The Japanese government is considering injecting at least a trillion yen, almost $13 billion, into the crippled utility to stave off a potential bankruptcy. And that money won't even account for all the environmental damage that will stem from the radiation from the Fukushima plant.

So much for the Japanese nuclear industry's world-leading earthquake-resistant construction standards. Japanese firms have been selling that perception for years, at home and abroad. The industry's safety record, though, tells a different story. While it took the largest tsunami in more than a century to trigger the event, the Fukushima disaster occurred in an industry where decades of safety breaches and cover-ups pointed to a major accident just waiting to happen.

The policy fallout from Fukushima is reaching well beyond Japan. While the earlier meltdowns at Three Mile Island and Chernobyl put the brakes on most nuclear expansion, the few reactors that were built after those disasters were far more costly because of new mandatory safety features. Naturally, the mounting costs of new reactors only added to big power companies' growing aversion to the industry.

When you get right down to it, generating tremendous amounts of nuclear power from a very small amount of fissile material, like enriched uranium, isn't all that expensive. The real costs are found in the safety and containment systems needed to prevent deadly radiation from leaking into the atmosphere. More safety means higher costs, which only makes the power generated that much more expensive.

After each nuclear disaster, the bar is set that much higher for safety. Reactors built between Three Mile Island and Chernobyl cost 95 percent more than those built before 1979. Compared to existing nuclear facilities, the power generated in plants built after Three Mile Island was 40 percent more expensive. After

Chernobyl, the cost curve went up again. Additional safety and containment measures sent construction costs up more than 85 percent, while prices for nuclear-generated power increased by another 40 percent.

For the nuclear industry, the biggest cost wasn't found in the reactors that were built, but in the ones that were scrapped after each accident. Plans for hundreds of reactors were shelved as communities around the world said *not in my backyard*. And it wasn't government regulators that provided the check on the industry, but the market. Wall Street, for one, couldn't find investors willing to finance nuclear expansion. With no access to capital and spiraling costs, the power industry turned to alternatives, including hydroelectric, natural gas and, of course, coal.

Fukushima is having the same impact right now. In Japan, it may take decades before people return to the area around Fukushima. And TEPCO's unwillingness to acknowledge the scale of the disaster is hardly helping win back the hearts and minds of the public. Japanese citizens have learned only too well that when something goes wrong inside a domed building down the road, the local utility operator doesn't have the answers.

Germany was one of the first nations to react to Fukushima. A big nuclear player, Germany has dragged its feet on the issue of new reactors. It's been reluctant to license new plants, but willing to extend the operating permits of existing facilities. That same practice is par for the course in North America, where plants with expired due dates remain in service to help hold down electricity costs. Fukushima struck a raw nerve with the German public. Faced with new polls showing that more than 70 percent of the population was against nuclear power, the government did an about-face on a decision to extend the lives of its aging fleet of seventeen nuclear power plants until 2036. Chancellor Angela

Merkel, historically a strong proponent of nuclear power, immediately decided to close seven of the oldest reactors pending a safety review. Two have been permanently boarded up. Germany then made the bombshell announcement that it will shutter all of its nuclear power plants by 2022, some fourteen years ahead of its previous schedule.

The big issue Germany now faces is how to replace the lost power from these reactors. Nearly 30 percent of Germany's electricity comes from nuclear, roughly the same proportion as in Japan. While Germany will undoubtedly boost the contribution from renewable sources, an area in which it already leads the world by a wide margin, few believe solar and wind can make up the gap. The more likely substitute is natural gas.

But for Germany, going to natural gas means greater energy dependence on gas-rich Russia. Germany already gets almost a third of its gas supply from Russia, an amount that is increasing with the opening of the Nord Stream, a giant pipeline under the Baltic Sea. A reliance on Russian gas will extend Moscow's influence farther into Europe, a geopolitical leverage the EU can't be happy to see.

Other countries are also reconsidering nuclear power. Switzerland is now looking to phase it out altogether. In the United States, home to the most reactors in the world, the construction of a new plant in the state of Georgia was regarded as the first stage of a nuclear renaissance. Prior to Fukushima, fourteen more states were considering proposals for new nuclear power plants. But as Americans watch the environmental and economic fallout from the Japanese disaster, the country's nuclear revival looks as if it will be nipped in the bud.

In today's environment, public anxiety will make building new facilities nearly impossible. A recent Gallup poll found that seven out of ten Americans were fearful of a nuclear accident. A CBS poll found support for nuclear power had slipped to 43 percent, lower even than in the aftermath of Three Mile Island.

The nuclear industry is feeling the effects of Fukushima nearly everywhere except in China and India. That's where power needs are the greatest, and it's why both countries are, by and large, holding the line on ambitious nuclear plans that were announced prior to Fukushima.

As might be expected, China's nuclear energy plans are aggressive. Currently, twenty-five reactors are under construction, which will be added to the fourteen the country already has in service. The buildup will offer a fivefold increase in China's nuclear power generation capacity by 2020. The burgeoning fleet of nuclear facilities is a pillar of the country's objective to obtain a fifth of its energy from non-hydrocarbon sources within the next decade. Reaching that goal is a cornerstone of China's plan to lower the carbon intensity of its economy.

Will China meet its nuclear goals? Like Japan, China is no stranger to devastating earthquakes. A magnitude 7.3 quake in Tangshan killed a quarter of a million people in 1976, and at least 87,000 perished in a quake in Sichuan in 2008. Following Fukushima, China ordered a full review of its nuclear agenda, but whether it will make any changes to that agenda remains an open question.

India's plans are nearly as big. More than half of its 1.2 billion people still need to be connected to an electrical grid. The country will have to find the energy from somewhere. India's oil consumption is already roughly three times its domestic production. And thanks to demand spurred by record auto sales, the country's fuel bill is only heading higher.

Fukushima or no Fukushima, it appears that India's plans to order as many as twenty-one nuclear reactors will charge ahead.

India's politicians are paying ample lip service to the idea of nuclear safety, but the proof will be in the pudding. Construction on
two 700-megawatt atomic power plants in Rajasthan is expected
to be complete by 2017.

While India's and China's nuclear plans could go ahead undeterred, public sentiment toward nuclear power in Japan is now
overwhelmingly negative. Unsurprisingly, the Japanese people
want even less to do with nuclear than the Germans. They want
their government not only to scrap plans for any new reactors but
to shut down facilities currently in operation.

In an apparent reversal of national energy policy, the clock
is ticking on the operational lives of Japan's fleet of nuclear reactors. Since the Fukushima disaster, only 2 of the country's
reactors are back on-line. No fewer than 48 remain shuttered
until upgrades on the other plants are able to meet new tougher
safety standards.

Local governments in Japan have the power to withhold permission for the nuclear power stations to restart. Sensitive to the
huge shift in public sentiment against nuclear power, Tokyo is
backing them up. In the course of roughly a year, Japan may go
from a country drawing nearly a third of its power from reactors to
a country that's nearly nuclear free.

A permanent loss of 30 percent of the energy in the electrical
grid means Japan will have to tap other sources, which means
imports will need to rise. Whether it's oil, natural gas or coal, Japan is about to add to the demand for global resources. Japan's
10 regional power companies, for instance, have boosted their
consumption of fuel oil and crude oil by more than 60 percent
post-Fukushima. Already the world's largest importer of lique-
fied natural gas, Japan's LNG consumption is also up, reaching
a record high in 2012.

Japan's nuclear accident makes the world's reliance on hydro-carbons that much greater. At the same time, oil and coal prices are telling us those resources have never been scarcer.

—

It took a once-in-a-century tsunami to trigger the Fukushima disaster. On the surface, that could seem like a singular occurrence unlikely to be repeated. Yet in the big picture of the energy world, these one-off events are happening with surprising regularity. It was only a few months before Fukushima that BP's Macondo well was gushing millions of gallons of oil into the Gulf of Mexico. Are Macondo and Fukushima just a tragic coincidence, or is nature trying to tell us something?

It's certainly not a message most of us want to hear. Fukushima and the Deepwater Horizon rig are both products of an insatiable demand for energy, which compels us to harness ever more costly and tricky sources of supply. The more our economies grow, the more energy and power they need, prompting the development of even riskier resources, from the deep waters of the Arctic to environmentally hazardous shale oil in America's heartland.

Will the prices needed to pull these new sources of supply out of the ground actually end up killing the world's appetite for it? In some places, that's already happened.

CHAPTER 5

THE KEYSTONE CONUNDRUM

I LOVE TO FISH. OVER THE YEARS, I've been lucky enough to fish some pretty spectacular waters. Selwyn Lake, a remote glacial lake that straddles the 60th parallel on the Canadian Shield, is a spot that really stands out. Two-thirds of it is in the Northwest Territories; the rest, including the fishing lodge, is in northern Saskatchewan. That's where I flew last summer, along with my regular fishing buddies, Murray, Harvey and Maurice.

Fishermen from around the world are drawn to the Canadian north by the prospect of hooking a giant lake trout. These fish, which find enough food to grow in the short time each year when the water is ice free, need cold, clear, deep lakes to survive. Left undisturbed, they can reach world-record sizes. Some of the fifty-pound monsters lurking in northern Canadian lakes have been swimming in those same icy waters for up to a hundred years. Landing a trout anywhere close to that size is the treat of a lifetime for a fisherman.

At Selwyn, like most northern lakes, the standard practice for sport fishing is catch and release, which fisheries experts figure is the best way to maintain fish stocks. Intuitively, it seems to make sense. Releasing fish for others to catch means more fish for everyone.

Or so I thought. While there is a strict limit at Selwyn Lake on how many fish you can keep, there are no restrictions on how many you can catch. In the space of one morning, for instance, Murray and Maurice landed no fewer than 101 lake trout. On another part of the lake that same morning, Harvey and I caught 40 more. The two fish we kept made for a delicious shore lunch. At the time, I didn't give much thought to the 139 we let go.

In the back of my mind, I suppose I liked to think they all swam happily away, feeling lucky to get a new lease on life. I figured that eventually those trout would grow to become the thirty-pound brutes that keep remote fishing lodges in business. But though we caught a lot of fish on our trip to Selwyn, we never saw any even close to that size. It wasn't until I got back to Toronto that I found out why.

Not long after we returned home, Harvey's wife, Hindy, sent an email about barotrauma. My previously clear conscience about the other 139 trout quickly clouded over. Barotrauma, I learned, is a condition that affects fish caught in depths greater than 60 feet. When these fish are hauled out of the water, nitrogen gas contained in their swim bladders begins to expand. The amount of swelling is proportional to the depth. Pulling up a fish from 100 feet can cause a swim bladder to triple in size. Under natural circumstances, the swim bladder controls buoyancy and gradually adjusts as a fish rises to the surface. But when a trout is yanked into a boat, there's no time for the bladder to adjust. The effect of the sudden ascent resembles the bends that hit a scuba diver who ascends too fast. Unlike divers, though, trout don't get to recover in hyperbaric chambers.

In extreme cases, the force of a swelling swim bladder can push it out of a fish's mouth. These fish are usually goners. But even those without visible signs of distress, such as those protruding swim bladders or bulging eyeballs, can succumb to pressure-related internal injuries within weeks of being caught and released.

Our fish finders showed that we hooked nearly all of the trout in at least 60 feet of water. Some were as deep as 100 feet. It's almost certain that every fish we hauled up was put through some degree of barotrauma. If the mortality rate was even 20 percent, that would mean in just one morning we needlessly killed almost thirty fish. Some research suggests the mortality rate due to barotrauma runs well north of that figure.

Over the course of a couple of days on the lake, the four of us released more than 300 fish. Our guides said a larger group had just caught over 600 fish. How many ultimately survived the ordeal is anyone's guess.

At Selwyn Lake, the vast majority of the fish we caught were around five pounds. The trip and the rugged landscape of northern Saskatchewan were outstanding, but I must admit to being a bit disappointed that we didn't see anything close to trophy size. After reading up on barotrauma, though, I couldn't help but think that this could be the explanation.

A month later, I had a chance to take my son Jack to another remote fishing lodge, this one located on an island off the coast of British Columbia. King Pacific Lodge is on Princess Royal Island, a 1,000-square-mile jewel in the heart of the Great Bear Rainforest. The island is framed by coastal mountains and blanketed by virgin woodland that contains some of the world's oldest trees. Some grow for up to 1,500 years and tower 300 feet above the ground. Peering at the forest through the primeval mist that often covers the island is like stepping out of a time machine into a prehistoric age.

Ecotourists come from around the world to see the wildlife,

which ranges from bald eagles to rainforest wolves to the endangered marbled murrelet, a member of the auk family. The island is also a sanctuary for the spirit bear, a rare type of North American black bear endowed with white fur that is found nearly exclusively in the rainforests of British Columbia's Pacific coast. For centuries, members of the Gitga'at First Nation have safeguarded the spirit bear. When the fur trade came to British Columbia, the Gitga'at, who don't hunt the bear, never spoke about it to outsiders in order to shelter it from European trappers.

The Gitga'at aren't the only protectors of the delicate ecosystem on Princess Royal Island; distance is also a friend. More than 500 kilometers separates the island from Vancouver and the bustle of BC's lower mainland. Unfortunately for rainforest conservationists, the island is also less than 100 kilometers from the town of Kitimat, which is the proposed terminus for a new pipeline that would carry crude from Alberta's tar sands. Dubbed Northern Gateway, the proposed pipeline will cost $5.5 billion and ship some 525,000 barrels of oil a day. I figured Jack and I had better do our salmon fishing before that pipeline ever gets built. The industry is quick to assure anyone who will listen that Northern Gateway will adhere to the highest standards of environmental safety. All ships that enter the port, for instance, will be pulled by tugboats and guided by land-based radar. Only double-hulled tankers will be allowed into the terminal. I don't doubt that the industry will fully deliver on these safety measures, but it only takes one *Exxon Valdez* and Jack and I won't have a chance to fish those pristine waters ever again. And neither will anyone else.

Opponents of the proposed pipeline don't have to look far for a cautionary tale illustrating the likelihood that human error will someday enter the equation. Even now, the *Queen of the North*, part of the BC Ferries fleet, is resting underneath 1,400 feet of water

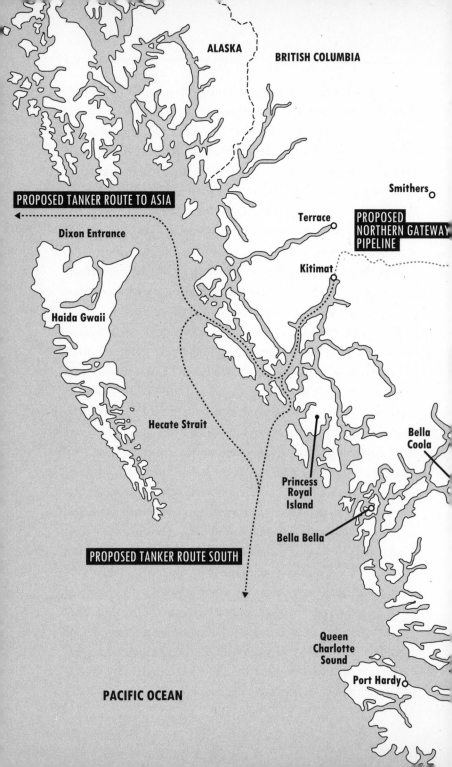

not far from the northern edge of Princess Royal Island. The ferry sank a few years ago when it scraped its hull against a small island in a channel on the way up to Prince Rupert. Locals from the nearby village of Hartley Bay scrambled into boats in the middle of the night and saved 99 of the 101 people on board. The wrecked ferry still holds thousands of gallons of diesel, and every day a bit more seeps out of its fuel tanks and into the surrounding water. That spill is bad enough, but it's a pittance compared with the 2 million barrels of oil that a supertanker would carry from Kitimat. If the pipeline goes ahead, every year hundreds of tankers will need to safely negotiate the same passage that sank the *Queen of the North*.

Even though Northern Gateway has yet to receive regulatory approval, Jack and I are happy we made it to Princess Royal Island when we did. The salmon run was amazing. We also encountered pods of whales on nearly every outing. Watching a humpback whale lunge out of the water is a truly majestic sight.

Among the many differences between fishing for salmon on the west coast and angling for lake trout in northern Saskatchewan are the rules governing the catch. Instead of catch and release, the standard for salmon fishing in BC is catch and kill. King Pacific Lodge will even send your catch to a local fish processor, which will fillet and package your fish to your liking.

In contrast to the hundreds of fish we pulled out of Selwyn Lake, salmon fishing on Princess Royal Island is conducted within strictly prescribed limits. In a three-day trip, each person is limited to eight salmon, four coho and four chinook. And these rules aren't for show. Canada's Department of Fisheries patrols the waters to make sure no liberties are taken with the salmon run. We experienced that firsthand when we were intercepted in the middle of nowhere. Officers searched our boat to make sure our catch was within the legal limit and that we were using the proper barbless hooks, which do less harm to fish that are hooked but get away.

Over three days of unforgettable fishing, Jack and I caught our limit. And once we had each reached our maximum, we were done. Not only did we stop catching fish, but we stopped casting our lines altogether. Once you stop hooking fish, it naturally follows that you aren't risking killing them anymore.

The fish Jack and I took home from BC were a fraction of the number my buddies and I inadvertently killed at Selwyn Lake. We all want to live in sustainable ways, but sometimes what seems like the sustainable solution can actually have the exact opposite effect.

WHAT DIRECTION WILL OIL FLOW?

Catch and release or catch and kill? Which one is really better for the environment? It's a question lobbyists would have done well to ask before mobilizing against TransCanada's proposed Keystone pipeline. The $7.8-billion pipeline system would take crude from Alberta's tar sands down through the Midwest and on to Texas, where Gulf Coast refineries are eagerly awaiting the new feedstock.

The project was thrown into limbo by environmental politics at the highest level. In the run-up to the 2012 election, President Barack Obama delayed a decision on the line until after the race was over. It was a smart move, considering the weight that local politics carry in an election year. And Keystone had become a political hot potato, particularly in Nebraska where a major aquifer that supplies water to eight surrounding states turned out to be a major flashpoint of opposition. In early 2013, Nebraska's governor, much to the chagrin of environmental advocates across the country, approved the project after it was rerouted to skirt the aquifer. That put the decision in the hands of new Secretary of State and noted climate hawk John Kerry. His decision is expected as this book goes to print.

Arguably even more interesting than whether the project goes ahead is the magnitude of the discussion about the line. Pipelines are a relatively sleepy business. Or at least they were. Keystone, it's safe to say, has become the most talked about pipeline project in history. Just like fishing in northern Saskatchewan, though, I wonder if environmentalists, if successful, would come to find that an apparent victory over Keystone actually did more harm than good for the environment.

If the aim of anti-pipeline demonstrators was to keep Trans-Canada from building the 1,600-mile Keystone line, then, regardless of the result, they deserve well-earned credit for raising public awareness for their cause. But if the agenda was to fight global carbon emissions by hindering the expansion of Alberta's tar sands production, then little has changed. It's catch-and-release politics. A win for Nebraska's farmers simply increases the risks to the pristine rainforests along the BC coast. When supertankers are navigating the narrow inlet into Kitimat, I wonder if the environmental lobby would have regretted that Keystone didn't find an acceptable route through the network of highways and byways that already exists from Montana to Texas.

Output from Canada's tar sands, currently about 1.9 million barrels a day, is forecast to nearly double by 2020. Keystone was tagged as the best option for getting new production to world markets. In the long run, though, several new pipelines will be needed to handle the extra volume coming from the tar sands. There's a massive economic incentive to get those lines built. If it's not Keystone, then it might be Enbridge's Northern Gateway project. And if not

ALBERTA SASKATCHEWAN MANITOBA

Edmonton

Hardisty

Calgary

ONTARIO

MONTANA NORTH DAKOTA

MINNESOTA

WISCONS

SOUTH
DAKOTA

WYOMING

IOWA

NEBRASKA

ILLIN

Steele City

MISSOURI

COLORADO

KANSAS

St. Louis

Cushing

Oklahoma City

OKLAHOMA ARKANSAS

TEXAS LOUISIANA

Port Arthur

Houston

EXISTING KEYSTONE PIPELINE

PROPOSED KEYSTONE EXPANSION

Gateway, then TransCanada is already talking about a new line that will ship oil 3,000 miles to the Atlantic coast, where it will make its way to Gulf Coast refineries by tanker.

Canadian oil companies have all the motivation in the world to fast-track another pipeline out of Alberta. The bulk of the province's tar sands output currently ends up in refineries clustered throughout the US Midwest. An increase in volume from the tar sands, combined with prolific production from North Dakota's Bakken play has created a supply glut at those refineries. As it stands, Canadian oil only makes it as far south as Cushing, Oklahoma, the terminal point for the pipeline system. The plan for Keystone extends the system another 435 miles to the Gulf Coast, effectively connecting landlocked Cushing to world oil markets. Gulf Coast refineries also hold more spare capacity than those of any other refining region in the United States. The proposed Keystone line would facilitate an ideal marriage between Texas refineries hungry for more supply and new Canadian oil in need of a home.

A surplus of oil backing up at Cushing has turned into a sweet deal for Midwest refiners, and it's why West Texas Intermediate crude (WTI) has been trading at a discount to world oil prices by anywhere from $10 to $30 a barrel for the last several years. Without a new pipeline, Midwest refiners will get to keep paying a discounted price for Canadian oil.

Considering that Canada exports more than 2 million barrels of oil a day to the US market, getting shortchanged by, say, $20 on every barrel sold is no trifling matter. It works out to some $40 million a day or roughly $1.25 billion a month in foregone petrodollars. And it's not just Canadian oil producers that take a hit to the bottom line. The royalties collected by Alberta's provincial government shrink right along with the price of WTI, as do the corporate taxes collected by Canada's federal government.

Unfortunately for Canada, comparing the gap between domestic oil prices and WTI is only part of the story. The discount between Canadian oil and world prices is even greater. A barrel of Brent crude fetches between $30 and $50 more than many of the barrels flowing out of western Canada. At the high end, that means Canada is getting short-changed by upwards of $100 million a day. That's more than $30 billion in the course of a year.

If it's not going into Canadian pockets, where exactly does the money end up? US motorists certainly don't get a break at the pumps. By and large, American drivers pay the same price no matter where in the country they live. No, the big winners are the oil companies that own the Midwest refineries; they've been pocketing huge profits on the back of abundant supplies from Canada.

In the refining business, the difference between the cost of feedstock, such as bitumen from Alberta's tar sands, and the price charged for end products, such as gasoline and diesel, is known as the crack spread. A wide crack spread means refiners are making a lot of cash. In Cushing, crack spreads have been as much as five times wider than margins for refineries in other parts of the United States. On the Gulf Coast, for example, refineries pay the going rate for Light Louisiana Sweet crude, which trades near the same price as Brent crude, the benchmark world oil price. The story is much the same for refineries on the Pacific and Atlantic coasts. Refineries in the Midwest, in contrast, get to fatten up at the expense of Canadian oil exporters. Until a major new pipeline is constructed, Keystone or otherwise, crack spreads in the Midwest will remain wide open. But just as water doesn't flow uphill, it's unnatural for oil to keep flowing to places where it gets sold at a discount.

If President Obama were to find the flow of oil from Canada's tar sands too hot to handle, the Chinese would certainly have no qualms about taking it off his hands. In the event that Enbridge gains approval from Canada's National Energy Board to build Northern Gateway, a zero-sum world will only tilt that much further in China's direction. Once oil tankers load up at Kitimat and hit the high seas, their cargoes will go to the highest bidder. In all likelihood that means China. Before building a new pipeline, companies like Enbridge secure commercial agreements, known as shipper commitments, to make sure the pipe will be filled with product. It's an open secret in Canada's oil patch that members of the Asian market are part of the group that's already secured space on a potential new line to the Pacific coast.

Turn back the clock only five or six years and the thought of Alberta oil heading directly to China would have been unthinkable. Why ship oil across an ocean when the world's best customer lives next door? The historic ties between Canada's oil patch and the United States run deep. It's no accident that Calgary is often described as the most American city in Canada. The neighborhood of Mount Royal, where many of Calgary's oil patch millionaires now live, was originally dubbed American Hill due to the number of wealthy Yankee businessmen who settled there early in the last century. One of the city's most influential players, Imperial Oil, is nominally based in Calgary but is controlled by ExxonMobil, which owns 70 percent of the company. When it comes to the history of Canada's oil patch, the commercial compass in Calgary has always pointed south to Houston.

When I was still making regular stops in Calgary as chief economist of CIBC World Markets, the circuit often included visits with Alberta's ministers of energy and finance. During a number of these meetings, I remember being told in no uncertain terms that a direct investment in the province's tar sands by a state-owned company would be wholly unwelcome. State-owned companies, the ministers would suggest, don't play by the same commercial rules as the good old boys from Texas.

How times have changed. China National Offshore Oil Corp. (CNOOC) just completed the largest ever overseas acqusition by a state-run Chinese company. It was a $15.1-billion deal for, you guessed it, a Canadian oil sands player, Nexen. That buy followed China's state-owned refining company, Sinopec, which in 2010 paid $4.65 billion for a 9 percent stake in Syncrude, which runs the largest of Alberta's four tar sands mines.

Before that deal, Chinese companies had already picked up stakes in a number of early-stage projects that have yet to reach commercial production. A year earlier, PetroChina, one of the country's state-owned exploration companies, spent $1.9 billion for a 60 percent share of a project being developed by Athabasca Oil Sands Corp, and paid another $680 million for the remaining stake in early 2012. Prior to that, Sinopec and CNOOC each picked up ownership positions in smaller players with big plans on the drawing board. And China's interest in Canada's oil patch isn't limited to the tar sands. Sinopec in 2011 paid $2.9 billion for Daylight Energy, a midsized exploration and production company with operations in Alberta and BC. Suffice to say that Alberta's stance on China has changed since the province's cabinet ministers were telling me that national oil companies should stay home.

Money talks, and China has a lot to spend. Regardless of the rhetoric I was fed by its politicians, Alberta is now clearly open for business. Canadian tar sands players angling for a generous buyout would much rather think about what to do after the check is cashed than worry about who's writing it. Likewise, Calgary's investment bankers are never ones to turn down a potentially juicy commission. Local rainmakers are undoubtedly picking up some Mandarin to help grease the wheels for future transactions.

China's deep pockets have also obviously made an impression on the Alberta government. That's not hard to do when you're willing to pay world oil prices that are as much as $20 a barrel higher than Canada's one-time favorite customer to the south. The pull of the Chinese market is also being felt in Ottawa, where politicians are taking a long look at the merits of giving the go-ahead to Northern Gateway. A regulatory decision on the project is expected sometime in 2013.

It's tough to refute the benefits of opening up new markets for Canadian oil, which is currently being held hostage by US refiners. If Washington were to ultimately scuttle Keystone, Canadian politicians would be quick to shift focus from winning US congressional support to fast-tracking a different project that would take oil out of Alberta.

Of course, even a rock-solid business case for building Northern Gateway still doesn't mean it will see the light of day. The pipeline already faces fierce opposition from conservationists who are worried about what the project will mean to the ecosystems on the Pacific coast. And that's only part of the battle. The project faces an even stiffer test in persuading members of the First Nations that a new pipeline is in their best interests. The pipe will cut across lands that are traditionally claimed by First Nations groups, and these unresolved land claims are a potential quagmire that could derail Enbridge's hopes for the line.

Native land claims clashing with grand plans for pipeline projects are a familiar story in Canada. The Mackenzie Valley Pipeline project, intended to bring natural gas from the Arctic to southern markets, was held back by land claims for decades. When natural gas prices were flying high a few years ago, the line looked like it might finally go ahead. By the time years of hearings brought an agreement to hand, natural gas prices were in the process of cratering, which killed the financial incentive for the pipe. Northern Gateway is dealing with different land claims in different economic times, but it's still an open question whether Enbridge will be able to successfully negotiate its way through the tangled issue.

That said, oil is Canada's number one export. At current prices, pipeline economics make for a powerful political force. Northern Gateway would move more than half a million barrels a day of very precious oil. A new line would also end the supply glut in the Midwest, which would help boost the price of WTI at Cushing. All told, a new pipeline would lift the revenues of Canadian oil companies by billions of dollars. More cash flow means more profits, which means more revenue in government coffers and eventually back to Canadians. The stakes are high enough that Enbridge and Ottawa won't hesitate to cut some big checks to gain the support of local interest groups.

Ottawa has the incentive to do everything it can to make a proposed pipeline a reality as soon as possible. If Northern Gateway ever sees the light of day, the big loser will be the US economy. Even with the Bakken shales and other tight oil plays, President Obama knows full well that the United States needs as much Canadian oil as it can get. If the political winds don't shift soon, America's loss could turn into China's gain. Maybe Obama should have joined Jack and me on our fishing trip to Princess Royal Island. He might have learned that catch and kill, despite how it looks, is a better option in the long term than catch and release.

If the Keystone project were to be shelved, what's bad for TransCanada and Alberta's royalty revenues would turn out to be even worse for Princess Royal Island and the rest of Canada's pristine North Pacific coast. There would, however, still be one ray of hope: the end of growth. The same triple-digit oil prices that would bring Chinese tankers halfway around the world to fill up on oil extracted from tar could soon deep-six the global economy. If China's economy stops growing at its current clip, maybe it won't need to import oil from the tar sands. The twists and turns of the Inside Passage will be left for salmon to navigate, not supertankers.

That's one of the silver linings of a static economy. A new world of slower growth will certainly usher in some painful changes, but it also might save one of the largest remaining temperate rainforests in the northern hemisphere. That's good news for the spirit bear—and the salmon run. As for the rest of us?

We all might find ourselves in that world of no growth much sooner than we ever could have thought.

[CHAPTER 6]

THE DANISH
RESPONSE

THE FIRST THING I NOTICED ON A FLIGHT into Copenhagen a few summers ago was a ring of wind turbines surrounding the city. Not far from the city's harbor, the sweeping arc of offshore windmills is a hard sight to miss. I found out later that this is exactly what the Danes have in mind. The gleaming white windmills, which rise more than 100 meters above the deep blue waters of the Øresund strait, are intended to be an unmistakable symbol of Denmark's commitment to renewable energy.

The rest of Denmark's bona fides when it comes to green living are also tough to ignore. In the last two decades, Denmark has cut its carbon dioxide emissions by 13 percent. That makes for a remarkable contrast with North American emissions, which have increased by 30 percent since 1990, the baseline year for the Kyoto accord. The credit for reversing greenhouse gas emissions is often given to eco-friendly initiatives like the wind turbines I saw dotting the Copenhagen seascape. It's a success story the Danes are literally selling to the rest of the world. Denmark, which in 1991 became the first country to set up an offshore wind farm, now garners 11 percent of its exports from sales of energy technology. At home, wind power accounts for an impressive 20 percent of domestic electricity generation.

Denmark clearly has plenty of good reasons to be proud of its environmental track record. From the moment I glimpsed the wind turbines from my plane seat, though, I couldn't get away from a niggling curiosity about how the country generates the rest of its power. At the conference I was attending, a speaker from a local power company presented on Denmark's world-leading green technology. I tracked him down after my own talk, figuring he was just the person to ask. He hemmed and hawed, but when I pressed him, he reluctantly told me how his country generates the other 80 percent of its power.

Coal.

I was floored. The first thought that crossed my mind was "Something is rotten in the state of Denmark!" For a country striving to be completely independent of fossil fuels, Denmark couldn't have picked a worse way to generate electricity. Coal is 20 percent dirtier than oil and twice as dirty as natural gas. With big dollars at stake selling green energy technology around the world, I can understand why Denmark wants to showcase its offshore wind farms instead of its coal-fired power plants. But the cold hard truth is that it is smokestacks, not wind turbines, that allow most Danes to turn on the lights.

Coal's share of power generation, I found out, is the same in Denmark as it is in China. Where China's carbon footprint now dwarfs every other country in the world, though, Denmark's is actually shrinking. How can this be?

To answer this energy riddle, you need to look past how power is generated in Denmark and into the prices Danish citizens pay for electricity. Households in Copenhagen pay roughly 30 cents per kilowatt-hour for power. That's two to three times the average price in North America. In Denmark, government-regulated power prices are laden with carbon taxes, which means electricity isn't cheap, whether it's wind powered or coal fired. Not surprisingly, Danes use a fraction of the power that North Americans consume.

All those world-famous windmills, it turns out, aren't behind Denmark's falling emissions. The real reason for its smaller carbon footprint is its high electricity prices, which put a huge damper on power demand. The coal that *doesn't* get burned because power is so expensive is more important to the level of Denmark's carbon emissions than the coal that does get burned.

That's good news for the planet's future. Despite its offshore wind farms, Denmark shows that carbon abatement isn't limited to places with ideal conditions for wind power—or solar or hydro-electric, for that matter. Higher energy prices are a tactic that can be applied anywhere. The market is oblivious to whether the wind blows or the sun shines. Charge enough for power in any country in the world and people will use less electricity. It's basic economics.

If capping carbon emissions is the goal, the solution isn't to rush out and build wind turbines; simply raising prices will do the job. Consider, for instance, the state of Montana or the province of Alberta, both of which have huge coal reserves. What's more, citizens there consider energy abundance a veritable birthright, so few think twice about burning as much of it as possible. Even in those places, though, I bet charging 30 cents per kilowatt-hour would cut the demand on the local power grid in a hurry.

To lower carbon emissions, you don't need to build a single wind turbine or invest even a dollar in so-called clean coal technology. Just charge more for power and emissions will come down as a result.

WHY ARE SO MANY DANES RIDING BIKES?

Denmark's track record of environmental success also has a lot to do with cars. Or I suppose I should really say a lack of cars. Cyclists are everywhere in Copenhagen, which boasts some of the best bicycle lanes in the world. They even have their own traffic signals. And it's paid off. No matter where you go in Copenhagen, nearly everyone seems to get there on a bike.

When you see so many physically fit, rosy-cheeked, good-looking Danes peddling around the city, the first thing you think about is renewing your gym membership. After that you can't help but appreciate how an entire population seems to be so environmentally conscious. It's admirable, no doubt, and Danes should certainly be proud. But once again, the economist in me, ever on the lookout for price signals that explain human behavior, felt compelled to ask more questions.

It turns out that driving a car in Denmark, much like turning on the lights, is a very expensive proposition. The biggest cost isn't even at the pumps. While fuel is more expensive in Denmark than it is in Canada or the United States, gasoline prices in Copenhagen are largely in line with the rest of Europe. Yet few other major European cities have the same volume of bike traffic as Copenhagen.

What differentiates Denmark from its neighbors is the cost of buying a car. Danish car buyers pay a tax ranging from 100 to 180 percent of the vehicle's sticker price; the exact amount depends on the size of the engine. For the cost of one vehicle with a gas-guzzling V-8 in Denmark, for instance, you could buy up to three cars in North America. If my fellow Torontonians had to pay those prices, the number of bikes on the road might start to rival Copenhagen.

Of course, ending a hundred-year-old love affair with the automobile won't come easy. A few years ago, for example, Toronto's city council passed a new annual vehicle registration tax that cost Toronto car owners the princely sum of $65 a year. That was too much for Torontonians to stomach. Facing disastrous pre-election polling numbers, the incumbent mayor headed for the exit. One of the first acts of the new mayor, Rob Ford, was to announce that the city's war against the car was over. He and his new council canceled the tax.

Defenders of North America's car culture will also argue that the sprawling landscapes of cities such as Los Angeles, Phoenix and Calgary make Copenhagen-style bike usage impractical. Getting to work every day certainly can't be like training for a triathlon. And frigid winter temperatures in some cities are also clearly unsuitable for year-round cycling. Those are fair points, but what the Danish model shows us is that prices influence demand. The Danes have crafted policies that encourage conservation. There's nothing stopping civic governments in North America from doing the same.

The world won't always look the way it does now. The sprawl that defines many North American cities is a result of cheap oil that makes it affordable for suburban homeowners to commute to work. Replace inexpensive oil with triple-digit prices and cities will eventually shrink back to their original bike-sized urban cores. When gasoline prices move high enough, you can also bet that suburbanites and city-dwellers will start agitating for better transit options. High fuel costs will force these types of changes on all of us before you know it. Denmark is meeting this pending reality on its own terms. The rest of us would be wise to consider how that country is doing it.

Copenhagen's trademark windmills act as a smokescreen that obscures a more important takeaway than the mere viability of green energy. The power the Danes use is not much greener than anywhere else. Denmark is green because the Danes have learned how to use less power.

I'm sure a good number of Danes would take issue with me. They'll point to their coal plants, which are among the most carbon efficient in the world. They'll rightly note that those same power stations do double duty, generating heat as well as electricity. While all of that is true, it misses the fundamental point. Prices are what have made the difference. Prices are what matter.

Of course, selling green technology around the world is far more lucrative for Denmark than simply showing the rest of us how to use less energy. That's why the offshore wind turbines are in full view of the capital city and why Denmark has put its environmental branding front and center. But the real lesson we need to take from Denmark is how to curb our energy appetite. If we don't, we'll be at the mercy of fuel prices that are only marching higher. Wind and solar are welcome additions to the power grid, but the world still runs on hydrocarbons. What's more, a focus on new sources of energy supply only considers half of the equation; the other half is demand. And here, conservation is a practical solution that's available right now.

Someday, economically viable fuel alternatives will unseat hydrocarbons from the top of the energy pyramid, freeing our electrical grids and our gas tanks from the clutches of high prices. But that day isn't today. In the here and now, our economic success in the face of triple-digit energy prices will hinge on burning fewer hydrocarbons. That means we all have to learn how to use less energy.

That's exactly what the Danes have done. In Copenhagen, households use nearly a third less energy than in North America. Expensive power is all the motivation Danes need to switch off lights when they leave a room. Or don a sweater in the winter instead of cranking up the thermostat. In the summer, Danes spend more time in the fresh air and less time straining the electrical grid by cooling their houses with air-conditioning. Compare Copenhagen with a city like Houston. To escape the summer heat, Houstonians move from air-conditioned houses to air-conditioned cars to air-conditioned offices and back again. Copenhagen doesn't face the same oppressive summer heat as Houston, but the stark differences in energy usage between the two cities are worth considering. Are Danes worse off for living in smaller houses and cutting back on air-conditioning? Is Copenhagen turning into an abandoned wasteland, strangled by punitive energy costs?

Far from it. Copenhagen is one of the most attractive cities in Europe to visit. Tourists come from around the world to enjoy its charms. And it's not like Danes are flooding foreign embassies in a desperate attempt to emigrate to places with cheaper power. Surveys show Danes, who enjoy one of the highest standards of living in the world, are among the happiest people on earth. As could be expected, the amount of out-migration in Denmark is negligible.

As much as Denmark is a living, breathing example of environmental success, it's only fair to note that the battle against carbon emissions is easier there than it is elsewhere. Denmark has no significant hydrocarbon reserves of its own, which means its politicians don't need to worry about appeasing a carbon-intensive energy industry. In the same spirit, the country also doesn't have an auto sector to speak of. In Denmark, no one needs to worry about currying favor with autoworkers to get reelected.

Getting ahead of the curve on the environment is a whole lot easier when you don't need to undermine key parts of your economy to do it. When Denmark slaps a sky-high tax on new cars, it only hurts some other country's auto exports. And it's not like German autoworkers get to vote in Danish elections. Contrast Denmark's situation with the pressures faced by the government of my home province of Ontario. While this may surprise people south of the 49th parallel, Ontario actually produces more cars than any state in the union. When the global recession sent automakers reeling toward bankruptcy, Ontario, along with Canada's federal government, spent billions of taxpayer dollars to help keep General Motors and Chrysler solvent. Across the border, politicians in Washington doled out even more money to those same companies in order to safeguard high-paying manufacturing jobs.

Likewise, the oil industry also gets billions in subsidies from governments in the United States and Canada. In the United States, government tax breaks for Big Oil are wrapped in the rhetoric of promoting energy self-sufficiency and reducing the country's dependence on imported oil from faraway lands that could become unfriendly at any moment. In Canada, subsidies are granted under the guise of protecting one of the country's leading exports.

Danish politicians don't have to contend with the powerful lobbying efforts of Big Auto or Big Oil. Nor does Denmark have to worry about penalizing hard-working coal miners or assembly-line workers. The country is politically free to impose what are, in effect, huge carbon taxes that encourage energy conservation. While admirable from an environmental standpoint, for a country that's forced to buy oil and coal from foreign producers, slashing energy consumption also makes a tremendous amount of economic sense.

Half a world away, the Japanese are coming to the same conclusion.

WILL THEY BE RIDING MORE BICYCLES IN TOKYO?

Like Denmark, Japan is largely devoid of domestic hydrocarbon reserves. That forces the country to import nearly every last drop of the 4.5 million barrels of oil its economy burns every day. As we saw in the last chapter, in an effort to reduce its oil imports, Japan turned to nuclear energy, which before the Fukushima meltdown accounted for nearly a third of the country's power generation.

Japan has no obvious substitute for its lost nuclear power. Practically and economically, that makes for a country highly motivated to adopt Danish-style energy conservation. Finding ways to save oil is nothing new for Japan, which became a pioneer in energy efficiency after the OPEC oil shocks of the 1970s and 1980s. Without hydrocarbon reserves, Japan had few choices at the time. Today, the Fukushima disaster is forcing the country to draw on that experience.

The new catchword in Japan is *setsuden*, or electricity conservation. These days, the concept is evident almost everywhere. Office dwellers are going without air-conditioning, while factory workers are switching off lights and machinery when they're not needed. In stores, escalators are becoming staircases. And households across the country are being encouraged to scale back power usage by as much as 20 percent. Even Japanese businessmen, renowned for their conservative attire, are being asked to wear casual clothes to work rather than dark suits, the idea being that dressing in breathable material will reduce the strain on office air-conditioning.

Are Tokyo's streets soon to be filled with businesspeople in cream-colored open-neck shirts riding bicycles?

In another sign of the times, Toshiba is about to launch a new flat-screen television designed specifically for countries, like

Japan, that are experiencing frequent electricity blackouts. The TV can run for three hours on a rechargeable battery, so no one has to miss a favorite program due to a power outage. Nissan and Mitsubishi are advertising that electric cars aren't just for making routine trips to work or the grocery store. The manufacturers are now considering boosting the capacity of electric car batteries to enable motorists to power hot plates with their vehicles. No power in the kitchen? No problem. Dinner can be cooked using the family sedan.

Other firms across the country are even changing the hours of the workday. The Tokyo Stock Exchange, for one, is starting work earlier in the morning to cut down on air-conditioning needs. The Exchange has also turned off its electronic stock price ticker, and has even closed the visitors' gallery to avoid having to light and cool the room.

Setsuden is defining the new contours of an energy-constrained Japanese economy. Similar changes may soon decide the shape of your economy as well.

A magical new power source isn't waiting in the wings to solve Japan's energy problems. Instead, the country is figuring out that the alternative to building more nuclear reactors is using less electricity and closing the energy gap in other ways. Here, the cost of fuel will actually turn out to be one of Japan's best friends. High prices enforce an economic discipline that will naturally curtail energy use.

Certainly other steps will help along the way. More electric vehicles are bound to be on roads in Japan, and around the world, before too long. Wind and solar power will continue to become more affordable and more efficient, which will add to the role they're able to play in supplying tomorrow's power needs. And more inventive measures are being found all the time. In Paris, an ambitious car-sharing service using electric vehicles has been launched. The French are hoping the new communal car plan will meet with the same success that a similar bicycle-sharing scheme did a few years ago. Other cities are bound to follow suit.

But the really big changes that will come in an energy-constrained future won't have to do with the type of vehicles we drive or how we generate electricity. Instead, what will matter most is the energy that's *not* used. The real energy savings, as Denmark knows, happen when fewer cars are on the road and less power is used at home.

Of course, that still leaves us with one very large concern. Higher energy prices will undoubtedly get us to use less energy. But if economic growth, as we found out in chapter 1, is a function of energy consumed, what kind of an economy is possible in a world of energy conservation? Can the global economy continue to expand without using more and more energy? And if not, what does a static economy look like?

PART
TWO

CHAPTER 7

ZERO-SUM WORLD

THE BLACK SEA SHIPYARD IN THE Ukrainian port city of Niko-
layev was established by a Belgian-owned concern in the late
1890s as the Nikolayev Shipbuilding, Mechanical and Ironworks.
Since then, it's gone by many names: the Andre Marti Shipyard,
Nikolayev South Shipyard and Soviet Shipyard Number 444.
Among other notable vessels, the yard launched the battleship
Potemkin. A mutiny on board the *Potemkin*, made famous by an
eponymous silent film, was a key event in the Russian uprising
of 1905, a precursor to the 1917 revolution that overthrew Czar
Nicholas II and ushered in the Soviet Union.

If you visited the Black Sea Shipyard in the mid-1990s, you
would have come across the rusting remains of the *Varyag*. When
shipbuilders laid down the keel for the *Varyag* in 1985, the massive steel hulk was to become the Soviet navy's second Kuznetsov-
class aircraft carrier. But that was before the fall of the Berlin Wall.
Construction of the *Varyag* halted in 1992, after the Soviet navy
stopped making payments to the shipyard. Following the breakup
of the Soviet Union, ownership of the *Varyag* was transferred to
Ukraine. Instead of becoming the pride of the fleet, the *Varyag*,

which was 70 percent complete, was stripped of her engines, electronics and rudder, and left to rust.

Originally projected to cost $2.4 billion, the ship was put up for auction in 1998 and sold for the bargain-basement price of $20 million. As part of the sale, Ukraine stipulated that the *Varyag* couldn't be used for military purposes. That was fine with the buyer, a small Chinese tourism company, Chong Lot, which said it planned to turn the boat into a floating casino off the coast of Macao.

The boat spent the next few years being towed around the Black Sea, as Chinese diplomats worked to get Turkey's permission to let the steel carcass through the narrow straits of the Bosporus. It took until 2001, but the *Varyag* eventually made it into the Mediterranean. Denied access to the Suez Canal for safety reasons, the *Varyag* set out on the long haul through the Strait of Gibraltar, around the Horn of Africa and back up through the Indian Ocean to China, a trek that cost millions in fuel and labor and took more than a year and a half to complete. But the ship's saga didn't end there.

Instead of docking at Macao, the tugboats made for Dalian, a naval port on China's northeast coast. Once there, the *Varyag* slipped off the radar. It reemerged in 2005, painted the distinctive gray of the People's Liberation Army Navy.

Only twenty aircraft carriers are currently in service around the world, according to *Jane's Fighting Ships*, the definitive guide to the world's warships. The US operates eleven, Italy two, while Spain, Russia, France, Brazil, India, Thailand and the UK have one each. The *Varyag*, which was commissioned in September 2012 and landed the first aircraft on its deck a few months later, is now China's first aircraft carrier and the flagship of its navy. Chinese officials, who sidestep questions about the floating casino cover story, are plainspoken about the carrier's future role in protecting the country's foreign interests—oil being at the top of the list.

—

Bill Clinton once said, "When word of a crisis breaks out in Washington, the first question that comes to everyone's lips is, 'Where's the nearest carrier?'" America's role as global superpower rests on the back of its aircraft carriers, the most powerful military assets in the world. China has now joined the club, a development that has the full attention of its neighbors. The Philippines, Singapore, Indonesia, Malaysia, Cambodia, Thailand and Vietnam are all running into problems with China and its territorial claims to most of the oil- and gas-rich South China Sea.

China's years of practicing a good-neighbor policy appear to be coming to an end. It's getting more aggressive in pressing its rights, recently sending an unmanned submarine to plant a flag on the ocean floor of the South China Sea to act as a symbol of its military capability and regional dominance. China reportedly planned to call the *Varyag* the *Shi Lang*, after a 17th-century admiral who conquered Taiwan—a not so subtle nod to its plans for the craft. Ultimately, though, the carrier was renamed the *Liaoning*, after the northeast province where it was refitted.

China's energy interests span the globe, meaning the *Liaoning* could end up off the coast of Africa or in the Middle East. It could also sail to South America, where China is looking to get more and more of its future oil supply. A burgeoning relationship with Venezuela could lead to more barrels being shipped from the Faja, the country's heavy oil belt, directly to Chinese refineries. That would be unwelcome news for the United States, the current destination for more than half of Venezuela's oil exports.

How many tanks of gas Chinese drivers burn never used to pose a threat to anyone in North America, or anywhere else for that matter. In the early 1980s, China's oil consumption was a modest 2 million barrels a day. Now, its daily intake is much less humble, verging on 10 million barrels. Fortunately for China's ever-increasing fuel needs, world oil production grew so robustly in the last three decades that the extra demand was easily handled.

But when global fuel demand is increasing faster than global supply, something has to give. China's appetite for more oil will come at the expense of someone else's oil diet. Economists use the concept of "zero sum" to describe this type of situation. In zero-sum conditions, one party's gains are offset by another party's losses. When it comes to energy, that means every time you fill up at the gas station, you take away a tank of fuel from someone else.

In a zero-sum world of global oil supply, China's demand for fuel will come at the expense of the United States. Americans consume roughly 20 percent of global oil production while producing less than 10 percent. That's a big gap that the United States currently bridges by importing oil from foreign countries. If China's economic growth continues to outpace the United States', China will gain a comparative advantage in the global competition for more barrels.

Consider each country's relationship with Venezuela, home to the world's largest oil reserves, according to OPEC statistics. An oil tanker takes less than two days to travel from Venezuela to the US Gulf Coast, where refineries are set up to handle the country's supply of heavy crude. Proximity alone makes the United States the natural destination for Venezuelan oil. By comparison, a journey across the Pacific takes much longer and costs much more. Yet since 2005, Venezuela's exports to China have more than tripled, to 125,000 barrels a day. Over the same time frame,

Venezuela's oil exports to the US have steadily fallen, to less than a million barrels a day from more than 1.5 million. China also recently lent Venezuela $20 billion to ramp up petroleum production, and you can bet the intention behind the loan wasn't that Venezuela would send more oil to the United States.

China's relationship with Venezuela will become even more of a concern to the United States if a proposed pipeline is built to carry oil from the Faja across Colombia to the Pacific coast. Colombian president Juan Manuel Santos considers the new pipeline an economic priority for his country. If constructed, the new South American pipeline, a conceptual mirror of Enbridge's Northern Gateway proposal, would give China a direct connection to the world's largest oil reserves.

A pipeline to Colombia's Pacific coast wouldn't spell an end to the trading relationship between Venezuela and the United States, but it would certainly mean more barrels heading to China and fewer to the Gulf Coast. In a zero-sum world of global oil supply, if the United States is forced to reduce its oil consumption, American drivers will bear the brunt of the decrease. More than two-thirds of the oil burned by the US economy is used as transit fuel, whether for gas-guzzling cars, diesel-burning trucks or jet-fueled airplanes.

To see zero-sum dynamics already at play, you need only look at the global auto industry. In the United States, auto sales fell as low as 10 million units during the last recession and, even after a strong rebound, still lag the sales tally in China by several million vehicles a year. And China isn't the only Asian country seeing explosive growth in its auto sector: in the last decade, annual sales in India have quadrupled, to 2.7 million vehicles.

Chinese motor vehicle sales, according to auto industry experts J.D. Power and Associates, are expected to double to 35 million units by 2020. Sales in India, meanwhile, are expected to more than triple to 11 million vehicles over the same time frame. Those may seem like gigantic increases, but the growth is only an extrapolation of what's already happened in those markets in recent years.

Soaring Chinese auto sales have sent worldwide auto registrations to unprecedented heights. Global vehicle ownership reached the one billion mark in 2010, according to *WardsAuto World*, a key source for industry statistics. Globally, that equates to one vehicle for every seven people. A 30 percent increase in Chinese registrations in 2010 pushed the total past the billion-vehicle milestone. Vehicle registrations had already doubled between 2006 and 2010. At over 100 million, China is now home to the second-largest vehicle fleet in the world, surpassing Japan and trailing only the United States.

Yet even with the sharp increase in the number of drivers in recent years, only one out of seventeen people in China owns a car. In India, that ratio is one in fifty-five. By comparison, a total fleet of 240 million vehicles in the United States means more than one vehicle exists for every licensed driver in the country. As economic conditions in China and India continue to progress toward the standards enjoyed in OECD countries, growth in their domestic auto markets is inevitable and seems relatively boundless. If you're a General Motors or an Audi, it's not too hard to figure out where you'll be breaking ground on your next factory. And of course, new car plants in China and India mean new jobs, which will keep a zero-sum world of GDP growth tilted toward Asia and away from North America.

Although vehicle sales in emerging markets will definitely be robust to say the least, they aren't likely to come even close to the heady forecasts from outfits like J.D. Power, since their projections leave out a crucial element: fuel. If predictions for vehicle usage in China and India come to pass, the extra fuel needed to power those vehicles will put even more strain on global oil supply. The increase from today's consumption levels alone would be more than half the total amount of gasoline and diesel fuel currently burned in North America.

In theory, I suppose it's possible that in the next decade half of the North American auto fleet will be replaced by vehicles that run on electricity or natural gas. But considering that the latest numbers from the US Department of Energy show there are still fewer than a million alternative-fuel vehicles on American roadways, I wouldn't want to bet on it. Nevertheless, in the coming years we know that more drivers in China and India will be on the road than ever before. When it comes to consuming oil, China and the United States will soon be trading places.

WHY CHINA CAN AFFORD TRIPLE-DIGIT OIL PRICES WHILE AMERICA CAN'T

Most fans of business television are familiar with *Squawk Box,* a daily morning show on CNBC that runs prior to the New York Stock Exchange's opening bell. The hosts talk fast and a bit too loudly, I suppose to mimic the energy of a trading floor. It's not a bad program, if you're into that kind of stuff. Back in 2007, I'd just released a research report at CIBC World Markets predicting that nearly all of the future growth in world oil consumption would occur outside the United States and other OECD markets. A CNBC producer called wondering if I would talk about the report on his show. I was happy to oblige since I would already be in New York speaking to clients.

The producers set me up in a camera-crammed studio above

the floor of the exchange. Right out of the gate, I could tell that the interviewer had already written off the report. Did I really believe, he asked, that starving peasants in China would be filling up their gas tanks while motorists in Manhattan wouldn't be able to afford to drive? I tried to manage the tone of my response, attempting to counter his sarcasm with what I hoped was a more thoughtful note (though a matching touch of derision may have snuck into my answer). The upshot was, yes, absolutely, the numbers show that's exactly what will happen, I said. I couldn't help but point out, moreover, that not everyone in China was starving, and certainly not the folks that I expected to be buying cars. But the interviewer, and probably most of the audience, wasn't buying what I had to say.

Persuading North Americans that their oil-guzzling days are over while people with a fraction of their average national income will be filling up at the pumps was a hard sell back then. And despite recent demand numbers that tell the same story, it still is. But to close your eyes and hope the world stays the same is really just sticking your head in the sand. Change in world oil consumption isn't coming—it's already here.

Growth in oil demand is heavily skewed toward emerging-market economies and away from advanced industrialized countries. Consumption in China and India is increasing at roughly 10 percent a year. In 2010, China added almost a million barrels to its daily oil intake. And it doesn't seem to matter what's going on in the rest of the global economy, those countries are only getting thirstier for oil. During the last recession, for instance, nearly all of the demand destruction that occurred for oil happened in OECD countries, such as the United States and Europe. Just prior to the recession, in the winter of 2007, OECD oil demand reached 50 million barrels a day. At the bottom of the recession in the spring of 2009, that consumption had fallen to 45 million barrels. On a peak-to-trough basis, the OECD shed 5 million barrels a day in oil demand. In contrast, oil consumption in China and other emerging-market economies barely dipped over the same period. Since the economic recovery took hold, oil-demand growth in China has resumed at its prerecessionary pace of around 10 percent a year. OECD countries, meanwhile, continue to see consumption flatline or even decline.

The numbers show that oil demand in emerging markets is far less sensitive to triple-digit oil prices than demand in more traditional oil markets. When energy analysts, who are still in a US-centric mindset, attempt to explain why higher prices aren't affecting demand the way their theoretical models suggest they should, the first reason they reach for is state subsidies. In the big picture of global oil demand, however, that's a pat answer that falls well short of capturing what's actually going on. In India, for example, the state's total annual subsidies for gasoline and diesel amount to less than $10 billion a year. That's not much more than American taxpayers used to shell out to fund corn-based ethanol production. Indeed, when it comes to subsidies, the definition is very much in the eye of the beholder.

In some countries, determining the shape of a fuel subsidy is straightforward: governments step in and regulate prices at the refinery, a classic form of subsidy that directly cuts fuel costs for citizens. In the United States, refineries are free to sell their products at market prices, but that doesn't mean subsidies don't exist elsewhere in the system. The United States has some of the lowest fuel taxes in the world. While most Americans wouldn't consider low fuel taxes a hidden subsidy, low taxes mean cheaper fuel, which lets drivers burn more gasoline and diesel; the effect on consumption is the same. You don't have to look any further than our bike-riding

Danish friends in the last chapter for evidence of the relationship between taxes and consumption. High fuel taxes mean Europeans have been paying the equivalent of triple-digit prices for years. And their declining fuel consumption bears witness to how tax-driven pump prices can change transportation habits.

The biggest reason why fuel consumption in places such as China and India is so resilient in the face of triple-digit oil prices has little to do with subsidies and much more to do with what's driving demand. Oil consumption in emerging-market economies is much more sensitive to income growth than to pump prices. Many auto purchasers are first-time drivers who have only recently made the jump from living off the land to earning a regular paycheck in a city like Beijing or Mumbai. Turn off the road from any of those new superhighways in China and you don't have to travel far before the familiar trappings of the developed world fall away. Instead of seeing an Audi whiz by on a paved road, you're more likely to pass an oxcart on a narrow dirt track leading to a village. That's the world from which China will recruit its future drivers. If you've never owned a car before, changes in the price of gasoline aren't going to determine how much fuel you will burn. If you can afford to trade in your bicycle for a new car, then it's a safe bet your income has just gone up by leaps and bounds.

In China and India, incomes are growing several times faster than in North America, western Europe or Japan. Static income growth in OECD countries means that higher gas prices have a meaningful impact on household budgets. Spending more money on fuel means there's less money to spend on everything else. When incomes are rising as quickly as they are in China and India, then on a relative basis everything is much more affordable. The faster your income grows, the cheaper cars become, and the more you have the wherewithal to fill up your tank at whatever the world oil price happens to be.

If incomes were still growing in OECD markets at the same pace they are in China and India, vehicles would be flying off car lots in those countries as well. But they're not, and they're not likely to anytime soon. Give North American households, which typically own several vehicles, the kind of income growth that's happening in emerging markets and the extra money would buy a yacht, not another car. In China and India, a brand-new car isn't replacing an older vehicle with too many miles on the odometer; it's taking the place of walking or riding a bicycle. For people who were living as peasants less than a generation ago, earning a regular wage is a transformative development in the way life is lived.

The use of oil-fired power generation also separates emerging economies from most developed nations. With the notable exception of post-Fukushima Japan, few OECD countries generate a significant amount of electricity using oil. In North America, coal, natural gas and hydroelectric do the heavy lifting for the electrical grid. In China and India, power generation can still consume a significant amount of oil. China's fleet of coal-fired power plants handles most of the country's electricity needs, but when coal supplies get interrupted, the country falls back on its network of diesel-fueled power stations to make up the shortfall. That's exactly what happened when floods hit Australia a few years ago, shutting down most of the country's coal exports to China.

Fundamental differences exist in oil consumption trends between the developing world and OECD countries. The OECD is becoming the junior market for oil, a situation that becomes more apparent with each passing year. Oil consumption in those countries peaked right around the time oil prices first hit $70 to $80 a barrel. In the United States, the quintessential car-loving nation, oil consumption has dropped more than 10 percent, about 2 million barrels a day, from its prerecession peak. The US economy is still the world's fuel hog, gobbling up more than 18 million barrels a day, but consumption is clearly heading lower. After the next recession, the US economy's daily oil intake could drop as low as 15 million barrels a day. Over time, it will drop even more. Indeed, in a zero-sum world, such a decline is actually inevitable if economic growth in China and India is to continue. That's the picture I was trying to paint for CNBC's audience a few years ago. Today, that landscape is much easier to see.

OIL IS REDRAWING POLITICAL AND MILITARY ALLIANCES

A zero-sum relationship in global oil markets casts a long shadow over current international relations. Economic growth demands oil, which makes petroleum reserves a vital strategic asset for every country in the world. Access to oil, already a key driver behind political and military decision making, is also becoming essential to the new economic relationships currently being forged.

The *Liaoning* (ex-*Varyag*) is the most visible symbol of China's efforts to develop a blue-water navy capable of navigating across the world's largest oceans. One day China may need to defend critical oil shipping lanes in the Middle East. When that happens, it wants the option of sending the *Liaoning*, or another carrier, to safeguard its interests.

China's ties to Venezuela also bear watching. Ideologically speaking, shared socialist values make the pair natural trading partners. The relationship defines the changing face of world oil markets. China is emerging as the world's most important oil customer, while Venezuela's heavy oil reserves are the largest in the world. It's a logical fit that's now a growing concern for the United States.

The proposed pipeline to the Pacific coast represents a significant challenge to America's traditional sphere of influence in the western hemisphere. For nearly two hundred years, US foreign policy in South America has been guided by the Monroe Doctrine, which essentially means that America doesn't take kindly to foreign nations playing in its backyard. The United States boasts a long and often dubious track record of intervention, with a list of notable hits that include a CIA-sponsored coup in Guatemala in the 1950s, the attempted Bay of Pigs invasion in Cuba during the 1960s, the Iran-Contra affair in Nicaragua, and the 1983 invasion of Grenada. If China starts siphoning off even more oil supply from Venezuela, history suggests the US will try to take steps to maintain the status quo.

I'll save those scenarios for Tom Clancy to describe in his next thriller. What history shows us is that wars can be won or lost on the issue of oil supply. The Germans found that out in the Second World War when they lost access to oil and had to start manufacturing it out of coal. Without oil, the world's mightiest armies grind to a halt. Tanks don't run. Jet fighters don't scramble. And frigates stay in port instead of patrolling the high seas.

The world's militaries, which guzzle an astounding amount of oil, have good reason to be concerned about their reliance on fossil fuels. Few are more aware of fuel's cost than the Pentagon. The US military is the world's single largest industrial user of oil, burning around 350,000 barrels a day. If it were a country, the United States Armed Forces would be the 38th-largest oil-consuming nation in the world, slotting in just below Sweden. That makes its operating budget especially sensitive to the price of oil. Every $10 increase in the price of a barrel costs the Pentagon about $1.3 billion. These are operating costs that Washington would love to shave as it grapples with its trillion-dollar budget deficit. Whether the Pentagon will be successful in decreasing its oil addiction is up in the air. The United States Air Force, for instance, burns roughly 2.5 billion gallons of jet fuel a year. It knows it needs to safeguard itself against a disruption to foreign oil supplies and is attempting to wean its fighters and bombers off oil by switching to biofuels. Homegrown biofuels offer some certainty that future supply will be there when needed, but there's a catch: right now, the best available biofuel substitute costs about $35 a gallon, roughly ten times the price of conventional jet fuel.

As oil supplies become scarcer and fuel more expensive to burn, the impact on economies, markets and politics will be even more profound. In a world of triple-digit prices, economic and political power shifts from major oil-consuming countries to major oil-producing countries. That heightens the importance of net exporters such as Canada and Russia, but it's a scary prospect for the global stature of net importers such as the United States and Germany. For countries that depend even more heavily on imported energy, such as Japan, the likelihood of increased energy scarcity promises to put already vulnerable economies on an even shakier footing.

Conversely, nations with abundant energy resources become more powerful and affluent. Few countries are in better shape in this regard than Russia, which is using the clout of its massive oil and gas reserves to extend its influence across Europe. The security that comes from a steady stream of petrodollars also allows Venezuela to thumb its nose at the United States and stoke anti-American sentiment across Latin America.

The rise of sovereign wealth funds and state-owned oil companies can also be traced to the money that triple-digit oil prices have sent coursing into the global petro-economy. In the coming years, even more of the world's petroleum supply will be controlled by state-run actors. Companies such as Saudi Aramco, Rosneft, Indian Oil, Sinopec and PetroChina already rank among the heavy-weights of the world oil industry.

As these companies get even bigger, more oil will be traded on a state-to-state basis, leaving fewer barrels for the open market. State-run companies in China and India already have long-term supply contracts with Saudi Aramco. Indeed, half of Saudi Arabia's crude exports now go to China, which has surpassed the United States as the kingdom's largest customer.

Over time, these types of state-to-state deals will spawn a new network of international relationships. Alliances between nation-states will increasingly revolve around the security of energy supply rather than shared political or economic values. We are already seeing that on today's world stage. The global balance of power is undergoing a seismic shift, and geopolitics are at the epicenter. Consider Germany's announcement that, in the wake of Japan's nuclear disaster, it would become nuclear free by 2022. That declaration brought a broad smile to the face of Russian leader Vladimir Putin. Whether or not most Germans realize it, their country just became a lot more dependent on Russian gas.

European natural gas production is rapidly depleting. It fell by about 6 percent between 2005 and 2010, and it's expected to decline at roughly the same rate for the next several decades. Russia, meanwhile, has massive stores of natural gas just waiting to be tapped. As European demand grows, Russia is ready to fill the void. Europe already imports about half of its natural gas supply, an amount that's expected to increase to more than two-thirds in the next few decades.

The opening of the Nord Stream, the world's longest subsea pipeline, is a flashpoint for concerns about Russia's growing influence in Europe. The Nord Stream, which began to flow in late 2011, runs for more than 1,200 kilometers under the Baltic Sea, connecting the Russian city of Vyborg, near the Finnish border, to Greifswald in northeastern Germany. Russia is already the source of about a third of German gas imports, a number that will only go up as nuclear plants come off line and the Nord Stream reaches full capacity. The more gas Russia sends to Germany and the rest of Europe, the more Russia can use its energy exports for political and economic leverage.

Ukraine knows full well how that story can play out, having had its gas supply from Russia cut off several times over the last decade. Roughly 80 percent of the natural gas that Russia sends to Europe gets there via Ukraine. In exchange for cut-rate prices on natural gas, Ukraine has long given Russia a sweet deal on shipping costs. But this relationship is hardly harmonious. When Russia periodically pushes to collect more money for its gas, Ukraine counters with a demand that Russia pay more for pipeline access. The situation last came to a head in 2009, when Russia turned off the gas supply just as Europe was facing a wave of freezing winter temperatures. The dispute was eventually settled with the help of loans from the International Monetary Fund and the World Bank. The larger disagreement, however, remains unresolved. Indeed, part of the motivation for building the Nord Stream is to circumvent Ukraine. The Baltic pipeline lessens Russia's dependence on the transit routes that run through eastern Europe and effectively increases its clout with wealthy European nations.

The United States is keenly aware of Russia's newfound importance to Germany, the largest economy in Europe. It hopes the emergence of shale gas plays in eastern Europe might mitigate Russia's growing influence. Poland, for example, is in negotiations with energy giants such as Exxon to develop its gas reserves. The same advances in directional drilling technology and fracking practices that have opened up shale reserves in Canada and the United States can be used to exploit Polish reserves, which are estimated to contain as much as 5.3 trillion cubic meters of gas. But just as shale drilling has inspired environmental opposition in North America, it's also stoking controversy in Europe. Poland has lobbied hard within the EU against the adoption of any European-wide rules that would ban fracking.

France is driving much of the opposition to shale gas. The stance isn't surprising, considering nuclear-powered France would love to step in to help Europe with its future power needs. The French government recently passed legislation banning both fracking and the production of shale gas. If France is successful in pressing its case in the rest of Europe, Paris-based Areva, one of the world's biggest nuclear energy companies, will be a prime beneficiary.

That economic self-interest drives government agendas isn't news. But as chess pieces are moved around the board, it's becoming ever more apparent that energy is dictating political, economic and military strategies.

HOW CURRENCY SHIFTS AFFECT OIL CONSUMPTION

When it comes to gaining a larger share of the world's oil diet, sometimes the checkbook can be mightier than the sword. In the competition for more oil barrels, China's central bank carries far more clout than the military threat posed by its nascent blue-water navy ever could.

If China wants to muscle away oil supply from the United States, an arms race is the last thing it needs to pursue. Oil, like most internationally traded commodities, is priced in US dollars. That means when the dollar falls against other currencies, it takes more greenbacks to buy every barrel of oil. That reality cuts two ways. For Americans, it means oil gets more expensive. If you live in a country with a currency that goes up against the greenback, then oil becomes cheaper. If the greenback were to plunge against the yuan, the decline would effectively transfer millions of barrels of oil consumption from the United States to China.

So what is the likelihood that the US dollar falls against other major currencies? With the eurozone debt crisis still in the middle innings, it's understandably hard to envision how the greenback might suffer a significant drop as well. After all, currency markets are also a zero-sum game. If one major currency is going down, another major currency must be going up.

If Europe's currency union eventually breaks apart, though, a realigned euro would rally against the US dollar. A currency backed by the strong northern European economies of Germany and France would quickly attract global capital flows. And when the reformulated euro went up, the greenback would go down.

The United States government, as we saw in chapter 2, is heavily dependent on the savings of other countries to pay its bills. China, of course, is at the top of this list. Oddly enough, few in Congress see it that way. The prevailing view is that the People's Bank of China has nowhere else to invest its massive foreign reserves but in US treasuries, arguably the safest and most liquid market in the world. That belief takes the urgency out of curbing America's borrowing habits. Why bother to cut spending or raise taxes if you know your banker has no choice but to continue to lend you more money?

Folks on Capitol Hill and Wall Street need to recognize that China's central bank isn't motivated by the same goals as other market participants. China isn't like a retail investor looking for a fund manager to deliver a few extra percentage points to juice a portfolio's return. China's state-owned foreign reserves don't go into US treasuries because they offer a better rate of return than other investment options. No, China pumps its billions into US treasuries because that's what it takes to hold down the value of the yuan against the US dollar. The amount of foreign reserves that need to be invested and the return they fetch is incidental to that task. To date, an undervalued yuan has supported China's economic growth by making its goods more affordable in the US market. But as we have already explored, that dynamic is changing with the economic awakening of 1.3 billion Chinese consumers.

If the People's Bank of China decides that holding down the yuan is still an economic priority, then so be it; China has the cash and there is certainly no shortage of treasuries to buy. But what happens if China's central bank suddenly gets very different marching orders? Can a stagnant American economy continue to be a primary driver of China's economic growth? Triple-digit oil prices are already squeezing profits on merchandise that needs to make a long trip across the Pacific to get to customers. And when Chinese goods arrive, they're entering a market that isn't what it used to be. Debt-laden US buyers are still hungover from a decade-long spending binge. Consumers are pulling in their horns while there are some 5 million fewer jobs in the US economy then there were four years ago. Not exactly a promising combination for Chinese exporters.

If China saw fit to torpedo the greenback, it certainly wouldn't take much. One call from the politburo in Beijing to the People's Bank of China could trigger a long slide for the dollar. The ramifications of a weaker greenback would quickly ripple through to energy markets, allowing China to stand back and let its beefed-up purchasing power redistribute world oil supply accordingly.

GROWTH IS ZERO-SUM TOO

If I told you that one country quadrupled its oil consumption in the last decade while another was using fewer and fewer barrels, which do you think would be posting stronger economic growth? The first one, right? Welcome to the new world order. China's ability to consume a larger share of the world's oil supply translates into a bigger share of global economic growth. Looking ahead, the gap between the world's two economic heavyweights will only get wider.

In a zero-sum world, if Chinese oil consumption doubles over time, the number of barrels going to the United States could be chopped in half (or something close) since the energy pie is only so big. It's a simple notion that will soon become a stifling reality for the United States and other OECD countries.

If oil is the fuel that drives economic growth, and oil consumption is a zero-sum game, then so too is economic growth. Ultimately, that might be all the reason China needs to abandon its cheap yuan policy and turn its back on US treasuries. Instead of a cheap yuan facilitating export-led growth, China will let a rising yuan power domestic growth.

Only a decade ago, America was the engine of the global economy, a role that China has now assumed. With the notable exception of oil, China uses far more resources than the United States. Whether it's coal or copper, China now accounts for nearly half of global demand. That's why commodity markets these days are taking more cues from the People's Bank of China (and fewer from the Fed) than at any time in the past. A slowdown in China's economy, which is chugging forward at roughly 8 percent a year, is much more important to global commodity demand than whatever happens in a US economy that's hard-pressed to expand at a fraction of that pace.

Economic growth has always been competitive, but never to this point has it been zero-sum. Triple-digit oil prices are an unmistakable sign that we're entering a very different world from the one we've known. In the past, an abundance of resources allowed for much more economic growth than is possible today. Even if China's economy expanded at twice the pace of the United States' economy, what really mattered was that both were getting bigger. Mutually occurring growth was feasible in the last decade because we were not yet in a zero-sum world. Now, zero-sum conditions (or something closely resembling that state) are just around the corner. That means growth in certain regions of the global economy will dictate that other economies no longer grow—or, even worse, shrink.

Emerging economies such as China's and India's will still be affected by rising oil prices, but the effect will be much more muted than the impact of high prices on the mature economies of the OECD. Between them, China and India have 2.5 billion consumers just waiting to spend newly earned paychecks. Rising commodity prices might cut China's annual economic growth to 5 percent from 8 percent, but the country's economy will still be expanding. This won't be the case for other countries. Whatever rate of economic expansion China and India are able to sustain will come at the expense of growth elsewhere in the world. If you live in an OECD country, chances are your economic growth is about to get squeezed.

WHERE WILL THAT LEAVE THE WORLD'S POOREST COUNTRIES?

Some people think a touch of comeuppance for the developed world wouldn't be such a bad thing. Organizations from the

United Nations to Oxfam have long wanted to redress the imbalance between the world's haves and have-nots. Advocates for poor countries have called upon richer nations to forgo economic growth in favor of greater global equity.

While a noble goal in principle, the promise of an economic slowdown is unlikely to win the hearts and minds of voters when polls open in the United States, Canada or the United Kingdom. Much to the contrary, deteriorating economic conditions in OECD nations will make wealthy countries even less eager to share resources with the rest of the world. At first blush, it may appear that under zero-sum conditions an economic slowdown in OECD countries will free up vital resources for developing countries. A closer look, though, shows that not every emerging economy is created equal.

If karma had a vote, static growth in North America, western Europe and Japan would make more resources available for the poor countries of sub-Saharan Africa and south Asia. In practice, it's debatable how much oil, fertilizer or grain will be left for those countries after global giants such as China, India and Brazil take their share.

Unfortunately, a zero-sum world will be no more liberating for the world's poorest countries than economic conditions were in the last century. The closer Chinese and Indian households come to achieving first-world lifestyles, the higher their extra resource consumption will drive commodity prices, limiting the access to those resources for the rest of the developing world. As we will see later, those dynamics are already apparent in today's food prices. The cost of basic staples such as wheat, rice and corn is heading ever higher, increases that are creating shortages in places that need food the most.

In the developed world, the situation will be much less dire.

We'll all still be fed and reasonably clothed. That said, we will feel the presence of the emerging economic giants keenly. More and more, foreign and economic policy will be tilted toward establishing stronger ties with new superpowers such as China and India. That's really what Canada's proposed Northern Gateway pipeline is all about. And that's just the tip of the iceberg. When stagnant growth becomes the norm across the OECD, the few economies that are still expanding will represent a lifeline that other countries will be desperate to catch. At the same time, triple-digit oil prices will make our economies feel ever more distant from those faraway centers of growth. As China and India march inexorably into the future, our own economies are about to take a hard turn back to the past.

CHAPTER 8

THE STATIC ECONOMY

AVIS RENT A CAR RUNS A DEPOT out of the parking lot of my former office building in downtown Toronto. Unlike the acres of room that rental agencies have at airport locations, space is at a premium in the heart of a cramped city. A limited number of parking stalls forces Avis to perform a constant balancing act between cars ready to be rented out and the steady stream of vehicles being returned.

Over the years, I noticed a funny thing about the employees at Avis: many of them started to have gray hair. I doubt these pensioners figured they'd spend their golden years jockeying cars around an underground lot. Still, most of them seemed to have a pretty good time doing it, at least if the banter I caught on my way into work was anything to go by.

Whether it's as rental-car jockeys or Wal-Mart greeters, more and more seniors are staying in the workforce longer. And this trend, clear in the employment statistics, doesn't look as if it will change anytime soon. The number of seniors working past retirement age, according to the US Bureau of Labor Statistics, is forecast to increase 85 percent between 2006 and 2016.

The demographic challenge facing North America is well known. As baby boomers reach retirement age, government and corporate pension plans are straining to keep up with an unprecedented number of retirees. At the same time, increases in health care expenses and the cost of living mean retirement savings aren't going as far as they used to.

For many senior citizens, part-time work at places like Avis is the ticket to help close the gap between the money coming in and the cash going out. In the United States, the White House is considering raising the retirement age as a way to help curb the federal deficit. In Canada, the Harper government just raised the retirement age to 67 from 65. Until recently, such an option would have been politically untenable. Now, though, it points toward the type of changes that are in store for North America's job market and its workforce.

In a static economy, it won't just be GDP growth that languishes; so will job creation. This is where the ramifications of a zero-growth economy really hit home. Unless you're an economist, the idea of GDP may just be an abstract number you see dutifully reported in the business pages. Jobs, on the other hand, are as real as it gets. When you don't have one, you don't need a statistician to tell you that you're unemployed.

In the United States, unemployment rates have nearly doubled in the last decade, making job creation a battle cry for politicians across the country. In the recent presidential race, some of the most intense and highest stakes sparring between the two candidates occurred over their dueling plans to create jobs. Now that Obama is back in the White House, he's named rebuilding the country's middle class as one of the top priorities for his second term.

Beneath the political rhetoric, plans to put America to work share a common denominator: the idea of growth. Get the economy growing again and jobs will follow. But those plans don't account for a new world of higher energy costs that will prevent the economy from growing at the pace achieved in the last decade, when it pumped out a steady stream of new jobs every month. Time will show that those were the good old days. What do you do about job creation now that the economy's potential growth rate has downshifted into a much lower gear?

Huge budget deficits aren't the answer, and neither is printing money. Rather than boost payrolls, those measures just increase the national debt and ultimately stoke inflationary pressures. At the same time, few voters are willing to back a government that stands by passively while more and more people find themselves out of work.

Regardless of political stripe, everyone understands that a sustained period of rising joblessness can cause a country to crumble. Tax revenues go down, public services are cut, infrastructure falls apart, crime rates increase, and so does homelessness. It's a downward spiral. If we're to manage the slowdown in growth and avoid its worst consequences, the notion of what constitutes full employment needs to be recalibrated to account for the new economic reality. Just as oil trading at $20 a barrel is a thing of the past, so too are jobless rates in the low single digits.

Although jobs may become scarcer, at the same time we may also see fewer people looking for work.

CLOSING BORDERS

History suggests that rising unemployment in any country results in tighter border restrictions. A crackdown on immigration goes hand in hand with slower economic growth. All too often, such policies are shaded by xenophobia and even outright racism. In economic terms, though, the equation is straightforward: when the pie isn't growing, cutting fewer slices means everyone at the table gets a larger portion.

Since the recession of 2008-9, immigration quotas have shrunk in many of the world's richer nations. The lingering fallout from the economic slowdown for national jobless rates is making new immigrants less needed and, of course, less welcome. Whether they are fording the Rio Grande into the United States or crossing the Mediterranean into Europe, migrants will find it more difficult to gain access to places such as North America and western Europe. Countries in the OECD are slowing the flow of legal migrants by lowering immigration quotas. Meanwhile, other steps, such as the physical walls erected along the US border with Mexico, are attempting to curb illegal migration. In Arizona, police now have the authority to ask anyone they suspect of being an illegal immigrant for identity papers. The controversial legislation has echoes of France's recent deportation of groups of Roma (gypsies) to eastern Europe.

In Europe, borders are suddenly reappearing where they haven't been seen in nearly two decades. One of the consequences of the Arab Spring is a new wave of migration out of North Africa. In the past, Spain and Italy struck deals with Arab dictators such as Moammar Gadhafi to prevent migrants from crossing the Mediterranean and illegally entering continental Europe. But when those strongmen fell, so did the tacit agreements. Tens of thousands of people have reportedly fled North Africa for greener European pastures.

The exodus has spurred France and Italy to resurrect old borders and to staff crossings with passport-inspecting gendarmes. Such measures violate the Schengen agreement, which eliminates many border controls and allows EU-member countries to act as a single state when it comes to international travel. Other countries are following suit. Denmark, for example, recently reintroduced customs agents and gave them the power to stop and inspect vehicles coming into the country from Germany and Sweden. In Holland, the Dutch government plans to install a network of video cameras at major border crossings with Belgium and Germany.

As the formerly borderless contours of the EU are reshaped along old lines, how much longer will EU member states support unrestricted worker mobility when countries are struggling to employ their own domestic labor force?

I saw the benefits of EU labor mobility firsthand when I had an opportunity to speak at an energy conference in Cork, Ireland, in 2006. At that time, the Irish economy was red-hot, an oddity that flipped the country's typical migration pattern on its head. Ever since the great potato famine some 150 years ago, migration has more or less been a one-way flow off the island, but in the middle of the last decade, people were actually moving to Ireland for jobs. I was staying at an upscale hotel where pretty much the whole staff seemed to be Polish. A few years later, Ireland's real estate market and its banking sector went bust, taking its economy along for the ride. I haven't been back to Ireland since, but I have a strong hunch that Cork's hotels are now staffed by more Irish workers and far fewer Poles.

In a zero-growth economy, the need to recruit labor from abroad evaporates. Instead, we're more likely to divvy up available jobs among people already at home.

WORK SHARING AND A GRAYING LABOR FORCE

A slowdown in growth can certainly bring out the ugly side of human behavior when it comes to immigration policy. On a much brighter note, lower rates of job creation also have the potential to foster a stronger sense of community as industries move toward employment models that promote job sharing.

In Germany, a job-sharing program known as Kurzarbeit helped the country weather the latest recession with resounding success. The thinking behind Kurzarbeit is that holding down part of a job is better than having no job at all. Instead of, for instance, three people working full-time and one person being unemployed, under Kurzarbeit four people divide the work of three jobs and split the paychecks. The government then tops up the wages of all four workers. The program isn't perfect, but it is credited with saving more than half a million jobs during the last recession.

The program has helped put Germany on a much better footing compared with other countries. More people going to work every day allows Germany to keep tax money coming in, while reducing the number of unemployed workers who depend on the state. It also allowed German companies to retain skilled workers during the economic downturn. All told, Kurzarbeit has worked largely as hoped. Not only did job sharing keep unemployment in check during the recession, but maintaining continuity in the workforce has helped the jobless rate fall quickly during the recovery. Among OECD countries, Germany is the only nation that can boast a lower jobless rate today than in 2008.

Of course, Kurzarbeit does come with one very large caveat: state subsidies. In 2011, Germany budgeted 5.1 billion euros for the program to help cover the lost income of nearly 1.5 million workers. Germany's economic success in the years preceding the recession gave the country the ability to support such a program. Not every country that could benefit from a Kurzarbeit-style program would have the same financial wherewithal. Indeed, for job sharing to be viable under static economic conditions, the program would have to be tweaked to become less reliant on subsidies. Still, the principles that guide Kurzarbeit are robust and not necessarily contingent on government support.

Originally designed as a temporary measure, Kurzarbeit is becoming a more permanent feature of the German labor market. Ángel Gurría, the OECD's secretary-general, suggested that the widespread adoption of similar programs in other countries would have blunted the impact of unemployment on as many as 25 million workers in the OECD community since the last recession. Instead, jobless rates throughout most OECD countries remain persistently high. For Kurzarbeit to work elsewhere, the program would need to be tailored to suit the specifics of different labor markets. In general, though, it's easy to envision job sharing becoming a standard practice that helps countries around the world deal with the fallout of a static economy.

As an economist, I'm continually intrigued by people's instinctive capacity to adapt to changing economic circumstances. When the exchange rate between the Canadian and US dollars swings one way or the other, shoppers on both sides of the border quickly head to whichever spot holds the most value for their hard-earned dollars. When fruit is in season, grocery stores lower prices and customers fill up their baskets. Homeowners who may not even consider themselves financially savvy lock in mortgage rates in anticipation of a central bank rate hike. Over many years of watching the economy, I've come to appreciate that people respond to all manner of economic signals. In a zero-growth economy, changes in the demand for labor will no doubt induce a range of responses from the workforce.

Tomorrow's labor market will navigate more than a few twists and turns as it adapts to slower growth. Our workforce, for one, will get older. When the job market weakens, youth unemployment is quick to go up. Entry-level jobs held by young people are often less stable, meaning that when the economy dips, they're among the first to disappear. Fortunately, young people typically have fewer commitments and more flexibility than their older counterparts. An option currently being taken up by more young people is staying at home. Rather than venturing into the cold world of landlords, empty fridges and utility bills, the so-called boomerang generation is choosing to stay with Mom and Dad until well past their teen years. This trend points to a big potential increase in postsecondary-school enrollment. If young people don't need to hold down jobs to pay bills, they still need to be doing something with their time; heading to college is something many parents are eager to support. Delayed entry into the workforce is one response to the diminished job prospects that come with slower economic growth. If twenty-somethings can't find jobs, school becomes an attractive alternative. For a country as a whole, more schooling will not only keep youth unemployment from heading higher, but over time it will also result in a better-educated labor force.

As one tail of the labor force is about to get shorter, the other tail is about to get longer. At the same time as fewer young people are entering the workforce, more older workers will be staying in it. Just like the car jockeys at Avis, tomorrow's labor force will see more people working well past what we now consider retirement age. The underfunded state of many private- and public-sector pension plans may leave many people with little choice but to keep working.

As the number of retired workers continues to increase, pension benefits are becoming more dependent on the investment returns earned by pension fund managers. The future of many pension plans is already threatened by huge looming actuarial liabilities. What that term means is that pension plans expect to pay out more in the coming years than they expect to bring in. When the economy was growing and the stock market was booming, pension funds were able to mitigate the potential shortfall brought about by an aging workforce by making savvy investments. In a static economy, though, the opportunities to notch stellar investment gains shrink considerably. Even public-service pension plans, typically the Cadillacs of the pension world, will be affected, as has already happened in bankrupt countries such as Greece.

A squeeze on pension income will provide all sorts of incentives for retirees to find part-time jobs. This trend may cause society at large to reassess how we think about retirement. In North America, economists consider the working population as those between the ages of 15 and 65. But that definition hasn't changed for decades, despite increases in life expectancy. People are living longer and are healthier than ever before. Most pensioners these days are capable of participating in the labor force well beyond their formal age of retirement. So don't be surprised if you see a lot more gray hair in tomorrow's labor force. You can also expect that some of the part-time positions held down by seniors will be created through Kurzarbeit-style job-sharing plans. That might just be the right prescription for retirees looking to top up shrinking pension checks while managing rising health care costs at the same time.

MORE MANUFACTURING JOBS IN A LOCAL ECONOMY

In tomorrow's static economy, job sharing may well become commonplace, but the jobs being shared may not be the type you expect. High oil prices won't just usher in slower economic growth, they will also increase the importance of local economies. In my first book, *Why Your World Is About to Get a Whole Lot Smaller*, I detailed how soaring fuel prices will change the dynamics of international trade by dramatically increasing transoceanic transport costs. In a world of triple-digit oil prices, distance costs money, pure and simple.

Connecting cheap labor in Asia with rich consumers in North America makes all kinds of economic sense when oil is $20 a barrel. But when oil prices escalate, it's less profitable to ship most goods across the Pacific. Changes in transport costs are radically rerouting global supply chains, bringing many of them much closer to home. Hauling iron ore from Brazil to feed Chinese steel factories and then shipping the finished product back across the Pacific to North America isn't economically viable when oil prices are trading in the triple-digit range. Instead, we could see iron ore from Labrador loaded on trains and shipped to factories in Rust Belt cities such as Pittsburgh, Cleveland or Hamilton, Ontario. Old steelworks may reopen to supply nearby construction companies with finished steel. Likewise, as I also pointed out in my last book, sending billions of dollars' worth of refrigerated food across an ocean makes little economic sense. Rather than importing clementines from China or strawberries from Spain, high oil prices will encourage us to buy fruit from local orchards.

More and more, we're hearing stories about multinational firms moving production back to North America from China. One example is Global Sticks, a Canadian company that's among the world's largest manufacturers of sticks used for ice cream treats and Popsicles. Global Sticks recently moved its manufacturing plant from China to Thunder Bay, Ontario. When oil was $20 a barrel, it made sense for Global Sticks to manufacture its products using low-cost Chinese labor and then ship them back to North America. Now, the cost of moving billions of wooden sticks across the Pacific to your neighborhood ice cream shop trumps the amount saved in low Chinese wages. The mass production of Popsicle sticks is precisely the type of low-margin manufacturing that used to be tailor-made for China. Once those businesses moved offshore, North American business leaders and politicians thought it was a given that they were gone for good. But that assumption didn't account for a fivefold increase in the price of fuel.

Rising shipping costs act like a built-in tariff by adding to the price of imported goods. The farther away you get from the end market, the higher the tariff. And distance isn't the only trade barrier now facing Chinese exporters. Climbing unemployment in North America and Europe is making those markets less receptive to goods made by foreign workers who toil for much lower wages in a faraway land.

Trade protectionism is on the rise around the world, meaning manufacturing is getting less mobile and more insular. Consider President Barack Obama's liberal use of nontariff barriers such as the Buy American provisions now in place for federal procurement. Obama's job creation plan requires materials used in federally funded infrastructure projects to be sourced in the United States. That's not only a big blow to Canadian exporters that would love to get a slice of Washington's stimulus spending, it's also a potential breach of the North American Free Trade Agreement.

As I mentioned earlier, by flooding the system with cash, the Federal Reserve's quantitative easing program is also working to devalue the US dollar. A cheaper dollar is both good for US manufacturing, making goods cheaper at home and abroad, and punitive to foreign producers trying to crack the US market. In a job-hungry world, even free market–loving America is becoming more protectionist. Globalization's so-called race to the bottom to capitalize on the lowest wage rate anywhere in the world is about to hit some big roadblocks in the static economy just ahead.

The contours of our economy are already changing, at least in North America. The lost manufacturing jobs of yesteryear are coming home. Over the next decade, manufacturing will account for a larger share of employment and a larger percentage of GDP. That shift is already apparent in the strength of the recovery in US manufacturing since the recession. According to a closely watched survey from the Institute of Supply Management (ISM), 62 percent of manufacturing companies expect revenues to continue to increase in 2013, extending the sector's winning streak. The ISM's semiannual report from December 2012 expects that US manufacturing, which has expanded in 36 of the last 40 months, will continue on this upward trajectory. Those looking for factory jobs in the US should keep tabs on the exchange rate between the dollar and the yuan. If China skips a few Treasury auctions, the greenback is primed to slide by 20 to 40 percent. That kind of sharp decline would cause North America's hollowed-out manufacturing sector to fill back up in a hurry.

Globalization ushered in a massive redistribution of income between countries. A huge pool of cheap labor brought companies, ranging from auto plants to call centers, to places such as China and India. The shift was a boon for those countries and the bottom line of multinational corporations, but someone always gets the short end of the stick. In this case, it was North American workers. Not only did they lose their jobs, but their bargaining power also took a hit each time another overseas factory opened.

The competition for jobs in a globalized world put governments in a tough spot. If a multinational company found that setting up shop in, say, South Korea was too expensive, it could always try Vietnam, India, Mexico or any other country willing to cut it a better deal. One country could always be played off against another. Attempts to better regulate companies or to increase corporate taxes are easily thwarted when there's a looming threat of production being moved to a friendlier jurisdiction. When capital is mobile and labor is not, the playing field tilts toward footloose multinational firms at the expense of local wage earners.

But the reverse is also true. The less mobility exists in the system, the more bargaining power shifts back to the local economy. That's why labor unions push for trade barriers while corporations clamor for free trade. When products are protected, so are domestic factory workers.

For North American workers, trade protectionism doesn't have to come in the form of a tariff. High oil prices will make it more expensive to get to work every day, but they'll also bring offshore jobs back home. In a world where distance costs money, unemployed factory workers will see a return of long-lost jobs and governments will regain the ability to increase corporate taxes. Just as cheap oil tipped the scales in favor of mobility, triple-digit oil prices will shift the balance of power back toward local labor and government.

WHITHER THE HEDGE FUND MANAGER
AND INVESTMENT BANKER?

In a zero-sum world, as we saw in the last chapter, if something is growing, then something else must shrink. If you're looking for the most likely candidate to counterbalance a rejuvenated manufacturing sector, a contraction in the number of financial services jobs is a good bet. No part of the economy has grown as mightily as financial services in recent decades. Figuring out why isn't hard. Even looking at my own career makes the reasons for the investment banking industry's rapid expansion abundantly clear.

I started in the industry more than twenty years ago as a young economist at Wood Gundy, a venerable blue-blood Canadian brokerage firm. Before that, I'd spent six years at Ontario's Ministry of Treasury and Economics, which is now the Department of Finance. Back then, the investment world was much different than it is now. Rather than working with the balance sheet of a giant bank or a publicly traded company, the money that most brokerage firms invested came from a firm's partners. That meant risk and reward were judged very differently than they are by today's investment bankers.

Making the wrong call on the market could cost you everything. It almost did for Wood Gundy. The firm had a long-established presence in London, England, dating back to the turn of the 20th century. At that time, Canada was growing and its cities and provinces needed money for infrastructure. Wood Gundy made a lot of money for itself and investors by selling provincial and municipal bonds out of its London branch. When Margaret Thatcher's privatization push arrived in the 1980s, Wood Gundy's established connections in London helped it win the right to be the Canadian distributor of the last tranche of the government's shares in British Petroleum. By rights, the deal really should have been a home run for Wood Gundy, but when the stock market crashed in 1987, BP's shares sank along with it. The firm almost failed, which would have been a financial catastrophe for the partners. (A former executive once confided to me that only a last-minute cash infusion from one of Canada's wealthiest families kept the sheriff from padlocking the company's doors.)

In the 1980s, the same tide of deregulation championed by Thatcher in Britain and Ronald Reagan in the United States swept across other OECD countries, including Canada. Until then, the financial services industry had been divided into four separate pillars: banks, trust companies, brokerage firms and insurance. Cross-ownership was prohibited. When the restrictions preventing banks from owning brokerage houses were lifted, the major Canadian banks jumped at the chance to get into the lucrative business of investment banking.

In 1988, the Canadian Imperial Bank of Commerce scooped up Wood Gundy and used it to build an investment banking platform. Like many in the brokerage industry, the Wood Gundy executives were a sharp and hungry bunch. It didn't take long for a sort of reverse takeover to unfold at CIBC. The bank's senior executive positions were soon filled with former Wood Gundy staff, who imported the same aggressive deal-making culture that worked in the brokerage business to the bank as a whole.

Even more important than the change in corporate culture was the transformation in the way deals were funded. Instead of relying on a limited pool of partners' capital, former Wood Gundy bankers could now cut deals using the comparatively limitless funds provided by the bank's balance sheet. That meant bigger deals and larger profits. The razor-thin margins earned by traditional deposit-taking and commercial banking operations paled in comparison with the spectacular returns notched by the investment banking arm, encouraging CIBC to give more of its balance sheet to the rainmakers from Wood Gundy.

By the late 1990s, the deal flow at CIBC shifted into overdrive. Backed by the capital of a major Canadian bank, the scale of deals soon dwarfed anything ever dreamed of at Wood Gundy. CIBC World Markets became the newly minted investment banking arm of CIBC. And for a while all seemed right with the bank's world. CIBC World Markets was in the top tier of Enron's banking group, a lucrative spot to be in at the time. The investment bank was hitting home runs on Wall Street, leading initial public offerings for sexy new technology plays such as fiber-optic cable provider Global Crossing. Everybody was cashing in (including me, by that point the investment bank's chief economist).

In this new world of investment banking, the rewards for chasing big deals far outweighed the consequences when something went sour. When CIBC paid $2 billion to settle a lawsuit stemming from its intimate involvement with Enron, it wasn't the partners' capital that was at risk, as in the days of Wood Gundy. Instead, CIBC shareholders absorbed the losses. Similarly, when CIBC wrote off billions as a result of its investment bank's exposure to the US subprime mortgage market, it was once again the bank's shareholders who took it on the chin.

The transformation of modest brokerage houses such as Wood Gundy into bulked-up investment banks was a story that played out across North America's financial services sector. Unlike in Canada, Wall Street brokerage firms didn't even need to be bought by large commercial banks in order to enlarge their capital base. Instead, they tapped the public market, turning private partnerships into publicly traded companies with huge valuations. After all, why use your own money to finance deals when you can use someone else's?

If access to public money wasn't enough to supersize Wall Street deals, American regulators also contributed to the trend, easing the rules limiting the amount of money investment banks could borrow, allowing banks to pile up debt that dwarfed their equity. At the same time, the Clinton administration made a quiet but profound decision to leave the financial derivatives market largely unregulated. This followed the repeal of the Glass-Steagall Act, which had maintained walls between the pillars of the financial services industry in the United States since the 1930s. At the same time, former executives from Goldman Sachs, such as Robert Rubin and Hank Paulson, were now running the Treasury Department. Not surprisingly, Wall Street got nearly anything it wanted in those days. What else would you expect when regulators are recruited from the ranks of the regulated?

By the time Lehman Brothers and Bear Stearns blew up, their leverage had climbed to more than thirty times equity. At that level of debt, even small adverse market moves could send an investment bank into insolvency. After years of deregulation, no one should have been surprised. Give investment bankers all the financial incentive in the world to borrow money, strip away most of the rules and consequences, and the real question is how these brokerage houses stayed afloat as long as they did. Wall Street's only salvation was that it had become too big to fail.

As brokerage houses expanded, so did the financial industry's importance to the economy. Since the Second World War, the finance, insurance and real estate sector (FIRE) has doubled in size, rising from 10 percent of US GDP to 20 percent. Similar growth occurred in Canada and other OECD countries. More capital led to bigger deals, which helped drive the stock market ever higher. A soaring market also generated a tremendous demand for all types of wealth management professionals, from brokers to financial planners to accountants.

The boom in the financial services industry, like all things, can't last forever. Government-sponsored bailouts of unregulated capital markets could be the final straw that leads to voters demanding change. The policy pendulum is already swinging from the self-regulatory extremes prescribed by free-market ideologues such as Alan Greenspan back toward a system of increased oversight that will rein in the reach and power of the financial sector. In Europe, regulators are considering new rules that will restrict the leverage allowed in the banking system, as well as the imposition of a tax on financial market transactions.

In the United States, changing the current system will not be as easy. Wall Street is in a seemingly unassailable political position, with deep ties to the Obama administration as well as to influential members of Congress. But Wall Street has held similar sway in Washington before only to see changing economic circumstances curb its influence. In the Roaring Twenties, Wall Street dined out on largely unregulated markets. Fraud and corruption were systemic. That all changed when the Depression struck. An epidemic of bank failures compelled Washington to pass the Glass-Steagall Act that I mentioned above, to erect barriers between deposit-taking institutions and investment banks. Under the act's regulatory yoke, the United States enjoyed a remarkably stable financial system for the better part of five decades. That era ended with the push toward deregulation advocated by Reaganomics in the 1980s.

The lack of oversight that led to the subprime mortgage crisis offers ample evidence that regulatory reform is long overdue. The last round of bailouts has also stoked pent-up public demand for change. If another round of bank failures leads to more public bailouts, no amount of campaign funding from investment banks will save politicians from the wrath of taxpayers who are still waiting to see any meaningful regulatory reforms for the industry. If financial institutions are now too big to fail, the solution seems simple: make them smaller. Returning to the divisions sanctioned under Glass-Steagall is a step in that direction. Regulating the derivatives market and reining in the industry's use of leverage are two more measures that will help shrink the size of the institutions and the financial sector's economic footprint.

REDEFINING THE ROLE OF GOVERNMENT

Governments will be compelled to wield a larger regulatory stick over financial markets, but their imprint on the rest of the economy will become fainter in tomorrow's static economy. Any way you slice it, most governments currently have a large presence in their national economies. In North America, government spending accounts for roughly a fifth of GDP. Whether that's too big or too small to suit your ideological preferences, governments in Europe and North America are facing a diminishing capacity to spend money.

A static economy will necessitate changes in the services governments can provide to citizens. Government will become less about ideology and politics, and more about what taxpayers can and can't afford. Without economic growth and the tax revenue that comes with it, governments will be forced to turn to the private sector. When that happens, private-sector outsourcing shouldn't be interpreted as a vote of confidence in the corporate ethos—far from it. Too many Wall Street scandals, and betrayals of trust by companies such as BP and TEPCO, have taken the bloom off the corporate rose. It's just that when you park ideology at the door and start designing budgets, the numbers show the private sector can deliver many services more cheaply than government. And when incomes are being squeezed by slower economic growth, cost resonates pretty loudly.

Cheaper, by the way, doesn't necessarily mean more efficient.

The average private-sector worker doesn't churn out three widgets an hour while lazy public-sector employees only turn out two. The rate of widget production isn't the point; what matters is wages. Private-sector companies pay workers less to do the same jobs as government employees. That's what allows the private sector to provide services cheaper than government. And that holds true for everything from office workers to garbage collectors.

When dollars need to be slashed from the budget every year, saving on wages can be the difference between offering a service and going without. While most of us don't want to fire civil servants per se, many folks would wield the ax themselves if the alternative was losing the service altogether. Take my hometown of Toronto as an example. A hot-button issue in the last municipal election was whether city garbage collectors should retain their union-negotiated right to eighteen paid sick days a year. Needless to say, when garbage collectors get paid to be sick eighteen days a year, they will be sick for exactly eighteen days each year. For a city facing a budget crisis, paying for workers to stay home eighteen days a year is a luxury that is hard to justify. The new mayor of Toronto hails from the suburbs, where trash collection has already been contracted out to the private sector. He's vowing to do the same for the city. The writing looks to be on the wall for Toronto's garbage workers, who could soon be replaced by lower-paid, and no doubt healthier, private-sector employees.

The substitution of cheaper private-sector workers for less flexible and more expensive public-sector labor won't be limited to garbage collection. I noticed that the last time I renewed my car's annual registration and picked up a new license plate sticker. For my entire driving life, I've made a once-a-year trek to a government office run by Ontario's Ministry of Transportation. But that annual ritual is a thing of the past. The service is now delivered at kiosks in places such as Canadian Tire, a national retail chain. They'll even collect money for unpaid parking tickets on the city's behalf. Instead of a civil servant making $50,000 a year plus benefits, a store clerk earning minimum wage processes my fees.

The private sector won't just take over garbage collection and issuing license plate stickers. Crumbling infrastructure is already a familiar sight in many North American cities. Whether it's a bridge collapsing over the Mississippi River in Minneapolis or concrete chunks falling from overpasses in Montreal, the public infrastructure that we all use is getting older. Unfortunately, infrastructure is expensive and these days governments only have so much money to go around. It's only a matter of time before decaying bridges and pothole-strewn roads are hived off to a private-sector consortium willing to return them to proper working order. Of course, once infrastructure is recapitalized, the public will need to pay to use it.

Toronto motorists who take Highway 407 already know that model firsthand. Skirting the city's northern edge, the privately owned expressway would never have been built with purely public money. The government has too many other priorities and not enough money in the kitty to go around. Instead, the toll road was privately financed and is run by a Spanish consortium that turns a steady profit for the effort.

The prospect of more toll roads is probably unsettling to those concerned about the consequences for low- and middle-income citizens. Such worries could ease if oil prices continue to march higher. If we stand back and let the market find its own equilibrium, then rising pump prices will ration demand for roadways. Something of a return to the days of Henry Ford's Model T could unfold. Back then, only the rich could afford to drive and everyone else found another mode of transportation. Does it make sense for everyone to pay for roads and bridges they won't be using? As the number of people on the roads shrinks, public officials will feel less pressure to spend scarce tax dollars maintaining highways. Instead of funneling money to public roads used by privately owned cars, governments may decide to invest in subways and other mass transit rail systems.

The effects of smaller government budgets won't just be felt on the roads. Other traditional government services will also take a hit. Torontonians got a preview of what's to come when the city's budget-slashing mayor took a run at public libraries. Canadian author Margaret Atwood, a national icon, quickly joined the battle over library closures, galvanizing readers across the country to come to the defense of Toronto's libraries. Her support helped stem the tide, but you can be certain the library budget won't be safe for the rest of the mayor's time in office.

As much as I love books myself, faced with the alternative of cutting essential workers such as firefighters, police or ambulance drivers, I may have to accept that a publicly funded library system is an expensive bricks-and-mortar institution that could become a thing of the past. Perhaps more people will download books from the Internet rather than visiting a public space. We'll lose the benefits of a communal gathering place, but other venues can emerge to fill the void. We may also see changes to the funding model. In the early 20th century, Andrew Carnegie's foundation built thousands of libraries across North America to the great benefit of generations of readers. Perhaps some other wealthy philanthropists are waiting to do the same.

Universities already rely heavily on private fundraising. I was recently invited to a gala at the University of Toronto to kick off a campaign to raise $2 billion for the school. It's the largest fundraising effort in the history of Canadian universities, but it certainly won't be the last. At a time when Ontario's provincial government is struggling with a record budget deficit, scooping up outside cash to bolster public funding will soon no longer be a luxury, but a necessity.

In the United States, Harvard, the world's richest school, boasts an endowment fund of more than $32 billion. Such a bounty highlights the gap that can develop between haves and have-nots. I'm sure most state-run colleges would give their eyeteeth for a fraction of Harvard's Ivy League largesse, just as small Canadian schools would love to tap the University of Toronto's alumni lists. In a perfect world, funding for schools would be more equitable, but under zero-growth conditions that won't happen.

In tomorrow's static economy, more libraries could be named after local tycoons who like the idea of having their name engraved on the front of a sandstone building. Trash collectors won't be getting eighteen paid sick days a year, and you'll more often deal with minimum wage clerks rather than civil servants. Contributions from rich alumni will help fund the colleges your kids attend. And those same kids, incidentally, are more likely to live at home much longer before eventually finding apartments and getting jobs.

For governments to maintain the same number of services when the economy is stagnant, or shrinking, as they offered when the economy was expanding, they're going to have to find cheaper ways to deliver those services. In many instances, the private sector will be the lowest-cost alternative. In a static economy, the more jobs a government can outsource, the more services it can provide.

THE NEW CONSUMER

In Canada and the United States, consumer spending currently accounts for about two-thirds of GDP. In tomorrow's economy, you can bet that shoppers will be curbing the spendthrift ways that retailers have come to know and love. Most customers will have less money to spend, but that's only the beginning. Changes to attitudes and lifestyle may soon affect spending more than a lack of income growth.

In an expanding economy, spending money becomes habitual. When an economy stops growing, a natural repercussion is that people spend less. Big begets big and small begets small. In other words, downsizing in one area has a cascading effect across the board.

Take house sizes, for example. The bigger the house, the more stuff you need to fill it up. Kitchen appliances, furniture, clothes—the list goes on. I lived in a semidetached house for nearly twenty years in Riverdale, a downtown Toronto neighborhood. The house was 2,000 square feet, not a bad size, but probably smaller than you would expect for the chief economist of a major Canadian investment bank. Our kids grew up there, they never wanted to move, and it was close to the city's financial district where I worked for two decades. A consequence of four people living in a relatively modest house is that you don't have a whole lot of space. Buying something new means chucking out something else to make room.

We saw in the last chapter how consumption of scarce resources such as oil will become a zero-sum exercise between competing countries. That's a macro example, but the zero-sum principle applies just as well to tinier areas—like my old clothes closet. Small houses come with small closets. Mine was jam-packed. If I bought a ski jacket, a new suit or even a pair of jeans, I needed to say goodbye to an older piece of clothing. In the fall, I put all my summer shirts away in a dresser to make enough room for my winter clothes. This is hardly a burden, but on the other hand I don't think it's something that most folks in oversized suburban homes ever need to consider. If everyone had to throw something out each time they bought a new shirt, I guarantee that people would buy fewer clothes.

What holds true for clothes closets is equally true for the rest of the house. My 2,000-square-foot inner-city home had less furniture than a 5,000-square-foot suburban house. When you downsize your home, you also automatically cut other expenditures at the same time. Smaller homes come with smaller utility bills and lower property taxes. They cost less to insure, and most importantly, they cost less to buy, which shrinks monthly mortgage payments. Sometimes small begets small in an effortless way.

I grew up in a modest postwar suburban bungalow that was bulldozed after my parents sold it to make room for a house twice the size. In a smaller world, these giant suburban homes will become as obsolete as the SUVs parked in their driveways. The suburban landscape is defined by energy-sucking McMansions. Before long, these storehouses of consumer goods will be demolished to clear the way for smaller homes better suited to the finite dimensions of tomorrow's economy.

A smaller home will be a blessing when income growth starts to slow. The need to buy less stuff will free up much-needed cash to pay for energy and food. Since the last recession, energy expenditures have spiked and now account for as large a percentage of OECD household budgets as in past economic slowdowns. Higher energy costs are flowing directly into food prices through the cost of the diesel fuel that runs tractors, the fertilizer that feeds crops and the gasoline needed to transport food to grocery stores. As food and energy prices push inflation higher, they also squeeze out other consumer spending. That's a drastically different world than the one we've come to know.

In a globalized world, the proportion of the household budget that was spent on food steadily declined as high-cost food grown locally was replaced by cheaper imports from around the world. Three decades ago, North Americans spent a quarter of the household budget on food. Today, that figure is down to about 10 percent. But food inflation is now running much faster than that of other goods. Food's share of household expenditures is heading higher, leaving less money for everything else.

Faltering income growth is inconsistent with the world most Western consumers have come to know. But having less disposable income may not be as painful as you think. A growing body of research shows that consumer satisfaction hasn't kept pace with increasing consumer expenditures. Similarly, other studies in OECD countries show that our sense of individual well-being lags behind increases in personal income growth.

In the United States, for example, real income per capita has more than doubled since the Second World War. Despite increased wealth, however, studies find that Americans are no more satisfied than they were sixty-five years ago. In polls that gauge well-being, citizens in countries with less personal consumption, such as Denmark, consistently score higher than Americans. An international study on life satisfaction conducted by Gallup ranked the United States 19th, a disproportionately low standing in relation to its per capita income and consumption. A similar trend is evident in Canada. According to the University of Waterloo's Canadian Index of Wellbeing, increases in GDP haven't resulted in commensurate gains in life satisfaction. Since 1994, the sense of well-being among Canadians has only improved at about a third of the rate of the country's economic growth.

Part of the explanation for the discrepancy may be found in what Thorstein Veblen, a 19th-century economist, termed conspicuous consumption. This type of spending is driven by a need to demonstrate social status. Instead of buying stuff you really want, you buy to keep up with the Joneses. Veblen theorized that conspicuous consumption sparked by the need to bolster status doesn't necessarily lead to increased personal satisfaction or enjoyment.

In the postwar era, conspicuous consumption has meant buying bigger houses, faster cars and more expensive suits. But what happens if society's values change along with the economic speed limit? If conservation and sustainability become the watchwords for a new generation of eco-conscious adults, maybe keeping up with the Joneses will mean building a rooftop garden or installing solar panels in your backyard.

A Rolex watch, to pick another example, has long been a token of wealth and status, but there's no reason that can't change. Judging by the protesters in the Occupy movement, a significant segment of our society has lost faith in the merits of unregulated capitalism. To them, a Rolex isn't a sign that the wearer is an investment banker worthy of respect. Instead, it signals that the person who owns it may be about to break another securities law or make millions engineering a Ponzi scheme that will bilk suckers out of their life savings. As always, virtue is in the eye of the beholder. If values change, wearing a diamond-encrusted watch may someday send the wrong message.

Consumer spending doesn't necessarily have to be conspicuous to be unsatisfying. As per capita income increased in the postwar era, it stoked expectations of ever-larger increases in future consumption. Consider your situation if you've never owned a car before. Even if your first vehicle is an underpowered subcompact, you're likely to be over the moon to have it. Every time you slip behind the wheel, you're grateful that you're not waiting at a bus stop in the driving rain. Instead of being jostled by strangers with questionable personal hygiene, it's just you and your car. You settle into your seat, turn on your favorite radio station and get yourself home after a long day at work. Now *that* is consumer satisfaction.

After four or five years, you may want to trade in your subcompact for something a little better. If your income keeps rising, chances are that every few years you'll keep trading up for something more powerful, sportier or more luxurious. But compared with the joy of owning your first subcompact, the marginal benefit from each subsequent trade gets smaller and smaller over time. Economists describe this condition as one of diminishing returns. This principle suggests you won't be much happier in a fancier car than you initially were in your subcompact. And what's true for vehicles also applies to a slew of other things that we buy every day but don't necessarily need.

My own twelve-year-old Audi helped me recognize a long time ago that buying something newer doesn't always mean getting something better. I love driving a car with a stick, and Audi stopped selling standards in Canada many years ago. If I traded in my car for an automatic version of itself, I know my level of consumer satisfaction would actually go down.

As we adapt to a world of static economic growth, less consumption could begin to look like a virtue. Could tomorrow's society embrace conservation the way yesterday's consumers grasped materialism? The end of growth doesn't mean the end of consumer society as we know it, but it could mean that we develop a new sensitivity to an increasingly finite world. Fewer material purchases will also reduce our energy needs—a critical consideration in the years to come.

A new generation of consumers is already forming in OECD countries. Younger people are eschewing their parents' materialism in favor of simpler lifestyles. If this intergenerational shift in values continues to gain traction, it couldn't be better suited to our changing economic environment.

We could all do a lot worse than make the best out of having less. If our incomes stop growing and jobs become scarcer, then at least our leisure time will grow. It won't be money that makes our world go around, but time. And we may learn to spend our time in ways that are more satisfying than simply looking for opportunities to spend money. Embracing leisure time could be a key part of adjusting to a world in which our economies are no longer expanding. Maybe the concept of diminishing returns will aid the transition away from consumerism. If more stuff doesn't make us any happier, then why not try less stuff for a while? I'm betting that most of us who live in OECD countries can learn to live with less and not feel poorer for it.

For others, the task could be far more challenging.

ALL BETS ARE OFF

THE MOST FAMOUS WAGER IN THE HISTORY of economics involves a biologist, the price of tungsten, and three of the four Horsemen of the Apocalypse.

Stanford professor Paul Ehrlich planted the seeds of the bet in 1968 when he published *The Population Bomb*, a controversial book in which he argued that rampant population growth would cause civilization as we know it to collapse. The earth, Ehrlich wrote, can only produce so much food and support so many people. If the global population expands beyond this capacity, it will trigger any number of horrific consequences—the war, pestilence and famine promised by the Horsemen—until balance is restored.

As you might guess, *The Population Bomb* is not a cheery read, but it sold more than 2 million copies and its ideas are woven into the fabric of the modern environmental movement. The 1960s and 1970s were a time of much soul-searching about the harm inflicted on the planet by human activity. Anxiety about the environment inspired, among other things, a new wave of thinking about sustainability. The Club of Rome, for instance, was founded in 1968 by an international group of scientists, academics, industrialists and politicians who shared a belief that people must take action to keep the world from heading off a cliff. In 1972, the club released a report called *The Limits of Growth*, which argued that pending resource scarcity would make it impossible for the global economy to grow at rates achieved in the postwar era. In the last forty years, the Club has distributed more than 12 million copies of the report, which also asserts that global society is likely to overshoot the planet's carrying capacity. Once that happens, the club contends, society won't be able to avoid a large-scale environmental collapse.

Prophets of doom have sounded similar alarms before. Some two hundred years ago, Reverend Thomas Malthus warned that population growth was an inexorable force that would exhaust the land's capacity to provide sustenance. He foresaw starvation and pestilence arising as an inevitable result of overpopulation, bringing about a dying off that would cull the number of people in the world. Along with epidemics that would increase the death rate, Malthus also believed that moral restraint was necessary to keep the birthrate in check. He advocated celibacy, particularly for the poorer segments of society who couldn't afford to raise children (critics have since taken Malthus to task for his own three kids).

Ehrlich is arguably the most famous contemporary apostle of a Malthusian worldview, foreseeing the mass starvation of hundreds of millions of people just around the corner as humanity loses the battle to feed itself. He and the Club of Rome weren't alone in issuing warnings; a series of similar doomsday predictions also appeared in the popular press. The survivalist current at the time even inspired a mini-boom in North American farm prices, as people took to the country to prepare to live off the land.

But an economist at the University of Maryland, Julian Simon, wasn't buying what Ehrlich was selling. Just as human ingenuity has thwarted Malthus's predictions for the past two centuries, Simon believed that innovation would continue to solve the problems posed by population growth. Economics taught him that when faced with a scarcity of resources, people get better at gathering raw materials, become more efficient and find viable substitutes to use instead. In short, humanity doesn't roll over when confronted by adversity; it adapts. Simon even argued that population growth will help to solve issues that arise from resource scarcity. Necessity being the mother of invention, he believed that increasing the sheer volume of people on the planet would inspire more innovation and spur technological progress. More human beings means more brainpower is available to tackle any problem, much like adding RAM to a computer.

Simon and Ehrlich came from completely different academic disciplines, which clearly shaped their attitudes to the issue of population growth. Simon completed his doctoral degree in economics at the University of Chicago in 1961. In his research, he was drawn to exploring the economic effects of population change. His free-market upbringing at the Chicago School clashed with Ehrlich's stance on demographics. Ehrlich, now head of Stanford's Center for Conservation Biology, did his graduate work in entomology at the University of Kansas, studying with renowned bee researcher Charles Michener. Along the way, Ehrlich's ecological interests dovetailed with demographics and the study of population.

Here's where the bet comes in. Simon believed that Ehrlich's environmental approach to the consequences of population growth failed to account for the way prices motivate human behavior. In 1980, he challenged Ehrlich to a wager, the outcome of which continues to resonate more than three decades later. Simon bet that a basket of five basic commodities (tin, tungsten, copper, nickel and chromium) would decline in value over the next decade as people adapted to changes in supply and demand. Ehrlich believed that with more people bidding for the same finite resources, prices would spike. Each professor put $200 on each commodity and the loser had to pay up at the end of ten years.

Simon won. As he predicted, new methods of resource extraction emerged, processing techniques improved and alternative raw materials were adopted. Prices for nickel and chromium fell as better mining and smelting methods were developed. Tungsten and tin became cheaper as the world began to use substitutes such as ceramics and aluminum. Similarly, the demand for copper wiring fell, as global telecommunications firms discovered the magic of fiber-optic cable.

When resource consumption put humanity to the test, ingenuity triumphed.

Economics was vindicated, a fact that was widely publicized, much to the glee of free-market economists who since then are quick to trot out the results of the Simon–Ehrlich wager whenever anyone calls future resource abundance into question.

Losing the bet made for a rough few decades for the Ehrlich camp. Nevertheless, finding answers to the challenges that come with an expanding global population is not as clear-cut as the wager's results might suggest. Ehrlich may have been wrong about commodity prices—and way off the mark on mass starvation—but he was right about population growth. With roughly 4.5 billion inhabitants in 1980, the world added nearly a billion people over the next ten years, the largest increase for any decade up to that time. Yet, instead of hundreds of millions of poor people dying in the developing world, as Ehrlich forecast, measures of human welfare have improved. People are living longer and healthier lives, overall child mortality rates are down and average life expectancy is up.

At the same time, the rate at which the population is growing has continued to increase. We recently topped 7 billion, and more people are coming into the world every day. Simon was right about falling commodity prices in the 1980s, but that doesn't necessarily mean the consequences of rampant population growth can be dismissed. The noted evolutionary biologist E.O. Wilson, for one, has memorably described the pace of human population growth in the last century as more bacterial than primate. Not only is the human biomass greater than that of any other large animal that has ever existed, but we've also altered the biomass of other species to suit our needs, causing a proliferation of cattle, pigs, chicken and sheep—the animals we eat. Meanwhile, the ranks of animals that eat us—lions, tigers and grizzly bears—have dwindled.

Our impact on the world's plant life has been even more profound. We've cleared and cultivated nearly 40 percent of the earth's ice-free land for agricultural purposes. More than half of the planet's flora is now tied to human activity. Moreover, plant life everywhere has become more homogenous at the expense of ecological diversity as the same crops are planted around the world to conform to current dietary tastes.

And we're transforming more than just the biological world; we're reshaping the physical landscape as well. In coal mining regions, we've reduced mountains to nubs to exploit the underlying ore. In the Appalachians, for instance, the mining industry has destroyed hundreds of mountaintops over the last century. We've drained inland seas for our irrigation purposes. The Aral Sea in Uzbekistan was once the fourth-largest lake in the world, but so much water has been diverted toward cotton farming that it is now essentially a desert. In northern Alberta, Syncrude's tar sands mining operation moves 30 billion tons of earth every year, twice the amount of sediment that flows down all of the world's rivers annually.

Humanity's presence is also altering the biosphere's natural cycles. The best-known consequence of our interference is global warming, which is melting glaciers and raising sea levels. But we're also aggravating other processes, such as the nitrogen cycle. Our agricultural needs prompt us to remove nitrogen from the air and apply it to the land through artificial fertilizers. Nitrogen is a game changer for farming and has allowed for a massive increase in the size of the human biomass. Artificial fertilizers boost farm yields and the size of livestock, allowing us to consume ever-greater amounts of food. In particular, protein—essential for growth and relatively scarce in nature—is now much more abundant thanks to fertilization. The results aren't as good for the world's oceans, though. The fertilizer-rich runoff that drains from farmland into rivers, lakes and eventually the sea creates perfect conditions for algae to flourish. The resulting algal blooms choke off other marine life and create coastal dead zones, which are now common around the world.

Our impact on the physical environment is leading some geologists to refer to the modern era as a new geological epoch. The preceding eleven thousand years are known as the Holocene, which roughly translates into "most recent era." Now they say we have entered the Anthropocene, or "age of man."

Geological nomenclature is of little concern to most economists, who don't pay attention to how we change the landscape or whether the human population increases at the same pace as bacterial reproduction. What matters is what markets tell economists through price signals. And for a long time, falling resource

prices—from oil to food to the items in Simon's commodities basket—signaled that population growth wasn't hindering resource
consumption.

But at the start of the last decade, things started to change.
Commodity prices began to rise. Not just a single commodity
or even a group of related materials, but prices for almost everything rose in unison. As the calendar changed to a new millen-
nium, the world woke up to find economic revolutions under
way in China and India. Demand for commodities spiked, and
the price for everything from wheat to copper to oil suddenly
became supercharged.

The industrial revolutions in China and India are a testament
to Simon's optimism about human ingenuity. In the last decade,
the world has achieved breakthroughs in resource extraction and
found ways to use raw materials more efficiently. But economic
growth is also pressuring global resource consumption as never
before. Essentially overnight, hundreds of millions of people
moved from leading quiet lives in rural villages to urban lifestyles
that can increase resource consumption by a factor of ten. The
resulting explosion in commodity demand is a greater test of our
ability to stretch the world's resources than mere increases in
global population. In other words, the planet can probably handle
7 billion people, but not 7 billion people adopting the consuming
patterns of a Western lifestyle.

Commodity prices are telling us that the rapid rates of economic growth achieved by countries such as China, India and Brazil
are unsustainable. Too much demand chasing a finite supply of
resources will continue to send commodity prices higher. We saw
earlier how rising resource prices are already choking off economic
growth in the world's fastest-growing economies. High prices stoke
inflation and trigger interest rate hikes, which stifle the amount of

money that's available to feed growth. When Simon and Ehrlich made their bet, conditions were considerably different.

An across-the-board increase in commodity prices over the last decade makes it worth revisiting the Simon–Ehrlich wager. Taking a longer view, we see that the bet's outcome changes depending on its start date. Commodity prices rose steadily through the 1970s. By the time the two men placed their bets, prices were ready to drop as economic signals spurred industry to increase supplies and find cheaper substitutes. If we recalibrate the bet to start in 1990, Ehrlich would have won in six of the decade's ten years. If the betting starts in 2000, Ehrlich also reaps a resounding victory.

Market prices are telling economists something very different today than in 1980, when Simon and Ehrlich locked horns. Human ingenuity will still make breakthroughs, but rising commodity prices point to a world in which technological innovations can no longer keep pace with the rate at which our economies are consuming key resources.

REBEL, MIGRATE OR DIE

History shows that hungry people have three choices: rebel, migrate or die.

These options are even more alarming considering how much of the world's population is getting hungrier. Population in developing countries is swelling, which means the world needs to produce more food every day. At the same time as populations in developing countries are increasing, OECD countries are starting to close their borders. Opportunities for people to move to wealthy nations that can better support a larger population are becoming scarcer. Even places with immigration policies that still encourage new arrivals, such as Brazil, will become less welcoming as economies cool. If migration is less viable, hungry people are put into the dismal corner represented by options one and three.

When you combine a static economy with rapid population growth, it's not hard to figure out what happens to per capita income: it shrinks in a hurry. More people dividing the same amount of money equals less cash to go around. For the 1.5 billion people who subsist on less than $1.25 a day, how much can per capita income fall before the death tolls and rebellion predicted by Ehrlich come to pass?

In the last forty years, the world has gone in the other direction, making large gains in life expectancy while reducing infant mortality rates. In the 1950s, global life expectancy was 48 years, a figure that's now at 68. At the same time, the infant mortality rate has fallen from 130 for every thousand births to fewer than 50 per thousand. More people living past infancy coupled with longer life spans are key reasons why the global population has nearly doubled in the last four decades.

But such impressive improvements were achieved when economies were growing rapidly. What happens if growth falters? How will the world's poorest people fare? Population increases in the last few decades are bringing the planet's carrying capacity back into question. If we want to ensure that Ehrlich's apocalyptic predictions don't come true, we need to recognize that per capita resource consumption can't keep increasing indefinitely.

How much will living standards in parts of the developing world be squeezed by the hundreds of millions of people in Asia who are moving toward OECD levels of resource consumption? A burgeoning middle class in China and India has the purchasing power to buy everything from oil and coal to wheat and rice. In a zero-sum world, people who lack economic clout will be priced out of the market. Will that mean they don't get to eat? Will the ascendance of China and India into the upper echelons of the global economy be achieved at the expense of other developing nations? It's a story that should sound familiar in Britain and the United States, both of which built empires on the backs of other countries' people and resources.

China, of course, would like to cultivate a different perception. Chinese leaders are quick to remind others just how much its economic growth benefits the rest of the world. If China falls on tough times, countries that depend on it for their own economic well-being would certainly suffer. But it's worth wondering how much conflict and social unrest is created in other places, such as the Middle East and Africa, by the enormous appetite for resources in China and India.

Does China's success come at the expense of other countries whose economies aren't growing fast enough to keep pace with rising food and energy prices? The impulse behind the Arab Spring was a lack of food, a problem that hasn't gone away. In countries such as Somalia and Sudan, to name just two, far too many people go hungry every day. When civil unrest can be traced back to hunger, it casts economic growth in a much harsher light.

It takes seven pounds of grain to raise a pound of beef. That ratio tells you that the more cheeseburgers are eaten in sprawling urban centers in China and India, the fewer rice bowls are filled in the countryside. New city-dwellers with steady paychecks can afford higher-protein diets. Grain that would normally feed poorer people in rural areas is thus being used instead to fatten up livestock. In traditional Chinese cooking, a little bit of meat goes a long way: chop up a scrap of pork, mix it with vegetables and rice, and it can feed a whole family. However, the numbers show that more folks in China are trading in their stir-fries for cheeseburgers. In recent decades, global meat consumption has grown at twice the pace of population growth.

And it's not just cheeseburgers. When China and India burn more oil and coal, that translates into fewer resources and higher power costs for other developing countries. Consider, for example, Pakistan, which lives in the shadow of India's economic success. It's experiencing the worst electricity crisis in its history. In the summer of 2011, half of Pakistan's power-generating capacity was off line, because utilities couldn't pay for fuel. Cities in Pakistan are routinely subjected to electricity outages that last upward of fourteen hours. In rural areas, the power rationing is even more extreme and blackouts can last even longer.

Energy shortages have not only turned off the power for millions of Pakistanis, they've also shackled the country's economic growth. Pakistan's income per capita is increasing at its slowest rate since 1951, and now sits at a quarter of the pace enjoyed by neighboring India. Faced with mounting power outages, multinational firms are pulling out of the country and the economy is collapsing. And social and fiscal conditions will only get worse as Pakistan's population continues to grow.

People in Karachi may be able to live without air-conditioning and even cars, but they can't go without food. For the developing world, food shortages are the biggest challenge arising from growing populations. Projections for population growth see most of it occurring in countries such as Pakistan, Bangladesh, Uganda, Ethiopia and the Democratic Republic of the Congo. The UN predicts the global population will increase by 3 billion people this century, most of whom will be born in the developing world. Higher food and energy prices can mean the difference between life and death in many of these places. It's potentially devastating that the most explosive population gains will be concentrated in the countries that can least afford it.

FOOD PRICES ARE THE GATEKEEPER
OF POPULATION GROWTH

When Malthus made his predictions two hundred years ago, he couldn't foresee how unlocking the power of hydrocarbons, first in coal and later in oil and natural gas, would boost the land's carrying capacity. Energy abundance not only powered the Industrial Revolution and the economic growth achieved since then, but it has also allowed for huge increases in food production and, by extension, population.

Energy has never been in higher demand than it is in today's world of commercial farming. The quantum leaps made in agricultural productivity in the postwar era were achieved by channeling greater amounts of energy into food production. Farming is now extremely energy intensive, whether the power is diesel for tractors, fertilizer for crops or electricity to run irrigation systems.

The more hydrocarbons we burn, the more carbohydrates we can grow. But there are other consequences to that equation: higher energy prices flow directly into higher food prices. In fact, world food prices are rising even faster than energy costs. The UN's food price tracking index reached a new record in January 2011, eclipsing the previous high set in 2008. Back then, soaring food prices sparked riots in the developing world. Turn the clock forward to 2011 and it should come as no surprise that countries in the Middle East and North Africa were again convulsing with social and political unrest.

Rising food prices have different consequences depending on where you live. For people in OECD countries who spend no more than a tenth of their income on food, more expensive grocery bills are an annoyance. But for the planet's poorest 2 billion people, higher food prices are the difference between eating two meals a day and trying to survive on one.

Poor harvests in key grain-exporting countries such as Russia, Canada, Ukraine and Australia are pushing wheat prices toward the historic highs set during the food crisis of 2008. A drought in Russia in the summer of 2010 caused the country to cut wheat exports entirely. The ban remained in place for nearly a year, until yields improved and wheat supply once again exceeded the demands of the domestic market. Prior to the ban, Russia, the world's third-largest producer of wheat, barley and rye, exported a quarter of its 97-million-ton grain harvest every year.

For countries that rely on food imports, dwindling exports from major suppliers can have sweeping implications. Dictators throughout the Arab world have seen how hunger can quickly turn into revolution. Egypt's ousted dictator Hosni Mubarak found that out the hard way, as did Libya's Moammar Gadhafi and Tunisia's Zine El Abidine Ben Ali. By the look of things, Syrian president Bashar Assad will soon be joining this club.

Rulers in the Middle East and elsewhere in the developing world are learning there's a direct correlation between keeping people fed and staying in power. Algerian president Abdelaziz Bouteflika picked up that lesson by watching the fate of his dictatorial brethren. When food riots broke out in his own country, his government ordered 800,000 tons of wheat to help keep the peace. And Algeria isn't the only country in the region to resort to food to head off popular unrest: Saudi Arabia followed Algeria's lead, announcing plans to double its wheat inventories.

But ordering food is merely a stopgap. The underlying issues faced by the developing world don't have an easy fix. Take Egypt, the most populous country in the Arab world. In 1960, fewer than 28 million Egyptians lived inside the country's borders. By the time Hosni Mubarak took power in 1981, that number had swelled to 44 million. Today, Egypt is home to 80 million people. Given its current birthrate, the country's population will double to 160 million by the middle of the century. I'm sure if Malthus were around, he would wonder how a country that averages only two inches of annual rainfall could possibly sustain a population of 160 million when it's already struggling to provide for 80 million people today.

As much as Egyptians welcomed the overthrow of the Mubarak regime, it doesn't change the country's dilemma when it comes to food. Almost all of Egypt's arable land lies along the banks of the Nile River. An area that accounts for only 3 percent of the country's landmass now needs to support a population that has nearly tripled in the last fifty years. The plight of Egypt wasn't helped by nearly three decades under the yoke of a dictator whose family and military cronies bled the country's treasury dry. But even with a government that doesn't steal billions from its people, Egypt will still struggle to feed its population.

As its numbers continue to soar, Egypt will be forced to import more food. That's a particularly tall order given that roughly 40 percent of its national food bill is already spent on imports, including 60 percent of its grains. Moreover, the price of those imports is going through the roof. When 30 million Egyptians live on less than two dollars a day, it's easy to see why the consequences of food inflation are so dire.

Changes to autocratic regimes can happen overnight, but countries such as Egypt have problems that can't be solved even if the populace takes to the streets. As time goes on, it will only become harder for Egypt to feed its growing number of citizens. Egypt has all the markings of a country with a population that has outstripped the carrying capacity of the land.

When food prices peaked back in 2008, the increase came after eight solid years of global economic growth. Now, only a few years removed from the deepest recession of the postwar period, prices are again at record levels. Higher energy costs have ushered in a new era for food prices, which is ominous news for people in the developing world who are already struggling to put food on the table.

WILL GLOBAL FOOD MARKETS CONTINUE TO WORK?

Unprecedented demand for energy and resources may simply overwhelm our capacity to keep pace with a constant stream of solutions and innovations. Record food prices signal that feeding 7 billion people every day will become an ever-harder job for the global economy to manage. The task will be even more daunting as more people look to adopt the protein-rich diets enjoyed in wealthy countries.

The challenge of feeding a growing global population doesn't get any easier when major food-exporting countries decide to curtail shipments. That's not how markets are supposed to work. Higher food prices should lead to more food production, not less. According to conventional economic theory, higher prices encourage producers to bring on more supply. But that only happens in a free market. Governments don't necessarily respond to price signals in the same way as corporations that are motivated by maximizing profits. Indeed, in some cases governments may head in the opposite direction.

That's precisely what happened during the food crisis of 2008, and it's something global food markets are likely to see again. Instead of soaring food prices leading to more exports, governments diverted food production to meet the demands of domestic markets. Food didn't go to the highest bidder, but to the citizens of the countries in which it was produced.

When prices for luxury consumer goods go through the roof, politicians aren't compelled to intervene in the market. But when the price of basic foodstuffs soars, governments know they could face rioting in the streets. At that point, you can toss out everything the textbooks say about supply curves.

Economic theory insists that during the food crisis of 2008, record grain prices should have pulled supplies out of world granaries as never before. Instead, no fewer than twenty-nine food-exporting countries banned exports and dedicated food grown at home to a hungry domestic populace. The increased scarcity sent global prices that much higher. Countries that could still import food began hoarding supplies in case the trend of exporting countries holding back crops became even more widespread.

Economists who believe in the unfettered workings of the free market certainly wouldn't approve of blocking food exports. But they don't have to win elections or stay in power. The experience of the last food crisis shows that relying on the market mechanism of higher prices can leave a country full of hungry people. If pushed, food-exporting countries won't hesitate to sacrifice foreign markets in favor of holding down domestic prices. That tendency is hardly reassuring to nations who import large amounts of food. Even countries in the Middle East that boast vast petro-wealth can't buy food when foreign governments cut off supply. That's part of the reason oil-rich countries such as Saudi Arabia are taking matters into their own hands and snapping up agricultural land in other places. According to Oxfam, foreign interests have purchased more than 125 million acres of land in Africa in the last decade. That's more farmland than exists in Canada's prairies, one of the world's major breadbaskets.

It remains to be seen whether that accumulation of land will be an effective hedge against future bans on food exports. If push comes to shove, the food grown on those 125 million acres of African land could stay put. Governments are happy to take Middle Eastern petrodollars when times are good, but if food becomes scarce, those agreements may not be worth the paper they're printed on. A hungry population, as recent uprisings show, will not stand idly by as domestic crop production leaves to grace dinner tables in another country.

THE YANGS' NEW WORLD

North America is home to 5 percent of the world's population, yet its ecological footprint is larger than any other continent's. When you pit the standard of living and consumption habits of Canadians and Americans against those of people elsewhere, it's not hard to figure out why we leave such an outsized imprint on the environment.

In China, for example, car ownership stands at 20 cars for every thousand people, or 2 percent of the population. In North America, 435 out of every thousand people own a vehicle, or 43.5 percent. On a per capita basis, North American cellphone usage is double China's. Similarly, 60 percent of North Americans own a computer, compared with 4 percent of Chinese. Perhaps not surprisingly, North America's annual per capita carbon dioxide emissions stand at 13 metric tons, compared with 3 metric tons in China.

All of the stuff we own—computers, cars, cellphones, fridges—is built using an enormous amount of raw materials. Take copper as an example. It conducts electricity and heat better than almost any other material, which means it's used practically everywhere you look. From air-conditioners to flat-screen televisions to the wiring in your electrical appliances, copper is all around you. Of course, that only holds if you're reading this book in North America or Europe. If you're in rural China, copper is nearly absent from your home.

What happens when more of China's farmers make the jump from village life to modern cities? I recently picked up a story by *Bloomberg Businessweek* that did a good job painting the picture. It begins with 76-year-old Yang Caiguan and his wife, who have just moved from a traditional mud-brick house in the country to a four-bedroom apartment in Daojiang, a town in Hunan province. The Yangs' industrious son, who built a fortune as a factory owner, transplanted his parents to the city. He spent more than $50,000 buying and outfitting their new apartment, which is located in a gated community about five miles from their old home.

The transition to urban living is full of revelations for the Yangs, and also for the future of global resource consumption. The couple, who cooked over an open woodstove for decades, have traded that in for a new gas stove containing 10 pounds of copper. Their new refrigerator, which allows for the simple pleasure of eating ice cream whenever the mood strikes, is good for another 4 pounds of copper. The washing machine has almost 2 pounds and the hot water heater another pound. Each of the two air-conditioners in the Yangs' condominium unit contains 13 pounds of copper. Add in the rest of the appliances and the wiring in the apartment and the Yangs' new home is using more than 85 pounds of copper, or about ten times the national average.

Needless to say, it's taking the couple some time to adjust to the amenities of modern living. They've never had a freezer before, or an electric-ignition stove. They rarely draw on the hot water tank in the bathroom, since they prefer to bathe in the same plastic tub they've used for years. In their old home, ventilation was a few holes punched in the wall near the roof, not double air-conditioners. And they didn't need much copper for plumbing, since the toilet at the back of the house was open air.

The Yangs aren't alone in making the transition to an urban lifestyle. Millions of Chinese have made the same jump, and millions more are waiting to follow them. China already accounts for 40 percent of global copper consumption. Its annual domestic copper use has tripled in the last decade to nearly 7 million tons, a number that's only going up as per capita consumption increases. In twenty-five years, China's annual copper consumption is projected to reach as much as 20 million tons. But there's a major hitch that will keep those forecasts from coming true: that annual total is more than the current annual output of all the world's copper mines put together.

The finite nature of copper resources means China's consumption simply can't continue to grow exponentially. After all, China isn't the only nation that needs the world's resources. There are another 5.7 billion people outside China who want to consume the same copper, potash and oil being gobbled up by the Chinese.

The resource consumption of China's burgeoning ranks of Yangs is already rippling through the rest of the world. In London, for instance, thieves made off with a life-size bronze statue of Dr. Alfred Salter, a social reformer who fought to improve the plight of the country's poor. The memorial figure sat on a bench in the Bermondsey district, the same neighborhood that had its former squalor immortalized in the pages of *Oliver Twist* (stealing the statue of a social crusader has a certain Fagin-like heartlessness befitting of Dickens). With copper prices at nearly four dollars a pound, the city will have to find a less costly way to commemorate Dr. Salter's good deeds.

High copper prices have British thieves breaking into everything from power stations to train yards in search of scrap metal. The UK scrap industry does billions of pounds' worth of business a year, much of it in cash, which makes it a magnet for criminals. Commuters have become used to transit delays due to the theft of copper cables from rail networks. Similarly, across the country thousands of households have experienced blackouts after metal thieves nicked power cables.

The theft of public statues and bits of railroad infrastructure underscore the finite nature of global resource supply. Fresh demand for copper is pushing prices higher, and the end is nowhere in sight. North Americans consume more than five times the amount of base metals, fresh water and protein as people in the developing world. A direct relationship exists between global consumption per capita and the number of people who can achieve OECD lifestyles.

The more Yangs there are in the world, the fewer people the planet can support.

WRESTLING DOWN GLOBAL BIRTHRATES

The United Nations estimates that the world's 7-billionth person was born on October 31, 2011, most likely in Uttar Pradesh, the poorest and most populated state in India. According to the UN, the child is unlikely to have access to electricity or in-door plumbing and has only a 60 percent chance of attaining literacy. Overall, the UN estimates that 2.5 billion people in the world lack basic sanitation.

The UN's forecast for the global population to reach 10 billion this century leaves you wondering how the planet will support another 3 billion bodies. What will be left of the earth's remaining forests, jungles, oceans, rivers and wildlife? Even if we sacrifice the environment entirely, what kind of quality of life can the world's 10-billionth person expect?

Population growth is widely recognized as the key reason for economic underdevelopment in poor nations. When we look to the future, a stagnant global economy is a grim backdrop for rampant population growth. Faltering economies will put the brakes on population increases one way or another. Sadly, we could see a reversal in some of the gains we've made in human health and life expectancy.

The demographic implications of rapid population growth were the impetus behind China's infamous one-child policy. The country's Communist government adopted this drastic policy in 1979 to keep family size in check and hold down the country's population. On that score the policy has worked, reportedly leading to 400 million fewer people in China as a result. But the totalitarian family planning practices also come with horrific costs, including female infanticide and forced abortions.

China continues to reject overtures from international organizations to end the policy, although demographic shifts may encourage Beijing to give more serious consideration to changing its stance. Just as birthrates have nose-dived in OECD countries, the same demographic trends are emerging in cities such as Shanghai, which have bridged the gap to Western living standards.

In the big picture of global population growth, however, modern industrialized cities in China are no longer the main event. Most of the world's new babies will arrive in developing countries in south Asia and sub-Saharan Africa. Unlike China and India, globalization has left these countries behind. For them, a leap forward into Western living standards isn't waiting just around the corner. But a leap of sorts is exactly what's required. Birthrates in the developing world must come down if the planet hopes to avoid the Malthusian consequences of out-of-control population growth.

In the early 20th century, Dr. Kwegyir Aggrey, an American-educated missionary and intellectual born in Ghana, worked to raise the understanding of Africa among people in the West. A brilliant orator by all accounts, Dr. Aggrey spoke passionately about the role that education could play in improving social conditions. He once said: "The surest way to keep a people down is to educate the men and neglect the women. If you educate a man you simply educate an individual, but if you educate a woman, you educate a nation." What was true for Dr. Aggrey a hundred years ago is still true today.

The ramifications of gender equality and female education ripple into every corner of society. For evidence, you don't need to look any further than declining birthrates in OECD countries in the postwar period. In fact, you can take my own family as an example.

I met my wife, Deborah, when she was a national television reporter for the Canadian Broadcasting Corporation. Work and life kept us busy, and we didn't have our first child until Deborah was thirty-nine. We now have two children, Jack and Margot. In Canada, two-career couples are a common story. Like us, many people don't have children until much later than was the case for previous generations.

That's part of the reason Canada's fertility rate is only 1.58. If not for immigration, Canada's population would actually be shrinking, as would the populations of most other OECD countries. In Japan and South Korea, fertility rates are below 1.25. Compare those numbers with Niger, which has a world-leading fertility rate of 7.6. Let that sink in for a minute: the average woman in Niger has more than seven kids. In Uganda the fertility rate is 6.69, and in Somalia it's 6.35.

The United Nations Population Fund has found that educated women are likely to marry later and have smaller and healthier families. As female education rises, studies show that infant mortality rates fall and family health improves. Children of educated mothers are themselves more likely to achieve higher levels of education, feeding into a virtuous cycle. An increase in female education also translates into more women in the workforce, which boosts household income and GDP. And none of that even begins to engage broader questions of morality, gender equality and social justice.

Consider the situation of a woman in Uganda working as a reporter for the Ugandan Broadcasting Corporation. She may decide, as Deborah did, to hold off on getting married until later in life. Along with being busy with work, she would also have the financial wherewithal to stay single. All of which adds up to a reduction in the number of years she is actively looking to have children.

Educated women are also more aware of reproductive choices, such as contraceptives. A study from Bangladesh shows that women with postsecondary degrees are three times as likely to use contraceptives as women with no formal education. These same women are also ten times more likely to stay single rather than marry. According to the World Watch Institute, two out of every five births result from unintended pregnancies. That figure seems high, but if it's even remotely close to the mark, its implications are staggering. If births dropped by 40 percent a year, the global population would stabilize and much of the demographic challenge facing the world would disappear.

But we're a long way from that becoming a reality. Universal education and gender equality are two of the eight pillars laid out by the UN as part of a campaign to end global poverty by 2015. The UN won't meet its goal, but at least it's moving in the right direction. According to UN estimates, more than a billion women live in unacceptable states of poverty, most of them in the developing world. Organizations such as the UN, the World Bank and even the US military's Joint Chiefs of Staff recognize that education holds the key to pulling countries in the developing world out of their current quandary. It may not be possible to fast-forward economic development in many poor countries, but support for female education does seem to be gaining critical mass, at least among intergovernmental agencies, NGOs and relief organizations.

In tomorrow's economy, global population growth, like everything else, will have to adjust. Just as birthrates have come down in the developed world, the same change must occur in places such as Bangladesh, Pakistan, Uganda and other population hot spots.

Could a static economy hold positive unexpected consequences for world population growth? A lower global economic speed limit just might, if it helps spark the empowerment of women in the developing world. Even brutal dictatorial regimes could soon recognize that explosive population growth and food scarcity is an untenable combination. The pragmatic instinct to head off popular unrest may lead to more progressive approaches to education and family planning than we have yet seen. A Chinese proverb says that women hold up half the sky. When high prices curtail access to raw materials, some countries may find that empowering the long-neglected female half of the population is the most practical way to negotiate the demographic challenges to come.

Stranger things can happen. Just consider what triple-digit oil prices have in store for the environment.

CHAPTER 10

WILL TRIPLE-DIGIT OIL PRICES SAVE THE PLANET?

BRITISH NOVELIST WILLIAM GOLDING published his first book, *Lord of the Flies*, in 1954. The story, as you may remember from high school, follows a group of schoolboys marooned on an island. Removed from civilization, the boys devolve into a primitive state of disarray as the forces of anarchy and brutishness clash with order and rationality. As countless English teachers have observed, the novel explores the duality of human nature, the fragility of society, and the relationship between morality and immorality. It may also be an allegory of the Second World War.

As it happens, in the 1960s Golding became a fellow villager of James Lovelock, an independent scientist and a pioneer of the environmental movement. In the early days of the space race, Lovelock was invited to work at NASA's Jet Propulsion Laboratory outside Pasadena, California. His work on atmospheric gases fit with NASA's hopes to detect life on other planets. Lovelock's research for the Mars project, which led to the Viking mission, set his imagination spinning. He started to think of Earth not as a collection of disparate parts inhabiting the same planet but as a single entity—a superorganism.

Lovelock sees Earth as a complex web of interconnected systems. Everything on the planet is related: flora, fauna, air, water, rocks and all the stuff in between. He hypothesized that Earth is a self-regulating system that keeps its climate and chemical makeup at the levels needed to maintain life. This superorganism, among other things, regulates global air temperatures, the amount of oxygen in the atmosphere and the salinity of the oceans. When one organism, humans primarily, throws the biosphere's delicate balance out of whack, the entire system adjusts to return conditions to a state of equilibrium. In short, everything is connected and everything affects everything else.

After returning home from his stint at NASA, Lovelock, on a walk with Golding to the village post office, explained his grand theory of the planet to his neighbor. Golding was captivated and proposed that such a big idea needed a sweeping name to match it. A Nobel laureate steeped in myth and metaphor, Golding marshaled his literary faculties and suggested that Lovelock call it Gaia.

The Greek goddess of the earth, Gaia is sometimes considered to be Earth itself. Also known as Ge, she provides the root word for "geography" and "geology." Unlike nurturing images of Mother Nature, Lovelock's version isn't always tender. When Gaia is threatened by a rogue factor, such as carbon dioxide emissions, she defends herself by purging the offending agent and restoring balance to the system. Lovelock believes such a response is unfolding right now through climate change, or global heating as he prefers to call it. In a prediction that would make even Malthus shudder, Lovelock forecasts that an increase in global temperature will unleash a climate shift that will wipe out millions of people around the world.

Lovelock's most pessimistic visions could come straight from the pages of a postapocalyptic novel. As great swaths of the earth transform into deserts, the climate will become too hot for plants to grow. Food will be scarce and millions will starve. The remaining bastions of humanity will gravitate to the polar regions and the few other remaining spots on Earth that can still sustain life. Lovelock is clearly not for the faint of heart.

To attempt to avoid this potential cataclysm, Lovelock has become an outspoken proponent of emissions-free nuclear energy (a stance that hardly endears him to parts of the environmental movement). He's also floated suggestions for ways humans could intervene in climate change through mass-scale planetary engineering efforts designed to lower global temperatures. Again, not measures typically embraced by most environmentalists.

Lovelock's ideas have polarized the scientific community for decades. He'd be easier to dismiss if he weren't so often right. He was way out in front of the pack on global warming, sounding alarms that other scientists scoffed at before they eventually had to capitulate to his views. His early work in atmospheric chemistry led to the discovery of the hole in the ozone layer. He was even right that planetary probes would fail to detect life on Mars, which flew in the face of NASA's hopes (and funding aspirations) at the time. And the mainstream scientific community is coming closer to Lovelock's view that global warming could unleash a climactic Armageddon if immediate steps aren't taken to reduce emissions.

The Intergovernmental Panel on Climate Change (IPCC), established by the United Nations in 1988, comprises thousands of scientists and is the largest publisher of peer-reviewed climate change research in the world. In 2007, the organization shared the Nobel Peace Prize with Al Gore for increasing public knowledge about climate change and laying the groundwork to counteract such change. In its latest comprehensive assessment report from 2007, the IPCC warns that human-generated emissions are causing global temperatures to rise. An increase of 4 degrees Celsius in the next hundred years, they say, would create devastating consequences for humanity. Droughts will cause global food production to fall. Low-lying coastal areas will be flooded as glaciers melt and sea levels rise. Bangladesh and Vietnam will be in serious trouble, as will major metropolitan centers such as New York, London, Tokyo, Hong Kong, Karachi and Calcutta. Up to half of the land species on the planet will be threatened with extinction. Among other consequences, mosquitoes will thrive, exposing billions more people to diseases such as malaria and dengue fever.

But the IPCC also says this disastrous outcome is avoidable. If we curb our emissions by burning fewer hydrocarbons and switch to cleaner energy sources, we can cut the expected temperature increases in half, sparing the world from the worst consequences of climate change. Of course, cutting back on hydrocarbons is easier said than done. In the 21st century, burning hydrocarbons is a catch-22. Burning more oil, coal and natural gas is critical to achieving the economic expansion that's needed to support the billions of new people who are projected to inhabit the planet. But chasing that economic growth could throw so much carbon into the atmosphere that it may undermine humanity's very survival.

Thankfully, there is another way to look at this dilemma. If the abundance of hydrocarbons in an industrialized world has brought us to the brink of catastrophic climate change, then the scarcity of those same resources could be what saves us from environmental disaster. The future of our planet's climate may soon be out of our hands—and that may not be such a bad thing.

As the stakes of the climate change debate continue to rise, it's hardly surprising that the issue is becoming ever more politicized. The environmental movement is no longer a backwater group of underfunded hippies. Instead, it's a well-financed lobbying machine, with high-profile players from Al Gore to Leonardo Di-Caprio. Environmentalists believe that critical changes are needed to government and corporate policies in order to put the world on a path to permanently reducing emissions. Green political parties around the world are mobilizing voter support for legislation that will change our carbon practices. If human decision making got us into this mess, the hope is it can also get us out.

On the other side, climate change skeptics, most of whom don't want costly new environmental policies to upset the financial status quo, are working to sway public opinion against the idea of global warming. Big Oil, for one, still isn't shy about casting doubt on the notion that humans are responsible for increases in global temperatures. Among other things, climate change deniers argue that global warming is a naturally occurring phenomenon, perhaps linked to an increase in solar flare activity from the sun. Skeptics also contend that naturally occurring emissions have an underappreciated influence on atmospheric carbon levels. When the Icelandic volcano Eyjafjallajökull erupted in the spring of 2010, global warming skeptics said it released more carbon into the atmosphere than all of the emissions savings mandated by world governments in the previous five years. Environmentalists countered that foregone emissions from grounded air travel more than offset the volcanic activity. (What I can say for certain is that Eyjafjallajökull cost me a trip to Portugal.)

The presence of large natural sources of carbon emissions hardly takes polluters off the hook. Just because nature can overwhelm us with a volcanic eruption at any moment doesn't mean our effect on the environment isn't just as profound. We can't excuse our contributions to the global carbon footprint because multiple sources of emissions exist. As the IPCC points out, our current rate of carbon emissions combined with the atmospheric buildup since the Industrial Revolution puts us on track to reach dangerous concentrations of greenhouse gases irrespective of random volcanic events.

The amount of carbon dioxide in the atmosphere is now greater than at any time in the last 640,000 years. The IPCC's 2007 report notes that eleven of the previous twelve years (1995–2006) were the hottest since instrumental readings of daily temperatures began in 1880. In the last century, the average world temperature increased by 0.7 degrees Celsius, with Arctic temperatures climbing at twice that rate over the same period. The evidence of global warming since the IPCC's last report is even more compelling. The United States' National Snow and Ice Data Center says the last ten years have seen the ten lowest readings for the Arctic's winter ice pack since satellites began tracking the data.

With the exception of hardcore climate change deniers, most folks find it hard to ignore the mounting evidence that human activity is warming the planet. Personally, I'm willing to accept the link between rising global temperatures and human-made carbon emissions. Think of all the smoke that's been belched out by factories from Victorian-era London to modern-day Beijing. Two hundred years of spewing filth into the atmosphere has to have had consequences for the biosphere.

At the same time, I'm not losing much sleep worrying about the worst-case scenarios from Lovelock or the IPCC. I find the IPCC's assumptions for economic growth—and, more to the point, fuel demand—hard to swallow. In its forecasts, the IPCC takes a business-as-usual approach to resource consumption. But projections that model the future by extrapolating from the quantity of hydrocarbons we currently burn are implausible.

The Achilles heel of the dire predictions for climate change is the computer modeling by IPCC scientists that assumes our hydrocarbon consumption will continue to increase at the same rate over the next few decades as it has in the past. Economic growth drives carbon emissions. When growth is shuffled to the back burner in a static economy, emissions will come down too, removing the need for stringent climate change policies. The pace at which our economies grow is far more important to the level of future emissions than any government-mandated carbon reduction schemes.

Like the central bankers and finance ministers we met in the opening chapters, staunch environmental advocates need to recognize that the global economy has downshifted into a much lower gear. And gearing down economic growth, as they'll see, is the most direct way to reduce carbon emissions.

The big question climate change scientists need to ask is where we'll get all the fuel needed to raise global temperatures to forecasted levels. The Exxons, BPs and Suncors of the world tell us they'll discover it, but as I've already pointed out, the real issue isn't locating resources, it's being able to afford to pull them out of the ground. Can we pay the cost of the new sources of supply that Big Oil is discovering? We only have to look at today's fuel prices for an answer. If supplies of oil and coal are abundant enough to fulfill climate change projections, then why are prices already so high? Soaring prices indicate scarcity. And if carbon-emitting fuels are getting scarce, how does that change the outlook for growth in carbon emissions and the nature of the climate change debate? Those are the questions policymakers need to ask before charging ahead with financially punitive plans for carbon abatement. If they don't, governments could squander billions implementing measures to help the environment that will ultimately prove unnecessary.

The specter of climate change takes on a very different shape in a world of fuel abundance and robust economic growth than it does when fuel is scarce and economies are faltering.

WHY EMISSIONS CONTROLS DON'T WORK

To date, attempts to regulate emissions have been driven by a belief that we need to decarbonize our economies. Therefore, governments try to reduce fossil fuel consumption by putting a price on carbon emissions. Some countries do this through carbon taxes, while others try to control pollution using elaborate cap-and-trade systems, which involve shuffling around carbon credits. The rationale behind these policies is straightforward: make emitters pay for emissions and they'll emit less.

The reasoning is sensible enough, but it hasn't worked in practice. So far, international climate change treaties have failed to gain universal acceptance or institute significant penalties around noncompliance. And without a globally agreed-upon price for emissions, carbon pricing schemes just won't work; emissions will simply migrate to jurisdictions where they cost less. That's the fundamental flaw in the Kyoto Protocol. By seeking to cap emissions in half the world, the international pact merely diverted emissions to the other half of the globe. Since there are no borders in the atmosphere, emissions from one country affect everybody's climate.

Hopes for the Kyoto accord were misplaced from the outset. Its design encouraged emissions growth to shift from rich nations to poor countries that are exempt from the protocol. And that's exactly what's happened. The developing world is responsible for 90 percent of the increase in global emissions since 2000. During that time span, China's emissions have doubled, pushing it past the United States as the world's largest emitter. Redistributing carbon emissions is not the same as actually reducing total global emissions, which are now 50 percent higher than in 1990, the benchmark year used by the Kyoto treaty.

To actually reduce global emissions, every country would need to agree to a global framework that included a universal price for carbon. That's why voluntary pacts, such as the post-Kyoto agreements negotiated at climate change summits in Copenhagen (2009), Cancún (2010) and Durban (2011), are meaningless. If emissions can simply move to another part of the world, then the difference made by voluntary commitments to reduce pollution is of little consequence.

So far, the rest of the world is showing little inclination to come on board for emissions controls. China and other developing countries argue that cumulative emissions are what counts when it comes to climate change. By that measure, they insist that countries such as the United States foot more of the bill. Since the Industrial Revolution, the United States has produced an estimated 27 percent of global carbon emissions, compared with only 9.5 percent for China. Although China's current emissions outpace America's, in cumulative terms the contribution from the United States is nearly three times as much. Neither China nor the United States currently puts a price on carbon, and neither appears likely to make a policy change anytime soon. As long as the world's two largest emitters won't pay for carbon, it's tough to persuade Canada, or any other country, to charge domestic industries and consumers for emissions.

One notable exception is the European Union. At least for the moment, the EU is taking the environmental high road and charging for emissions. But the system is far from perfect. It's put a low cost on emissions and offers a plethora of carbon credits, which gives the agreement little financial bite. And even the environmentally conscious EU is beginning to doubt whether its efforts are worthwhile if the rest of the world doesn't follow suit. In the absence of a global deal on carbon emissions, the EU's Energy Department is debating whether to continue with its transition to non-carbon energy sources. The continent's economic woes are undoubtedly throwing cold water on its environmental conscience. An attempt to show global leadership is commendable, but so too is looking out for a populace that's struggling under the weight of a financial crisis.

The prospects for establishing a global framework for carbon pricing are as remote today as ever. International summits in Copenhagen, Cancún and Durban failed to come up with any concrete measures that will help to meaningfully reduce carbon emissions. Meanwhile, plans by individual governments are also struggling to find traction. In the United States, the American Clean Energy and Security Act, also known as the Waxman-Markey bill, would have capped carbon emissions and established a trading scheme. But the bill died on the Senate floor in 2009.

The political fallout from the Fukushima nuclear disaster is also hurting the outlook for future reductions in carbon emissions. As plans to expand the capacity of nuclear power generation are canceled or delayed around the world, the prominence of hydrocarbons in tomorrow's economy only increases.

Japan has now backed off a pledge to cut greenhouse gas emissions by 25 percent from 1990 levels by 2020. With only two nuclear power plants up and running that goal is now considered unattainable. To replace its lost electricity generation, Japan is dusting off retired oil-fueled power plants. Reactivating the mothballed stations, including a mammoth facility south of Tokyo at Yokosuka, is helping Japan meet its domestic energy needs but it's also increasing its carbon emissions. The story is similar in

Germany, which is also veering away from nuclear power after the accident in Japan. To make up for the decline in nuclear energy, Germany has announced that it will need to build more coal-fired plants, in addition to importing more natural gas from Russia.

A weak global economy makes marshaling the political will to tackle climate change even more difficult. Measures such as carbon pricing are a tough sell at the best of times, let alone when an electorate cares far more about job creation than melting glaciers in Greenland.

In the United States, President Obama has directed the Environmental Protection Agency (EPA) to withdraw an air quality proposal that would have tightened pollution standards for US industries after Republicans complained the new federal regulations would kill thousands of future jobs and cost the economy billions. The President says climate change will be a priority for his second term. Much to the disappointment of climate hawks, though, his environmental agenda has so far taken a backseat to the immediate needs of the US economy.

North of the border too, economic imperatives are trumping environmental ambitions. Canada is backing out of the Kyoto Protocol just in time to avoid paying a huge bill for falling short of its commitments. Canadian carbon emissions are 30 percent higher than they were in 1990. Canada would have had to pay $14 billion to buy emissions credits from the rest of the world to comply with its obligations under the treaty. Instead, Prime Minister Stephen Harper decided to skip out on the deal and weather the heat from the global community. The South Pacific island nation of Tuvalu, for one, which is losing land to rising ocean waters, called the decision "an act of sabotage on our future." For Harper's Conservative government—never shy to remind Canadians it was the former Liberal regime that ratified Kyoto—the loss of international stature is outweighed by what else can be done with $14 billion.

HOW YOU REALLY STOP EMISSIONS

The simple unspoken truth is that a recession is the best possible way to tame runaway carbon emissions. An economic slowdown will stop the growth of emissions dead in its tracks. And the deeper the recession, the better it is for the atmosphere.

In fact, recessions do better than simply stop emissions growth: they actually reduce emissions levels. And, unlike the grand plans laid out at climate change summits, recessions don't take three or four decades to do the job; they do it nearly overnight. According to the IEA, in 2009 global carbon dioxide emissions fell for the first time since 1990.

The ripple effects from an economic slowdown elicit all sorts of environmentally friendly results. Consider, for example, the number of resource megaprojects that were canceled after commodity prices plunged during the last recession. In Alberta's tar sands alone, the oil industry canceled or delayed $50 billion of planned capital spending. The US environmental movement—backed by celebrity activists such as Robert Redford and Daryl Hannah—is deeply opposed to tar sands development. They can boycott the tar sands all they want, but on a practical level, falling oil prices carry far more consequences for the economic well-being of tar sands mines than any environmental protest.

Nevertheless, it's unlikely you'll ever hear politicians praising the environmental benefits of an economic recession. That message would be tantamount to political suicide. Instead, we hear political leaders babble about sustainable growth and commit to targets for reducing carbon emissions that are so far in the future most of them won't even be alive, let alone still in power. That makes for politically palatable greenwash, but it doesn't do anything about how much carbon dioxide the world is pumping into the atmosphere. Lower the economic speed limit, however, and emissions can't help but come down and lower the atmospheric thermostat at the same time.

Not surprisingly, it's tough to find any country in the world where voters are willing to forgo their own financial well-being in the interests of climate stability for people not yet born. No matter how compelling the scientific case for the adverse effects of climate change, or how much we profess concern for future generations, when the rubber hits the road, the vast majority of people are more concerned with the here and now. Curbing emissions will always take a backseat to the more tangible imperatives of job creation and personal financial stability. Just look at the Obama administration's decision to put the EPA's air quality proposal on the shelf. The White House undoubtedly believes the EPA's plan is good environmental policy, but that's a secondary concern when the economy is faltering.

Before we get too despondent about lax environmental standards, maybe we need to take another look at what environmental policies really accomplish in a world where oil costs more than $100 a barrel and coal more than $100 a ton. If the objective of climate change policy is to reduce carbon emissions, then that's exactly what's achieved by higher energy prices. And governments don't need to lift a finger. Throw a fossil-fuel wrench into economic growth and you also put the lid on carbon emissions. If energy costs are going to hammer the economy anyway, we may as well recognize the concurrent environmental benefits. Given the alternative of Lovelock's vengeful Gaia, perhaps we should even rejoice.

In a zero-growth world, governments don't need to step in with punitive carbon taxes or ineffectual cap-and-trade schemes, nor will we need to depend on the whims of environmentally conscious consumers or ecologically progressive companies. When our economies shrink, our carbon emissions will tumble without any legislative effort whatsoever.

Just look at what happened when the Soviet Union collapsed. The fall of Communism sent Russia's economy into a tailspin and lowered carbon emissions by a staggering 30 percent nearly overnight. And it's not like the Russian government made a policy objective out of carbon emissions; the Kremlin had more pressing concerns at the time than the environment. The latest recession had the same dampening effect on emissions. In the United States, energy-related carbon dioxide emissions fell 3 percent in 2008 and another 7 percent in 2009. That's more than was called for by the Waxman-Markey bill.

Of course, painful economic contractions don't come about by design—far from it. As we saw in chapter 1, governments threw the kitchen sink at the global economy in a bid to avoid a recession. That's why many countries now have so much debt that they're lurching toward bankruptcy. If persuading voters to put a price on carbon emissions is hard when economic times are good, try selling them on the benefits when the economy isn't growing.

That said, global warming is too large an issue to simply ignore. Governments know that voters want to see them do something about it—and that's where emissions intensity targets come in. Few countries will actually commit to reducing total emissions (Denmark being a notable exception), but many politicians around the world will sign up for emissions intensity targets. They demonstrate all the earmarks of environmental concern without hurting economic growth or, it should be noted, actually working to reduce emissions. In other words, adopting such targets is classic political greenwash.

Emissions intensity targets involve reducing carbon emissions per unit of GDP. When it comes to helping the environment, the emissions part of the equation is less of a problem than the GDP. The way these targets are set up, economic growth leads to a higher emissions threshold as GDP (the denominator of the equation) gets bigger. That means an economy can pump out more carbon while still staying on the right side of its targets. Each unit of GDP may be emitting less carbon, but the total amount of carbon emissions is actually going up. The faster economies grow, the more carbon they are allowed to produce. These are the types of environmental policies that politicians can live with. They look good to the public, but come with no real economic cost.

Similar intensity targets for oil consumption have proven to be just as ineffectual at curbing fuel intake. But you wouldn't know it by listening to the political rhetoric. In the United States, politicians like to flaunt the idea that America has cut its oil intensity in half since the first OPEC oil shocks. That may be true, but the United States economy is also much bigger than it was forty years ago, which means the country's total annual oil consumption has actually increased.

Intensity targets are even palatable for recalcitrant carbon emitters such as China. Over the next five years, China has committed to reducing carbon emissions per unit of GDP by 17 percent (a plan that depends on the massive nuclear expansion discussed in chapter 4). Of course, when China agreed to the targets, its annual economic growth was nearly 10 percent. At that rate, intensity targets are hardly the check on carbon emissions that Beijing would have you believe.

A plan with more bite would involve capping the total level of emissions. That's a path that China and India, among other countries, have steadfastly refused to take. They know that agreeing to hard targets for absolute emissions levels would result in an unacceptable reduction in economic growth. That would mean fewer citizens following in the Yangs' footsteps and making the transition to an urban lifestyle.

Furthermore, asking people in China and India to stop improving their standard of living in order to help save the world is more than a touch hypocritical when wealthy OECD countries won't reduce their own emissions to help do the same. It's a particularly tough request in light of China's position that cumulative pollution matters just as much as current emissions.

As it stands, agreeing to fruitless emissions intensity targets is a much more palatable option for governments than taking meaningful action to reduce global carbon output. But in a static economy, that could change. Slower GDP growth reduces the level of emissions allowed by such targets. In other words, in a zero-growth economy, emissions intensity targets can actually start to sting. Of course, governments may not let it come to that. As Canada has shown by reneging on Kyoto, once environmental agreements start to come with real economic costs, governments will pull the chute on voluntary international treaties with impunity.

Before that happens, however, higher energy prices are set to make emissions intensity targets even more superfluous than they are now. Indeed, triple-digit prices for oil and coal could relegate government emissions policies to the sidelines.

WHERE WILL WE GET ALL THAT COAL?

Higher energy prices will accomplish what politicians and environmentalists can't: a permanent reduction in carbon emissions.

Governments around the world have long thought that the path to a greener atmosphere begins with decarbonizing our energy systems—electricity generation in particular. Despite efforts to usher in more renewable power generation, however, the amount of carbon emitted per unit of electricity produced has actually increased by 6 percent globally in the last two decades. Even environmentally unfriendly coal still commands a 41 percent share of global power generation.

Regardless, when it comes to reducing emissions, altering the energy mix by adding more renewable sources is a red herring. What the world really needs to do is use less power. And that's exactly what is about to happen in tomorrow's economy.

Higher oil and coal prices are already putting the squeeze on economic growth and fuel consumption. In the last few years, power shortages have become commonplace in China, India and the rest of Asia. It is price and availability that is stopping these countries from burning more coal, not costly environmental regulations. As prices keep rising, it will only become more apparent how unnecessary international treaties and carbon taxes are for lowering emissions.

In China, power users aren't even paying full freight for the coal that's burned to keep the lights on. China's government has seen to it that coal-based power prices have only risen at a fraction of the actual increases in coal prices. That's a huge subsidy, and one that's unsustainable for a country burning more than 3 billion tons of coal a year. The Chinese Electricity Council warned that in the first four months of 2011 alone, the five largest power-generating groups in the country lost more than 10 billion yuan after they were forbidden from passing rising coal costs on to customers.

Chinese authorities can cap power prices for the time being, but that will only bankrupt the country's coal-fired utilities. At the same time, China's industries and consumers are living under a subsidized umbrella of false power costs. Eventually, resource scarcity will assert itself. Both China and India will have to ration power, which will put the brakes on economic activity. That process has already started with the rolling blackouts that are now a permanent feature of the economic landscape in those countries.

Few climate change experts take such economic considerations into account when making their big-picture forecasts. The IPCC, for example, released a series of models for the future of global carbon emissions in its benchmark 2007 report, presenting no fewer than forty different scenarios. The bottom line of the exercise was to conclude that unless immediate action on carbon abatement is taken, emissions would soon exceed critical levels and induce catastrophic climate change. More than a thousand of the world's foremost climate change scientists took part in the multiyear modeling exercise. In terms of the science behind global warming, I buy the group's declaration that a causal relationship exists between higher levels of atmospheric carbon dioxide and increases in global temperature. They say that if we can stabilize carbon dioxide levels at around 450 parts per million, then we can hold a temperature increase to 2 degrees Celsius and avoid some of the worst-case scenarios for climate change. That sounds good to me. But when we work backwards from the emissions projections contained in their models, we find something even better.

The amount of hydrocarbons that would need to be burned to fulfill the IPCC forecasts is staggering. The panel projects that oil consumption, for instance, will be greater in a hundred years than it is today. And that's not to say anything of coal, the largest source of human-generated carbon emissions. The majority of the IPCC scenarios see world coal consumption doubling over the next two decades. About 80 percent of the projected global increase is expected to come from China and India. But those forecasts are an extrapolation of current economic growth rates. The climate change experts who modeled the IPCC scenarios didn't ask where all that extra coal will come from—or, more importantly, what it will cost. And the projections are based on unrealistic expectations for hydrocarbon supply over the next several decades.

It's worth reemphasizing that the factor which most influences global consumption isn't the amount of resources contained in the ground but the affordability of those resources. As we discussed in chapter 4, there's a big difference between a resource and a reserve. How much oil and coal is left in the ground doesn't matter if our economies can't afford to burn it. For all intents and purposes, those hydrocarbons might as well not even exist. When we consider the price we'll need to pay to burn tomorrow's resources, humanity's chances of avoiding a climate catastrophe look a whole lot better than most IPCC models would suggest.

One outspoken critic of any model that assumes future resource abundance is Dr. David Rutledge, an engineering professor at Caltech. He estimates the total amount of coal available to be mined (past, present and future) at 662 billion tons. That's well short of the World Energy Council's calculations, which put that same figure at 1,162 billion tons. The maximum cumulative coal production assumed by an IPCC scenario, on the other hand, is 3,500 billion tons.

The discrepancy, according to Rutledge, arises from a lack of rigor around estimates for national coal reserves. Current estimates for US coal reserves, for example, are based on data that hasn't been updated since the 1970s. Once countries start paying more attention to estimates, reserves figures are consistently marked down. That's what has happened in mature coal-producing regions such as Germany and England. Whether or not Rutledge's numbers are exact is not the point. If his basic assertion that world coal reserves are consistently overestimated is accurate, the IPCC scenarios become much less frightening.

In a report to the German parliament, the Energy Watch Group, a Munich-based think tank, predicts that world coal production will only be able to increase 30 percent from current levels. And that assumes coal can be delivered to the places that need it the most, which is hardly a given. The cost of shipping coal, as we saw in chapter 4, means that only 15 percent of global production is currently being exported.

China is expected to hit peak coal production much sooner than the rest of the world, given its torrid pace of extraction. That's why it has sent its national energy companies on a global shopping spree to snap up available sources of supply. A major problem with this strategy is the lack of mines close enough to China to make it economically viable to ship coal back to the country. Unexploited coal reserves in Montana aren't any use to a thermal power station in Zhejiang. That could leave China scrambling for other energy options.

In the United States too, the outlook for coal consumption is cloudy. In the last decade, 90 percent of new applications for coal plants have been delayed or canceled, according to the Energy Department. Coal-fired power plants are still being built, but costs are increasing due to tighter emissions standards designed to reduce the negative effects of pollution on health and the environment. What's more, newly abundant supplies of natural gas from shale reserves make it a cheaper fuel than coal for power generation, signaling that more electricity will soon come from gas-fired plants.

A NEW HOPE

The world won't burn anywhere close to all the fossil fuels needed to realize the IPCC's dire climate change predictions. That's undoubtedly good news, yet environmentalists are unlikely to embrace the potential salvation offered by expensive energy. If higher commodity prices spare us from the worst consequences of global warming, the environmental movement could be marginalized.

If that happens, it would be an unfortunate step backwards for the world. Most of what green parties advocate makes a lot of sense, even if only considered within the context of energy costs. In a world of triple-digit oil prices, conservation measures that reduce fuel consumption are precisely what we need.

Nevertheless, governments still need to understand what higher energy prices mean for climate change. Many environmental policies are based on an assumption that future resource supply will be abundant, and while they may be implemented with the best intentions, they won't make any sense in the coming world of fuel scarcity. Given today's grim fiscal realities, we can hardly afford to make the wrong choices, implementing expensive environmental programs designed for a different world than the one we will be living in.

Why spend billions developing carbon capture and storage technology to trap emissions from coal plants if we're not going to burn all the coal necessary to make dire climate change predictions a reality? For that matter, governments need to ask whether we should really be burdening our economies by putting a price on carbon at all. Similarly, does it make sense to mandate auto manufacturers to increase fuel efficiency standards when pump prices will already be spurring drivers to burn less gasoline? When fuel costs $7 a gallon, as it does in Europe, you won't need policymakers telling you to drive a more fuel-efficient vehicle; prices will already have dictated the change.

I'm sure that many energy industry executives will agree with me—for all the wrong reasons. If you run a coal-fired power plant or operate a tar sands mine, why wouldn't you want to hear someone suggest you don't have to worry about the atmosphere or, more importantly, pay anything for your carbon emissions? For large industrial carbon emitters, maintaining the status quo is an inviting option.

I also don't expect the environmental movement to simply roll over and accept that slower economic growth will resolve the issue of global climate change. I doubt you could find any environmentalists willing to sit on their hands for a few decades, trusting that high fuel prices will quash demand and save us from catastrophic global warming. No one who takes the threat of climate change seriously would bet our planet's future on the accuracy of a twenty-year forecast for hydrocarbon depletion and higher energy prices.

I'm not expecting anyone to make that leap of faith, because I wouldn't either. Instead, just observe what triple-digit oil prices are doing to the global economy *right now*. The onset of high prices has already led to the deepest postwar recession on record, and their quick return is now threatening us with a double-dip slowdown from which there is no obvious path to recovery. Once we tip over that brink, just watch what happens to carbon emissions.

The reduction in emissions that's about to occur because of high costs is exactly the kind of adjustment environmentalists say we need. The green movement will get its wish, but it won't stem from forward-thinking government policies or altruistic voters worried about their grandchildren's future. Instead, it will result from a profound slowdown in economic growth, which we currently lack the tools to fix.

And we won't have to wait several decades for carbon emissions to fall; the wheels are already in motion. Economic growth is being hammered all around the world. The time frame for the next global recession isn't decades away—it could be mere quarters from now.

Of course, by definition recessions are temporary affairs. A slowdown could bring our atmosphere a brief respite, but won't emissions pick up again when the global economy comes back to life? It's fair to think that a recession-induced reduction in emissions would be a mere hiccup in the larger scheme of things. After all, during the economic recovery in 2010, global emissions rose by nearly 6 percent, one of the strongest increases on record. By historical standards, even the deepest downturns rarely last more than four or five quarters. But the next recession will be different from ones we've known in the past. This time around, we'll have to do without economic growth for much longer than a few quarters or even a year: we're about to face a permanent slowdown in growth.

As I've argued, the economic recovery since the last recession was predicated on an unsustainable level of fiscal and monetary stimulus. And worse yet, even the wobbly recovery we're now seeing has brought back the same triple-digit oil prices that sank us into a recession in the first place. Now that our petroleum-dependent economies are again under the yoke of high oil prices, what options do governments have left? As we saw in chapter 2, the last round of fiscal stimulus burdened world governments with debt levels that will take a generation to pay off. Borrowing rates are already at record lows, meaning little stimulus is left in the tank to spur growth. Indeed, rising inflation levels may force interest rates to go higher.

The environmental movement won't have to hold its breath very long to see what high fuel prices will mean for the atmosphere. Triple-digit oil prices are already here—and they herald the end of growth.

Like everything else, even our seemingly inexorable march toward environmental self-destruction is about to run out of fuel. If Gaia's vengeful climate change really is about to devour humanity, then triple-digit oil prices may just give us all a brand-new lease on life.

[CONCLUSION]

ON A HOT SUMMER NIGHT IN 1965, California Highway Patrol-
man Lee Minikus stopped Marquette Frye on suspicion of drunk
driving. It was a routine traffic stop, but what followed was anything
but routine. Frye was arrested, along with his stepbrother, who was
a passenger in the car, and his mother, who was in her house and
came outside to see what was happening. Neighbors and passersby
gathered to watch the ruckus, and more police soon arrived to dis-
perse the crowd. Shortly after that, bottles and bricks began to fly.

It was the spark that set off the Watts Riots, among the most
violent events of the civil rights era. More than a thousand people
were injured, thirty-four died, and at least six hundred buildings
were damaged or destroyed in the six days of rioting following
Frye's arrest. When the Los Angeles police couldn't bring the
rioters under control, fourteen thousand National Guard troops
were mobilized to help restore order. A section of south-central
Los Angeles covering forty-five square miles was cordoned off to
stop the rioting from spilling into other neighborhoods.

The riots became a defining moment of the 1960s. Unbe-
knownst to the people out in the streets, the civil disturbance also

quietly intersected with dire circumstances unfolding on the other side of the world. As the Watts Riots raged in southern California, India and Pakistan were falling into the grips of a famine. For thirty-five trucks that were stopped at the National Guard's cordon, the most pressing issue wasn't civil rights in the United States, but hunger in the developing world. The convoy, prevented from getting to the LA harbor by the guardsmen, was carrying seeds from an experimental agricultural facility outside Mexico City.

These particular seeds had been developed at the International Maize and Wheat Improvement Center by Norman Borlaug, an American agronomist who had been working on agricultural research in Mexico since 1944. Borlaug was born on a farm in Iowa in 1914. By the time he reached college, the Midwest was turning into a dust bowl and Borlaug, like so many others, could only watch as people around him went hungry. Graduating with a doctoral degree in plant pathology, the farmer's son dedicated himself to the art and science of growing food.

After arriving in Mexico to work on a hunger-fighting project funded by the Rockefeller Foundation, Borlaug made an agricultural breakthrough on the propagation of wheat that changed how the world feeds itself. Tall, majestic-looking stalks of wheat may have been inspiring, but he figured out that smaller plants actually produced better yields. The result was dwarf wheat.

Agricultural researchers at the time were using fertilizers to boost the amount of grain a plant produces, but the application led to top-heavy plants on long stalks that fell over due to their own weight. Dwarf wheat is a stubby, unimpressive-looking plant with a short stem that's strong enough to support much larger seed heads than its taller cousins. The simple insight that bigger isn't always better had a profound effect on crop yields, allowing wheat output on a given piece of land to quadruple on average.

Between the early 1940s and the early 1960s, Mexican wheat production increased sixfold. In 1963, Borlaug traveled to south Asia to try to persuade the governments of India and Pakistan that planting high-yield dwarf wheat could head off a famine. It took two years to win their support, but it was time well spent. What followed became known as the Green Revolution.

The thirty-five trucks stopped by the National Guard were carrying 500 million high-yield seeds bound for the subcontinent. The seeds eventually made it past the riot police and onto the ship. Once planted, they helped to increase yields in Indian and Pakistani wheat fields by more than half. The next crop was even better, and by 1968 Borlaug's high-yield agricultural techniques had helped Pakistan become self-sufficient in wheat production. India achieved the same status a few years later. By the early 1990s, Pakistan's wheat output had risen fourfold from levels in the mid-1960s, while India's production had increased fivefold.

Borlaug was awarded the Nobel Peace Prize in 1970. In presenting the award, the Nobel committee said of Borlaug, "more than any other single person of this age, he has helped provide bread for a hungry world." Credited with keeping hundreds of millions of people from starvation, Borlaug may have saved more lives than any other person in history. By one calculation, every day, half of the world's population eats a grain descended from the high-yield plants developed by Borlaug and the other agricultural researchers of the Green Revolution.

More than forty years ago, Borlaug and his colleagues found a way to expand the limits of a finite world. Today, we need to draw on the same spirit of ingenuity, innovation and tenacity to help us negotiate demographic pressures that will mount with renewed urgency in the coming years.

WHERE HAVE YOU GONE, NORMAN BORLAUG?
A NATION TURNS ITS LONELY EYES TO YOU

The American journalist George Will is attributed with saying that the future has a way of arriving unannounced. Whether we're ready for it or not, a world of static economic growth is almost here. The biggest question now is how well we deal with it.

Hydrocarbons have powered the world for more than a century. Fossil fuels aren't going anywhere anytime soon, but neither are higher prices. If we want the future to be as good as the past, our approach to economic growth needs to change, and that change needs to happen now.

Recognizing the ramifications of a lower economic speed limit is a necessary first step. Triple-digit oil prices, record budget deficits and potentially catastrophic levels of carbon in the atmosphere are telling us the same thing: endless economic growth is unsustainable. We can either listen to these warnings and adapt to their message or cling to past practices that are putting us on a collision course with scarcity.

We saw in chapter 1 how governments are pulling out all the stops to shock the global economy back to life. Interest rates are at rock-bottom levels, central banks are pumping money into the economy through quantitative easing measures, and governments are spending billions on stimulus packages. Add it all up and it means future taxpayers are being hamstrung with mountains of debt that will need to be repaid.

And for what? These policies are chasing a vision of the world that's already in the rearview mirror. Running up huge deficits to spur economic growth is the wrong move when high oil prices are inexorably pushing the global economy closer to a static state. Instead of fighting against the tide, we need to swim with the current.

Practical experience tells us that racking up massive amounts of debt is rarely a prudent fiscal choice. Just look at how things turned out for homeowners who bit off more than they could chew when interest rates fell in the last decade. We're still reeling from the consequences of the resulting housing crash. But those folks could have made different choices, just as our governments can today.

Rather than go further into hock, other homeowners chose to pay down their mortgages. That may have meant scrimping on some luxuries, but such restraint pays off when the rough patches inevitably come. That's the wonderful virtue of being debt free. Right now, our governments are like homeowners who are choosing to pile on expensive credit card debt while still carrying big mortgages.

No matter what stimulus measures are put in place, we can't make our economies grow at the rates they used to, because the energy that drives them now costs five times as much as it did only a decade ago. In economics, prices matter. Triple-digit fuel prices mean that our economies will slow down no matter how much stimulus we force-feed into the system.

Instead of trying to spur spending by keeping interest rates near zero, central banks need to ensure that inflation is held firmly in check. Rather than run huge budget deficits, governments need to get their fiscal houses in order, so we can pay for programs and services that will help us succeed in a new world of slower economic growth.

Governments must also stop trying to shelter their economies from higher energy costs. Prices are only a messenger; the real issue is the underlying scarcity they signal. If American motorists paid the same fuel taxes as drivers in Europe, the United States would care much less about geopolitical uncertainty in the Middle East or Venezuela. Similarly, if China forced power consumers to pay the full price for coal, the country would burn far less of it than it does now.

Other countries would do well to watch how Denmark and Japan are facing up to a world of higher energy prices. Denmark has demonstrated over the course of two decades that prices, not supply, are the key to energy conservation. Japan, in turn, is showing that *setsuden* is an economically practical and environmentally friendly alternative to burning more fossil fuels.

The steps being taken to blunt the pain of slower economic growth are only delaying troubles that will hit us eventually. Billions of dollars of stimulus spending may create a temporary upswing in employment, but it provides only a short-term Band-Aid for our deeper economic problems. What's even worse, the debt left behind, as Europe's fiscal crisis shows, can be crippling.

Slower economic growth means less job creation and higher unemployment. There will still be jobs, but many of us will need to adapt to changes in the type of work we do and how we do it. In chapter 8, we saw how the FIRE sector (finance, insurance and real estate) has doubled in size and now accounts for as much as 20 percent of economic activity in OECD countries. As the FIRE sector shrinks in a static economy, it will mean fewer job openings for stockbrokers, insurance salesmen and real estate agents. Folks currently in those jobs could face some tough times, but it's not as if they'll stay unemployed indefinitely.

As the contours of the new economy take shape, fresh opportunities will emerge. In a world where distance costs money, our hollowed-out manufacturing sector will fill up again. More of the products we buy will be made locally and sold regionally. If you're selling mutual funds now, you may soon be selling widgets from a local factory. You might even find yourself making them.

Or perhaps you'll join a reemerging agriculture industry. Triple-digit oil prices will make importing apples from South Africa prohibitively expensive, but it doesn't mean we'll stop eating fruit. The small orchards and farms that disappeared due to the cost efficiencies of globalization could be set to reappear. As farmland is reclaimed, people will need to grow the produce, sell the food and run the business of agriculture. Peddling fruit to local grocery stores may be different than pushing insurance to young drivers, but it can still provide a decent living.

Overall, we'll need to become much more nimble in our approach to employment. Instead of drawing a salary from a single job, more people could find themselves cobbling together multiple income streams through several different gigs. What we lose in stability, we could make up in variety and shorter workweeks. Job sharing could also become a much more common practice than it is today. Germany's successful experience with its Kurzarbeit program shows it's a viable option.

To facilitate the transition to slower economic growth, governments need to be financially flexible. That's what's so alarming about our current deficit spending. Instead of bailing out banks, governments should be saving their fiscal ammunition to foster initiatives such as job sharing and training programs. Many of us will need to embrace the idea of retraining to adapt our skills to the shifting needs of our national economies.

Older workers may learn something on this front by watching the younger generation. My kids are certainly growing up differently than I did. If you're under thirty, multitasking is a way of life. The generation coming up is much better equipped to handle the variable nature of the pending work world than people my age.

But we will all need to be open to the idea of change. Most of all, getting us to use less energy will be critical going forward.

Escalating resource prices are telling us that conservation has never been more important than it is right now.

There's one fact that should provide some comfort: the frightening predictions of doomsayers from the Reverend Malthus to Paul Ehrlich and James Lovelock haven't come to pass. When faced with big problems, we've always found ways to adapt, and there's no reason why we won't do so again. Human ingenuity shouldn't be underestimated. Even now, there are more Norman Borlaugs working tirelessly to help usher in a better future. Undoubtedly, some of these researchers will make breakthroughs in renewable energy that will help us transition away from our hydrocarbon economies. But that's still an eventuality. Right now, renewable sources are only a welcome part of the energy mix; they don't offer a panacea.

The demographic challenges we face can't be sold short. There are 7 billion people on the planet, and they all need to be fed—and the number goes up every day. In his 1970 Nobel lecture, Borlaug warned that even with more productive varieties of grain, rampant population growth was putting the world on a collision course with food shortages. What we need now is not a single Green Revolution, but a series of answers that will help us navigate a crushing demographic problem.

Recalibrating expectations for our future lifestyles is a place to start. In a static economy, we'll have less income growth, which will translate into us owning less stuff. Rather than fighting to retain our current degree of consumption, perhaps we can learn to appreciate what we gain on the other side of the ledger. We'll buy fewer things, but we'll also have more time to enjoy our lives. Does anyone really like the rat race? Maybe we all need to slow down and take a minute to breathe. Go for a walk instead of driving to the mall. Ride a bike rather than turning over an engine. Put on a sweater instead of cranking up the thermostat.

Sustainability isn't just an abstract notion; it's the governing idea behind the kinds of economies we need to foster. The world is full of helpful examples: bike lanes in Denmark, *setsuden* in Japan, Kurzarbeit in Germany. We need to embrace these tactics and make many other fundamental changes to the way we live.

We can still shape the future we want, but only if we're willing to relinquish the past we've known. As the boundaries of a finite world continue to close in on us, our challenge is to learn that making do with less is better than always wanting more.

THE TITLE OF "WORLD'S LONGEST RIVER" remains unsettled. In the previous century, most geographers gave the distinction to the Nile. More recently, scientists, armed with GPS technology and satellite imagery, have taken a sharper look at the exact location of the headwaters of the Amazon. Depending on who's talking, the Amazon, at somewhere between 4,000 and 4,350 miles, is now either in the top spot or just trailing the Nile by a slim margin.

What's not in dispute is the staggering amount of water the Amazon carries. The river accounts for a fifth of all the freshwater that drains into the world's oceans every day. During the wet season, the Amazon's floodplain covers some 135,000 square miles. That's like putting half of Texas underwater for part of each year. Meanwhile, the larger Amazon River basin, the area drained by the river and its tributaries, covers another 2,700,000 square miles, or about 40 percent of South America.

By any measure you choose, the magnitude of the Amazon practically breaks the scale. So do the river's fish. Freshwater dolphins, 400-pound catfish, giant eels: the Amazon's aquatic life is larger and more diverse than that of any other river system in the world. Thousands of identified species of fish call it home, and it's estimated that thousands more are yet to be classified. Of all those fish in the river, none captures my attention like the peacock bass.

Among the global fraternity of anglers, the peacock bass is arguably the most sought-after sport fish. By all accounts, it's unmatched among freshwater fish in terms of sheer fight. The violence with which it strikes a line routinely snaps rods and destroys tackle. Not only is it aggressive, but those who have fished South America's rivers also swear by its smarts. It makes sense that thriving in the Darwinian waters of the Amazon would take both grit and guile. How tough is this fish? It's known to swallow piranhas whole.

I didn't realize just how much I hoped one day to land a peacock bass until David Suzuki, of all people, regaled me with stories from his expeditions to the Amazon.

We're an unlikely match. Suzuki, it's fair to say, is an icon of the environmental movement. The longtime host of CBC's *The Nature of Things*, he's quintessentially West Coast, from his whale watching and climate change activism right down to his goatee and moppish white hair. My world is much more downtown Toronto, full of glass office towers, busy trading desks and vibrating BlackBerrys.

In the year and a half since this book was first published, one of the most pleasant surprises in my life has been discovering that Dr. David Suzuki, environmental paragon, has much more in common with this Bay Street economist than just respect and admiration for the peacock bass.

—

Well before I submitted the final manuscript of this book to my publisher, I was anxious about how the message of chapter 10, "Will Triple-digit Oil Prices Save the Planet?", would play with

the environmental movement. I doubted that many environmentalists would be willing to embrace the idea that expensive
oil might do more to mitigate climate change than decades of
political activism.

As it played out, this was one of those rare times when you enjoy
being wrong. After reading *The End of Growth*, Suzuki reached
out to my publisher to arrange a sit-down. Far from being upset
about my theory of the marginalization of the environmental
movement in a static economy, he was intrigued.

We soon set out on a series of cross-country speaking engage-
ments, with stops in Toronto, Montreal, London, Waterloo,
Guelph, Winnipeg, Saskatoon, Edmonton, Victoria, Ottawa and
Calgary. We called it the Eco Tour.

Eco is, of course, the root word of both *economics* and *ecology*.
Over the last century, these two ideas have come into conflict.
An exponential increase in economic activity has put our planet's
ecology in danger. But it doesn't have to be that way; the etymol-
ogy of the words tells us that much. *Eco* comes from the Greek
word *oikos*, which means house or household. *Ecology* is the study
of, or logic behind, where we live. *Economy*, meanwhile, refers
to the management of the household. In theory, the two notions
are quite complementary. In practice, unfortunately, evidence of
their harmonic roots is now buried under an antagonistic relationship. Too often, our choices are based on the premise that the
ideas are mutually exclusive.

As a pair, David Suzuki and I found that our message—and
quite possibly the planet's future—lies at the intersection of those
two terms. During our time together, we also discovered that
we're both convinced more hydrocarbons will stay in the ground
than most people think. Although we've arrived at the same place,
our rationales come from opposite poles.

From Suzuki's perspective, the world must get its act together on climate change because we have no other choice; the consequences of not taking steps to mitigate our burning of fossil fuels are so terrible as to be nearly inconceivable. To my way of thinking, the quantity of hydrocarbons we burn will be determined less by our environmental stewardship and more by economic practicality—specifically, the pace at which our economies grow.

US ENERGY INDEPENDENCE— BUT DOES IT REALLY MATTER?

Not long ago, the dynamics of North America's energy market seemed set in stone. But as the Greek philosopher Heraclitus points out, the one constant in life is change. The emergence of shale oil has reversed a bleak trajectory for US crude production, and the United States is producing more oil than it has in a decade. The IEA, as discussed in chapter 4, now sees US energy independence happening by 2035. It's a remarkable turnaround for a country that not long ago seemed inextricably bound to supplies in geopolitically tenuous spots such as Venezuela and Saudi Arabia. It would also seem to be an unequivocal boon for the US economy, as well as for President Obama, who made reducing America's dependence on foreign oil a priority for his administration.

Whether the IEA's forecast actually comes true, regardless of the agency's optimism, remains to be seen. The United States will certainly increase its daily oil production in the coming years, but by how much is still in question.

The surge in output from North Dakota's Bakken play has clearly been astounding. In 2007, statewide oil production was 115,000 barrels a day. Now, daily production stands at more than 700,000 barrels, an amount that's expected to double again over the next few years. By 2025, the IEA sees production from so-called tight oil plays in North Dakota, Texas, California and other states tallying more than 3 million barrels a day.

A trip to the boomtowns of North Dakota may cast a shadow over the likelihood of a continuing rapid increase in production. Like other gold rush towns, dots on the map such as Williston are scrambling to keep up with a surging population that's bursting it at the seams. The hallmarks of the boomtown syndrome are already on display: quadrupling rents, inflated food prices, oil workers sleeping in their cars in parking lots.

Relatively speaking, though, those issues are a sideshow. The larger concern for those banking on North Dakota's future oil production relates to costs, both economic and environmental.

What determines oil prices isn't whether crude is homegrown or imported. If the new barrels were cheap, that would be one thing. Swapping out politically vulnerable imports for affordable domestic production would be a prudent trade. But the new oil production coming from unconventional shale plays isn't exactly a bargain.

The crucial point for the US economy is the price of fuel, not its country of origin. The high costs of drilling for tight oil are already reflected in oil prices. Despite the surge in production from the shale revolution, which has delivered the largest-ever annual increase in US crude production, oil prices haven't come down. Shale oil means the US will be able to increase domestic production, but it's still not oil the country's economy can afford.

It's easy to see why. Drilling for tight oil is expensive. Each well in the Bakken can cost upwards of $10 million to complete. Those costs really begin to mount when so-called decline rates are taken into account. Production from a Bakken well comes on like gangbusters in the first year but, given the geological characteristics of most tight oil reservoirs, output soon falls off sharply and can drop by nearly half in the second year. It's a familiar story for global oil producers. Staying ahead of the decline treadmill, which requires running faster just to stay in the same place, is a defining part of the industry's day-to-day business.

What's more, future wells will undoubtedly be less ripe, given the oil industry's practice of plucking the lowest-hanging fruit when it first enters an area. As the sweetest spots of the Bakken play are drained, producers will continue to drill, but future output will come from more marginal reserves that will be less productive and more expensive to tap. For North Dakota not only to maintain but also to increase production means drilling several thousand new wells each year.

And then there are the environmental costs to consider. To drill and frack a Bakken well takes anywhere from 1 million to 3 million gallons of water. To put a million gallons in perspective, imagine digging a swimming pool 10 feet deep, 50 feet wide and about the length of a football field. To fill that pool would take a serious amount of water.

It's no surprise, then, that water trucks dotting the prairie landscape are the most visible symbol of North Dakota's oil boom.

If the most promising shale reserves in America were located beside an ocean, water would be much less of an issue. Unfortunately, North Dakota is in the Midwest, which is grinding through the worst drought in half a century. Another major US play, the Eagle Ford in south Texas, is in one of the driest areas of the country.

Drought and fracking don't mix. By far the largest users of America's water supply are its farmers. Ironically, many of those farmers are growing corn to feed the country's appetite for ethanol fuel (ill-conceived as that particular energy policy may be). Regardless of the crop, though, the oil industry's burgeoning need to pull water from underground aquifers as well as rivers, such as the Missouri, is already causing friction with the agricultural industry.

The IEA notes in its annual energy outlook that the sharp rise in shale drilling is pushing the limits of available water resources. Industry, it's warning, will be hard-pressed to secure enough water to keep America's oil renaissance on track.

—

It wasn't long ago that Prime Minister Stephen Harper was boasting to international audiences that Canada was an emerging energy superpower. You can't really blame him. When he began making those speeches in 2006, Canada's combination of proximity to the United States and massive tar sands reserves positioned us for decades of riches. That privileged spot is now looking much more precarious.

Canada's daily oil production comes to about 3.5 million barrels. Of that, the tar sands account for roughly 1.9 million barrels. Harper's dream of Canada one day joining heavyweights such as Saudi Arabia and Russia on the top rung of the energy ladder was largely based on expectations that tar sands output would double by 2020 and reach 5 million barrels a day by 2030. That would push Canada's total daily crude production to more than 6 million barrels. But these days, neither the Prime Minister nor anyone else is talking about pulling that many barrels from the tar sands.

Alberta, as considered in chapter 5, is landlocked. If an ocean were nearby, Alberta would have no end of markets in which to sell its oil. Being so far inland, however, has led to a reliance on a single customer. Exports to the United States account for about two-thirds of Canada's total production. To Canada's dismay, a relationship that was rock-solid for decades is now suddenly much more shaky.

When the world's largest oil market is right next door, it seems only natural to build a business model around slaking that thirst. But US oil demand isn't what it used to be. Not only is rising US domestic oil production moving into markets that were once earmarked for Canada, but US demand fell to 18.6 million barrels a day in 2012, its lowest level in sixteen years. As the US economy continues to stumble, its oil needs will shrink even further. Canada can take some comfort from the fact that the United States still needs our oil, but the timing of eventual production increases from the Alberta tar sands is now being pushed further into a much less friendly future. Between increasing US oil production and falling consumption, Canadian oil is getting squeezed on both sides of the supply-and-demand equation.

If the storm over the Keystone pipeline project makes one thing abundantly clear, it's the danger of putting your eggs in a single basket. An approval for Keystone, still in the hands of President Obama as this book goes to print, would see the pipe carry another 830,000 barrels a day to the US market. That would be a win for Canadian producers, as well as for Alberta's royalty revenues and federal tax coffers, but the added export capacity would still fall well short of getting tar sands production up to 5 million barrels a day.

Regardless of how the Keystone drama is resolved, the political bruising suffered by Obama has raised the stakes for other decisions on energy infrastructure. Future projects will need to negotiate past intensifying environmental opposition or risk being scuttled.

For Alberta to boost production from the tar sands, more pipelines will be needed to connect its oil to world markets. Industry is proposing a number of new routes, but making any of them a reality won't be easy, especially since hostility to pipelines isn't just an American pastime.

Enbridge's Northern Gateway project, as expected, is running into rigid opposition from First Nations groups and environmentalists. Indeed, I've put my public support behind the Coastal First Nations and the WWF in the campaign to stop Northern Gateway and find a more sustainable future for the pristine wilderness of the Great Bear Rainforest.

It remains to be seen whether the Houston-based pipeline company, Kinder Morgan, will have more success with its proposal to expand an existing line that runs from Alberta to BC's Lower Mainland. Built in the 1950s, the Trans Mountain pipeline is the only one that currently connects Alberta crude to tankers on the Pacific. Many of the same groups that are against Northern Gateway are already lining up to oppose the expansion.

Other proposals would see more western Canadian crude end up in eastern Canadian refineries, as well as export terminals that would get oil onto the Atlantic. So far, however, those projects, which involve reversing the flow of existing pipelines, aren't up for handling the volume of oil that Alberta wants to move out of the province.

Harper's belief that Canada was set to ascend into the upper echelons of the world's energy powers seems to have died on the vine. Of course, that might not be all bad. It certainly now looks as if more of the 170 billion barrels of oil trapped under northern Alberta's boreal forest will stay in the ground than was previously thought. The planet's climate may be grateful for that.

Canada's economy, however, is another matter. Western Canada is routinely described as the engine of the country's economic growth. As the flow of activity driven by the tar sands ebbs, Canada's already tepid GDP growth is set to shift into an even lower gear.

MONEY'S CHEAP—NOW WHERE'S THE GROWTH?

In the time that has elapsed since the hardcover edition of this book was released, governments and central banks have thrown untold billions at the global economy in an attempt to spur growth. In the United States, the twin stimulus of zero interest rates and trillion-dollar budget deficits is allowing the country's GDP to eke out a 2 percent gain. The future toll of this muted growth, meanwhile, remains to be tallied.

In the eurozone, a pledge by ECB president Mario Draghi to backstop the short-term debt of the shakiest countries helped calm the financial crisis and hold together the European Monetary Union. The eurozone debt crisis, though, remains far from over. What's still missing from the equation is economic growth. Without it, the eurozone's debt load is no more sustainable now than it was at the height of the crisis.

China's economic growth, meanwhile, is advancing at its slowest pace in more than a decade. Even Beijing admits its days of double-digit growth are over. China's GDP is still growing faster than that of OECD economies, but revisions to forecasts keep grinding expectations lower.

Some five years and counting after the financial crisis, it seems time for policymakers to take stock. What's been achieved? On the positive side of the ledger, the global economy has stayed out of recession and we've avoided another financial crisis. That's certainly comforting—but where's the economic growth? Given the unprecedented amount of stimulus being pumped into the system, if growth were going to come back, shouldn't we be seeing at least glimmers of a return?

Deficit spending and zero interest rates have certainly helped, but, by definition, they're short-term measures, not solutions for sustained growth. When the US government, for instance, takes its annual deficit from $200 billion to more than $1 trillion, all that cash can't help but move the country's economic needle. But what happens the second year? The year-over-year stimulus of another $1 trillion in deficit spending is zero. But the debt that's incurred certainly counts.

Although it's no longer adding any fuel to the economy, that debt still needs to be serviced and eventually repaid. Worse yet, when Washington starts to reduce deficit spending, economic growth too is effectively reduced. In relative terms, cutting the deficit from $1 trillion to $800 billion removes some $200 billion from the economy. Suddenly yesterday's stimulus becomes today's brake.

Similar circumstances unfold when interest rates stay low for too long. When rates drop from 5 percent to zero, the lure of cheap money pushes borrowing and spending into a higher gear. Households and businesses seize on the seemingly unique opportunity to borrow as much as possible. Purchases that were planned for the future are shifted into the present. If low rates become the norm, though, their capacity to induce people to borrow and spend diminishes.

Free credit also carries other economic costs. Beyond the clear risk that a prolonged period of low interest rates might reinflate asset bubbles, like the subprime mortgage–backed US housing market, keeping rates at zero comes with a long list of market-distorting consequences.

Japan found that out during its run of low interest rates in the 1990s. At that time, Japanese banks allowed struggling companies to roll over loans that wouldn't have been considered given normal interest rates. These companies were able to afford the artificially low interest payments, but they didn't have the wherewithal to repay the principal.

The practice of rolling over bad loans, known as evergreening, kept afloat companies that should have gone out of business. For the economy as a whole, the presence of these so-called zombie firms changed the competitive marketplace, limiting competition, altering investment flows and delaying innovation that comes with the emergence of new players. The Japanese economy is still paying the price for those distortions.

Certainly, Messrs. Bernanke, Draghi, Carney et al are well aware of the dangers of keeping interest rates near zero for a protracted period. No one suggests that Bernanke bump the Federal Funds rate to 4 percent overnight. Yet it must be recognized that zero interest rates are as unsustainable as huge budget deficits.

Central bankers and government policymakers need to understand that static growth is here to stay. Instead of countries throwing balance sheets behind a fruitless effort to achieve the economic growth of a bygone era, this financial muscle should be used to position national economies to cope in a world of much slower economic growth. Jobs are the first priority. Retraining, job sharing, youth unemployment: these are the issues that should be a preoccupation for economic decision makers.

The costs of denying the coming reality of much slower growth won't just be felt in the massive government debt that needs to be repaid. Chasing growth is also a dire policy prescription for our planet.

WHICH YARDSTICKS REALLY MATTER?

Climate change scientists say that if we can limit the increase in worldwide temperatures to 2 degrees Celsius, then we might avoid the worst consequences of global warming. By no means do they believe a 2-degree increase over preindustrial levels is ideal, but since temperatures have already risen, and will inevitably go higher, they were attempting to peg a round number that might mitigate the damage, while also being potentially achievable. Now, even that compromised hope appears out of reach.

In a hypothetical scenario where global governments adopt new policies that put climate change at the forefront, the IEA says there could be a 6 percent chance that temperature increases might be limited to 2 degrees. And that situation exists only in the IEA's imagination. Given current policies, the agency puts the chances of holding temperature increases to 2 degrees at 2 percent, to 3 degrees at 7 percent, and to 4 degrees at 17 percent. Those are some slim odds for the planet.

Such grim probabilities might suggest the world would now be poised to make some desperate changes to how we consume energy. Think again.

A big part of the problem is the countless billions already spent on our current infrastructure—the coal- and natural gas–fired power plants that produce our electricity. According to the IEA, existing infrastructure already accounts for 81 percent of the carbon dioxide emissions we can afford if temperature increases are to be held to 2 degrees. The rest of the emissions allowable under this scenario will be taken up by new power plants that will be built by 2017. That leaves the world precious little time and wiggle room to make the right decisions for the planet.

In order to keep pending hydrocarbon-burning infrastructure from getting built, the nations of the world would have to come together in a coordinated global action against climate change. How likely does that seem?

Consider the new action plan from the US Environmental Protection Agency. It's not hard to read between the lines and see the EPA has all but given up hope of curbing climate change.

Attention has quickly shifted from prevention to adaptation. The conversation is no longer about stopping ocean levels from rising, but instead about building seawalls high enough to contain flooding.

The same crowd that until recently denied any link between human-generated carbon emissions and climate change are skipping blithely past any further discussion and arriving at total capitulation. Having barely acknowledged that climate change exists, the argument now is that there's little we can do to mitigate it.

Not surprisingly, such logic is again flawed. Of course there are measures we can take to limit climate change. After all, if it's not us, then who else is putting emissions into the atmosphere?

By ending our dogged pursuit of economic growth, we can also simultaneously stop carbon emissions from increasing to even more dangerous levels. Still, no matter how closely our emissions profile—not to mention the rest of our environmental footprint—is tied to the pace of economic activity, it's not a connection that's easily accepted.

As a society, we're not climate change deniers, per se. After all, it's become incredibly difficult to ignore the empirical evidence of global warming. That said, we remain unwilling to make the economy accountable for its environmental impact—even when it's abundantly clear that our carbon trail is the flip side of economic growth. We find it much more convenient to believe that a reinvention of our economies is right around the corner. The key to environmentally sustainable living, we like to think, is switching our power sources from hydrocarbons to renewable options such as wind, water and solar. The allure of a post-carbon economy is that we can have our cake and eat it too.

Is it sensible to think we can consume ever-greater amounts of energy without compromising the environment? Do we really believe that our current material standard of living can be maintained without endangering our own sustainability on the planet?

How realistic is that vision within the time frame we have to act? And it must be asked—are we even heading in the right direction?

The answer seems to be a disheartening no. Instead of the global economy becoming less dependent on burning hydrocarbons, the reverse is true. Even more disturbing is the world's indiscriminate use of coal.

Coal is being shoveled into boilers throughout China and India at a record pace. Cheap power is critical to their developing economies, and coal fits the bill. More than 80 percent of the increase in global coal demand over the last decade has come from China. India isn't far behind. And with some 300 million people in India still living without power, there's no end in sight to how much coal it will eventually burn once the whole country is hooked to a grid.

The needs of China's and India's emerging economies are one thing, but when even supposed green-energy stalwarts like Germany are burning more coal, it makes an environmentally friendly global economy seem further away than ever. The Fukushima disaster is spurring Germany to turn its back on nuclear power, but renewable energy isn't what's picking up the slack. Germany is now relying more on coal and has designs on building even more coal-fired infrastructure.

When I tell David Suzuki about global coal demand, he shakes his head in lament. After spending decades fighting for the environment, he's frustrated at a world that, despite ample coats of political greenwash, continues to get dirtier.

The environmental movement may no longer be at the margins, but that still doesn't mean enough people or governments are willing to change their behavior to the extent, or at the pace, the planet needs.

We need to understand that less will actually mean so much more.

By the measures used by economists, the end of growth will leave us poorer. But GDP is only a number. As is consumption per capita, the Consumer Price Index and every other economic indicator.

At a few stops on the Eco Tour, Suzuki told a story about Bhutan. Sheltered in the Himalayas for centuries, when Bhutan decided to find out what lay beyond its borders, it sent young people to schools around the world. They returned and told the king what they had learned. To Bhutan, a standard such as GDP seemed illogical. Instead, the country chose to measure itself by a different yardstick: Gross National Happiness.

Juxtaposed against growth-chasing economies and rising global temperatures, it's a comforting story. Not everyone, it's worth remembering, sees the world the same way we do.

Economic growth is only one measure of well-being. And since it often comes at the cost of endangering our own survival, there are other standards we should take into account. The surprising thing is that if we look at it through a different lens, the end of growth will leave us all richer than we ever may have thought.

INTRODUCTION

p. 6: A copious amount of ink has been spilled dissecting the US housing crisis and subsequent stock market crash in 2008. For a particularly lively account of the bubble that developed for collateralized debt obligations and the emergence of the credit default swap market, see *The Big Short* (2010) by Michael Lewis.

CHAPTER 1: **CHANGING THE ECONOMIC SPEED LIMIT**

p. 32: For a broader take on how Reaganomics fostered the culture of deregulation that still persists in the United States, see *The Price of Civilization: Economics and Ethics After the Fall* (2011) by Jeffrey Sachs, director of the Earth Institute at Colombia University.

p. 36: Oil's usage has changed over the years. Today, it's primarily relied upon as a transit fuel, while being replaced by natural gas in other areas. In the 1970s, for example, a quarter of global oil consumption went toward power generation, a figure that's now fallen to less than 5 percent. In places such as North America, natural gas has largely replaced oil as a home heating fuel. Natural gas is also a ready substitute for oil as a feedstock in the production of petrochemicals. Unfortunately, the substitution of natural gas for oil ends there. Natural gas has yet to make an appreciable dent in the demand for oil as a transit fuel. That's one reason for the huge price spread between the two commodities, especially in North America, where the emergence of shale resources has sent natural gas pricing tumbling. It took a big jump in oil prices (the OPEC oil shocks) to get North Americans to switch from burning oil in their furnaces to burning natural gas, and it will take an even bigger jump to get them to switch their gas tanks over.

p. 41: Those old enough to remember the 1970s know that waking the specter of inflation is a scary prospect for any economy. Against a backdrop of historically low interest rates and expansionary monetary policy, it bears noting that the mandate of many of the world's central banks is to keep inflation in check. The Bank of Canada, for instance, has an inflation control target of 2 percent, the midpoint of a control range of 1 to 3 percent. Recently, the BoC's target inflation range was extended for another five years, until the end of 2016.

CHAPTER 2: **DEBT IS ENERGY INTENSIVE**

p. 57: The euro was launched in 1999, with the introduction of banknotes and coins following in 2002. Eleven countries originally adopted the currency: Belgium, Germany, Ireland, Spain, France, Italy, Luxembourg, the Netherlands, Austria, Portugal and Finland. Subsequently, Slovenia, Cyprus, Malta, Slovakia and Estonia joined the currency union. Collectively, these countries make up the euro area, also commonly known as the eurozone. Roughly 330 million EU citizens use the euro as their currency. The European Commission offers an extensive chronological account of the thirty-year process that led to the adoption of a single European currency at ec.europa.eu/economy_finance/emu_history/index_en.htm.

p. 59: Standard & Poor's cut the debt ratings of nine eurozone governments in January 2012. Among the downgrades, S&P removed the AAA status of France and Austria, cutting their ratings a notch to AA+. France's first-ever downgrade from S&P is particularly worrisome for the ECB, which depends on the large economies of France and Germany to backstop efforts to pull the eurozone out of its fiscal crisis.

p. 65: What makes the $2.3-billion trading loss at UBS even more disturbing is that Swiss taxpayers already paid a huge sum to bail out the bank in 2008, after UBS wrote down $56 billion in credit losses. Given that the combined assets of UBS and Credit Suisse, Switzerland's other major bank, are four times the size of the country's GDP, Swiss taxpayers have considerable reason to worry if financial markets take another turn for the worse.

p. 67: According to the US Treasury department, China holds roughly $1.5 trillion in American government debt. Japan is the second-largest buyer of US treasuries, holding about $885 billion.

CHAPTER 3: **THE ARAB REVOLT**

p. 77: For a detailed account of the countercoup that unseated Moham-med Mossadegh and reinstalled the Shah as Iran's ruler, see *All the Shah's Men: An American Coup and the Roots of Middle East Terror* (2003) by Stephen Kinzer.

p. 79: The size of Iraq's oil reserves are open to dispute. The US Geological Survey estimates only 78 billion barrels. The figure quoted in the text is from the US Department of Energy. The Iraqi government estimates Iraq's reserves at more than 300 billion barrels. That would make it the largest reserve in the world. But this claim, along with the Iraqi government's prediction that the country will ramp up current oil production of around 2.5 million barrels a day to a world-leading 12 million barrels a day, must be taken with a large grain of salt.

p. 80: Iraq's oil output is rising, but efforts to boost production face considerable hurdles, including widespread pipeline sabotage, such as an explosion of the Ceyhan pipeline in 2011. Other attacks on energy targets include a strike on the country's largest refinery, located in the northern city of Baiji. In addition, Iraqi crude exports are increasingly bouncing up against infrastructure constraints at key export terminals, such as the port at Basra.

p. 81: The US Energy Information Agency (EIA—not to be confused with the IEA, the International Energy Agency) identifies seven global oil transit choke points: the Strait of Hormuz, the Strait of Malacca, the Suez Canal, the Strait of Bab el Mandeb, the Turkish Straits (comprising the Bosporus and the Dardanelles), the Panama Canal and the Danish Straits. These narrow channels are part of shipping routes considered critical to global energy security. The Strait of Hormuz is the most important of these waterways. In 2011, roughly 35 percent of all seaborne-traded oil passed through the

Strait, or nearly a fifth of the oil traded globally (www.eia.gov/cabs/world_oil_transit_chokepoints/full.html).

p. 91: OPEC's Middle Eastern members are Iran, Iraq, Kuwait, Libya, Qatar, Saudi Arabia and the United Arab Emirates. The twelve-member group is rounded out by Algeria, Angola, Ecuador, Nigeria and Venezuela. The figures for the cartel's contribution to global oil supply can be found at www.opec.org/opec_web/en/.

p. 98: Saudi Arabia currently burns more than 3 million barrels of oil a day to meet domestic energy needs, which represents roughly a third of its production. According to *Arab News*, nearly half of that amount, some 1.5 million barrels a day, is used to power an extensive network of fuel-hungry desalination plants. In response to this growing drain on oil output, Saudi Arabia's national science agency announced a new initiative to begin building solar-powered desalination plants. Unfortunately, the scale of the efforts will be tiny. The first plant is expected to produce a mere 30,000 cubic meters of water, compared with the mammoth oil-fired Shoaiba plant (Stage 3) that produces 880,000 cubic meters of desalinated water every day.

CHAPTER 4: **HITTING THE ENERGY CEILING**

p. 102: Production of shale gas has more than its share of critics, many from the environmental movement. A 2010 documentary, *Gasland*, by filmmaker Josh Fox chronicled some of the environmental mishaps that have occurred as a result of drilling in the Marcellus formation in Pennsylvania, New York, Ohio and West Virginia. Hydraulic fracturing, the key process used to extract shale gas, was exempted in 2005 from the Safe Drinking Water Act (1974), a step that paved the way for a wave of drilling across the country and put a spark to much of the current controversy over fracking.

p. 107: The data on China's coal consumption is measured in short tons, a unit of weight equal to 2,000 pounds. The EIA calculates coal usage in short tons as opposed to long tons (2,240 pounds), the standard unit for measuring coal in the United Kingdom. Neither should be confused with a metric ton, also known as a tonne, which is 1,000 kilograms, or 2,204 pounds.

p. 109: If the International Energy Agency can be criticized for the size of some of its more recent downward revisions to expected world oil supply, those revisions pale in comparison with the haircuts that world coal reserve estimates have taken. Since 1980, world coal estimates have fallen by 50 percent. In some countries, reserve estimates have been literally wiped out. Coal reserves in Germany, one of the oldest coal-producing nations, were chopped from 183 billion tons in 1996 to 23 million tons in 2004—a 99 percent reduction in the span of eight years. Coal reserves in Poland, the EU's largest producer, have been halved since 1997.

p. 109: Another dramatic example of coal depletion is found in the UK. In the 19th century, there were more than three thousand coal mines in Britain. Today, there are six. At the turn of the last century, Britain exported almost a third of its total coal production. By 2010, the UK was importing almost 60 percent of its coal. Resource depletion in domestic coalfields was first documented in the 19th century by British economist Stanley Jevons. He's the namesake of the Jevons paradox, a concept that points out how an increase in the efficiency of resource extraction leads to an increase in resource consumption. For a discussion of the paradox, also known as the rebound effect, see pages 118–29 of my first book, *Why Your World Is About to Get a Whole Lot Smaller* (2009).

p. 120: Japanese regulations require reactors to close every thirteen months for maintenance and inspections. Normally, the process involves taking nuclear plants off line for two or three months. However, in the wake of the Fukushima disaster, only two of the reactors closed for inspection have been restarted.

p. 120: According to the Tokyo Institute for Energy Economics, even stepping up the amount of power generated from oil, coal and natural gas will leave Japan with a 10 percent shortfall in power supply if the country's nuclear reactors are permanently shut down. In that light, the energy conservation achieved through *setsuden* is set to loom even larger in Japan's future.

p. 120: Growing power shortages may also threaten Japan's industrial base. Hiromasa Yonekura, chairman of Sumitomo Chemical and head of the Keidanren, Japan's powerful business lobby, recently warned that power shortages could cause a stampede of manufacturing plants out of the country. His comments followed a number of high-profile announcements by Japanese manufacturers that decided to move plants elsewhere. The list of firms taking business offshore includes heavyweights such as Mitsui Mining & Smelting and Renesas Electronics.

CHAPTER 5: **THE KEYSTONE CONUNDRUM**

p. 125: The spirit bear, also known as the Kermode bear, is a contradiction in terms, a black bear with white fur. The reclusive bear, and the recessive gene responsible for its unusual coat, continues to fascinate and puzzle geneticists. For a deeper look at the ghostlike bears that inhabit Princess Royal Island, see Charles Russell's *Spirit Bear: Encounters with the White Bear of the Western Rainforest* (1994).

p. 127: The story of the *Queen of the North* was recounted by Bruce Barcott in the August 2011 issue of *National Geographic* ("Pipeline Through Paradise," ngm.nationalgeographic.com/2011/08/canada-rainforest/barcott-text).

p. 135: Enbridge hopes to complete a public and government review process for Northern Gateway by midway through 2013. Pending regulatory approval, ground will be broken in mid-2014 and oil will start flowing through the line in late 2017. However, as Trans-Canada's experience with Keystone shows, political, social and environmental forces can render corporate timelines for major infrastructure projects meaningless.

CHAPTER 6: **THE DANISH RESPONSE**

p. 137: Information about Denmark's environmental track record, including its level of carbon dioxide emissions since 1990, comes from figures available through the State of Green, a government-backed initiative to raise international awareness of the country's green credentials (www.stateofgreen.com).

p. 141: The argument for the relationship between urban population density and vibrant cities is well documented. Jane Jacobs, for one, argued convincingly against urban sprawl in her seminal work *The Death and Life of Great American Cities*, which has influenced thoughts on urban planning since its publication in 1961.

CHAPTER 7: **ZERO-SUM WORLD**

p. 154: The figures for Venezuela's oil exports to the United States come from the EIA. US oil imports from Venezuela reached a high of 1.77 million barrels a day in 1997. (www.eia.gov/dnav/pet/hist/LeafHandler.ashx?n=pet&s=mttimusve2&f=a)

p. 156: The figure for the number of licensed American drivers comes from the US Federal Highway Administration, an agency within the Department of Transportation (www.fhwa.dot.gov/ohim/onh00/onh2p4.htm).

p. 157: The number of Alternative Fuel Vehicles calculated by the Department of Transportation doesn't include hybrid electric vehicles or flexible fuel vehicles that run on an ethanol blend of less than E85. According to data from *Wards*, the cumulative number of hybrids sold in the United States surpassed 2 million in 2011. The Department of Energy says there are more than 8 million flex fuel vehicles on US roads, although many owners are unaware their vehicles have this capability. Most of the 2,400 fueling stations that offer E85 are located in the corn belt in the Midwest.

p. 159: According to the International Energy Agency's discussion of subsidies in its *World Energy Outlook 2011*, Iran and Saudi Arabia lead the world in fossil fuel subsidies. According to the IEA, fuel subsidies are most prevalent in the developing world. However, it should be noted that the IEA uses a narrow (and arguably self-serving) definition of what constitutes a subsidy. Tax breaks and incentives, loan guarantees, public money for research and development, and, most of all, very low fuel taxes are not considered subsidies by the IEA. If they were, we would find the incidence of subsidies much more frequent among OECD members such as the United States and countries in western Europe than current IEA numbers indicate.

p. 163: The figures for daily oil consumption of countries around the world come from the CIA World Factbook (https://www.cia.gov/library/publications/the-world-factbook). The United States is the world's largest oil consumer, guzzling more than 18 million barrels a day. Occupying the last spot on the list is the tiny island nation of Niue. On average, its 1,311 residents burn a cumulative total of 40 barrels a day.

p. 167: While it has yet to surpass the United States in oil consumption, China leapfrogged the USA in 2010 to become the world's largest energy-consuming nation, according to BP's *Statistical Review of World Energy*. Yet on a per capita basis, the Chinese consumer burns only a fraction of the energy consumed by the average American, pointing to a seemingly limitless potential for demand growth. Of course, triple-digit oil and coal prices will rein in Chinese energy demand, just as higher prices have curbed energy demand in OECD economies.

CHAPTER 8: **THE STATIC ECONOMY**

p. 177: For an in-depth consideration of how physical barriers, such as the walls erected along the US–Mexico border, divide our world, see *Walls: Travels Along the Barricades* (2012) by Marcello DiCintio.

p. 182: A study that explores the trend toward a graying workforce was released in 2010 by Boston College's Sloan Center on Aging & Work. Among other findings, the research study, *Working in Retirement: A 21st Century Phenomenon*, concluded that the linear progression of a traditional career path that begins at an entry-level job and ends in retirement no longer fits with current workplace realities. The emerging experience of workers of all ages suggests that multiple exit and re-entry points out of and into the workforce throughout one's working life are becoming more common. (familiesandwork.org/site/research/reports/workinginretirement.pdf)

p. 184: Global Sticks is by no means the only North American manufacturer that has recently come home from China. Not long ago, NCR decided to move production of its automated teller machines to Georgia, while toy maker Wham-O Inc. shifted half of its Frisbee and hula hoop production back to the United States. Caterpillar, which has operations around the world, has chosen Texas as the site of its next major manufacturing plant.

p. 200: A push-back against rampant consumerism is becoming more evident in corporate circles. Consider, for example, Patagonia's new marketing campaign. The outdoor clothing company is asking everyone who wishes to sell second-hand Patagonia goods on its new eBay venture to sign a Common Threads agreement. The pledge includes an obligation to buy only what is necessary, to reuse items and to purchase used products whenever possible. Has Patagonia already seen the face of tomorrow's consumer?

p. 200: Another sign of changing attitudes toward consumption and conservation in the developed world can be found in the design of Olympic Park, a sporting complex built for the 2012 Olympics in London. In a sharp departure from the massive edifices and monuments erected by past Olympic hosts, the motto of the London organizers was to "touch the ground lightly." Two-thirds of the structures built for the Olympics were temporary and were taken down when the Games ended, including an 80,000-seat stadium in London's East End.

CHAPTER 9: **ALL BETS ARE OFF**

pp. 219-222: For the full story on the Yangs and the implications for China's resource consumption see a November 2010 feature by *Bloomberg* reporter Fan Wenxin ("China's Rural Growth Spurs Copper Demand").

p. 222: Politicians have called scrap metal theft in the United Kingdom a scourge and an epidemic. The government is changing laws to allow for unlimited fines for people caught trading in stolen scrap metal and to ban cash transactions in the industry. The public uproar over this low-tech criminal endeavor is fueled by high-profile thefts from churches and public monuments. Police say a memorial is stripped every week in London.

pp. 222-223: To put the acceleration of population growth in perspective, consider that the human population reached the 1 billion mark in 1804. It took 123 more years for it to reach 2 billion, in 1927. We hit 3 billion people thirty-two years later in 1959. From there population doubled to 6 billion by 1998. A little more than a decade after that, the 7 billionth person was born. According to the UN's latest projections, the global population is expected to reach 10 billion by 2083, provided, of course, the world can produce enough food to feed the additional people.

pp. 224–25: The total fertility rate, which measures the number of births per woman, shows the potential for population change in a given country. In OECD countries, a fertility rate of approximately 2.1 is considered the replacement rate for a population; in developing nations, the replacement rate is around 2.3 to account for higher mortality rates. Rates below these figures indicate a population that is declining and growing older, while higher rates point to the opposite. A fertility rate of 2.06 makes the United States the only G8 country with fertility levels close to the replacement rate. Canada's fertility rate reached a high of 3.93 in 1959 and has since dropped steadily, bottoming out at 1.49 in 2000. The figures for global fertility rates come from the CIA World Factbook (https://www.cia.gov/library/publications/the-world-factbook/rankorder/2127rank.html).

p. 225: While fertility rates have fallen markedly in developed nations, they remain stubbornly high throughout much of the developing world. To get an idea of what fertility rates mean for population growth, consider projections for countries with the highest readings.

With a fertility rate of 7 children per woman, Niger's population is forecast to more than triple, from 16.5 million to more than 55 million, by 2050, according to the United Nations. Somalia's birthrate isn't far behind: a fertility rate of 6.4 means its population will nearly triple, from 10 million to close to 30 million, over the next four decades. With a fertility rate of 6.39, Mali's population will increase from 14 million to 42 million, while Uganda, with a rate of 6.38, will see its numbers swell from 34 million to almost 95 million by 2050.

p. 226: The proverb "Women hold up half the sky" is the inspiration for the title of a best-selling book: *Half the Sky: Turning Oppression into Opportunity for Women Worldwide* (2009). Pulitzer Prize–winning authors Nicholas Kristof and Sheryl WuDunn argue that the key to economic progress is the unleashing of the untapped potential of women. The treatment of women in the developing world, they contend, is the most pervasive human rights violation of our time. The book argues that investing in the health and autonomy of women not only moves us toward improving morally reprehensible circumstances but also leads to economic benefits that shouldn't be overlooked.

CHAPTER 10: **WILL TRIPLE-DIGIT OIL PRICES SAVE THE PLANET?**

p. 227: James Lovelock recounts his early days at NASA and the development of Gaia theory in *The Ages of Gaia: A Biography of Our Living Earth* (1988). Now in his nineties, Lovelock still conducts occasional experiments from his home laboratory in southwest England.

p. 229: The IPCC released its first comprehensive assessment report about the state of scientific, technical and socioeconomic knowledge on climate change in 1990. Other major reports followed in 1995, 2001 and 2007. The fifth assessment report is slated for completion in late 2014.

p. 234: Despite the Kyoto Protocol—which set an emissions reduction target of 6 percent below 1990 levels by 2012—emissions are on the rise. Global emissions have increased at an annual clip of 3 percent over the last decade, roughly three times the pace of the previous decade. The combustion of coal has accounted for more than half of the increase in global emissions during this time.

p. 249: According to BP's *Statistical Review*, total energy consumption rebounded at a blistering pace of 5.6 percent in 2010, the strongest annual growth rate since 1973. Nevertheless, total energy consumption in OECD economies remains roughly in line with levels of a decade ago. Over the same period, energy consumption in the developing world has increased more than 60 percent.

CONCLUSION

p. 253: The Green Revolution is not without its critics. Some environmental groups oppose high-yield agricultural techniques, believing the use of inorganic fertilizers, pesticides and controlled irrigation puts undue pressure on the environment. Other critics believe industrial farming techniques leave agriculture in the hands of corporate interests at the expense of small farms. For a broader discussion of the issues, see "Forgotten Benefactor of Humanity" in the January 1997 issue of *The Atlantic*. The story is by Gregg Easterbrook, a versatile journalist who, inter alia, also writes a column for ESPN.com under the moniker Tuesday Morning Quarterback. (www.theatlantic.com/magazine/archive/1997/01/forgotten-benefactor-of-humanity/6101/)

p. 258: Norman Borlaug may be the person most responsible for helping the world avoid the Malthusian fate predicted by Paul Ehrlich in *The Population Bomb*. Ironically, the pair's thinking is more aligned than a quick glance at history would suggest. In his Nobel lecture, for instance, Borlaug notes "the ticktock of the [population] clock will continue to grow louder and more menacing each decade." The full text of his lecture is available at www.nobelprize.org/nobel_prizes/peace/laureates/1970/borlaug-lecture.html.

[ACKNOWLEDGMENTS]

I have been very fortunate to work on this book with a great editor, Paul Haavardsrud, who did an outstanding job both on the page and with the research. *The End of Growth* evolved over the course of our many editing sessions at the Higher Ground Café in Calgary, where Paul lives, which is only fitting since oil plays such a pivotal role in the story.

I would also like to thank Nick Garrison, the equally great editor of my first book, *Why Your World Is About to Get a Whole Lot Smaller*, for telling me that it was time for me to write a sequel, a suggestion he delivered to me with much encouragement at one of our annual dates to see a Toronto Maple Leafs game.

Anne Collins, my publisher at Random House Canada, once again did a great job in quarterbacking the book through editorial rounds and a crash publication schedule. Likewise, Sharon Klein, my trusted publicist, has done another outstanding job on organizing the publicity and marketing of the book.

I'd like to thank Peter Victor of York University for the information he sent me on Germany's Kurzarbeit program, as well as David Foot of the University of Toronto for data on international birthrates. Also I would like to thank two of my former colleagues at CIBC World Markets: Benjamin Tal, Deputy Chief Economist, for information on potential growth rates in North America, and Karl Kainz, my old broker, for drawing my attention to the Anthropocene.

Lastly, I would like to thank my agent, Rick Broadhead, and once again my lawyer and friend Aaron Milrad, for his wise counsel and guidance.

© Greg Tjepkema

JEFF RUBIN was the chief economist at CIBC World Markets for almost twenty years. During that period, he placed first ten times in Brendan Wood's institutional investor ranking of top Bay Street economists. He was among the first economists in the world to accurately predict the onset and timing of triple-digit oil prices.

In 2009, Mr. Rubin left CIBC World Markets to publish his first book, *Why Your World Is About to Get a Whole Lot Smaller*. The book won the National Business Book Award in Canada, was long-listed for the Financial Times and Goldman Sachs Business Book of the Year Award in the UK, and has been published in French, Spanish, German, Italian, Portuguese and Chinese. Jeff Rubin's writing and commentary have been featured on CNBC, on CNN, on CBC radio and television, and in *The Globe and Mail* and *The Huffington Post*. He lives in Toronto.